MW00342345

The Grand Pattern of Development and the Transition of Institutions

The culmination of a long-lasting and impressive research program, this book summarizes the relationship between economic development with income on one hand and the evolution of institutions on the other; the transition of countries from one economic and social system to another. The author considers the transitions of two types of institutions: The first is external, namely, legal-administrative systems with staff and buildings. The political system and the economic system are considered. The second consists of traditions and beliefs. Here corruption and religiosity are considered. Contrary to the claim that institutions are causal to development, this book demonstrates that the main direction of causality is from income to institutions. As countries become wealthy, they develop into secular democracies with low corruption and a mixed economic system. In this impressive coda, Paldam shows that the evolution of institutions is not causal to the economic growth process but rather follows it.

Martin Paldam is Professor Emeritus in the Department of Economics and Management at Aarhus University.

The Grand Pattern of Development and the Transition of Institutions

MARTIN PALDAM

Aarhus University

CAMBRIDGE
UNIVERSITY PRESS

CAMBRIDGE
UNIVERSITY PRESS

University Printing House, Cambridge CB2 8BS, United Kingdom

One Liberty Plaza, 20th Floor, New York, NY 10006, USA

477 Williamstown Road, Port Melbourne, VIC 3207, Australia

314–321, 3rd Floor, Plot 3, Splendor Forum, Jasola District Centre, New Delhi – 110025, India

103 Penang Road, #05–06/07, Visioncrest Commercial, Singapore 238467

Cambridge University Press is part of the University of Cambridge.

It furthers the University's mission by disseminating knowledge in the pursuit of education, learning, and research at the highest international levels of excellence.

www.cambridge.org
Information on this title: www.cambridge.org/9781316515501
DOI: 10.1017/9781009025898

First published 2021

Printed in the United Kingdom by TJ Books Limited, Padstow Cornwall

A catalogue record for this publication is available from the British Library.

ISBN 978-1-316-51550-1 Hardback

Contents

Figures

Tables

Preface

This book is based on a set of papers from a long-lasting project that has led to a total of 12 papers listed in Table P.1. After a dozen years of work, I needed to take stock and put everything together. Once started, I came to rewrite, reorganize, update, and extend almost everything.

I stand as the sole author of the book, so I have to use first person. However, it is a boast for which I want to apologize. Ten of the "underlying" papers are joint work. No less than eight of the papers are coauthored by professor *Erich Gundlach* (EG) from the University of Hamburg. I tried very hard to convince him to be coauthor of the book, but he had involved himself in too many other duties. I shall not try to sort out what ideas are his – after such a long cooperation it would be impossible. Two of the papers had another coauthor: my colleague professor *Christian Bjørnskov* (CB), with whom I often discuss, and my daughter *Ella Paldam* (EP), who is postdoc at the Interactive Minds Center at Aarhus University. I am grateful to both of them for many fine discussions and good ideas. I also want to thank *Birgitte Højklint Nielsen*, who has been my eagle-eyed in-house editor.

The papers have been presented at guest lectures at a dozen universities, and at various conferences, notably at the annual meeting of the European Public Choice Society (EPCS). The papers have consequently benefited from comments from many colleagues and friends at the EPCS and elsewhere. They have also been through refereeing, often receiving useful comments. At the later stages of the process, it became rather

TABLE P.I. *The 12 papers: Column 2 is the coauthor*

1	EG	2008	Two views on institutions and development: The grand transition vs the primacy of institutions. *Kyklos* 61, 65–100
2	EG	2009	A farewell to critical junctures: Sorting out the long-run causality of income and democracy. *European Journal of Political Economy* 25, 340–54
3	EG	2009	The transition of corruption: From poverty to honesty. *Economic Letters* 103, 146–48
4	EG	2012	The democratic transition: Short-run and long-run causality between income and the Gastil Index. *European Journal of Development Research* 24, 144–68
5	CB	2012	The spirits of capitalism and socialism: A cross-country study of ideology. *Public Choice* 150, 469–98
6	EG	2012	A model of the religious transition: *Theoretical Economic Letters,* 419–22
7	EG	2013	The religious transition: A long-run perspective. *Public Choice* 156, 105–23
8	EP	2017	The political economy of churches in Denmark, 1300–2015. *Public Choice* 172, 443–63
9	EG	2018	Jumps into democracy: Integrating the short and the long run in the democratic transition. *Kyklos* 7, 456–81
10		2020	A study of triggering events: When do political regimes change? *Public Choice* 182, 181–99
11	EG	2020	A hump-shaped transitional growth path as a general pattern of long-run development. *Economic Systems* 44(3), article 10825
12		2021	The transition of corruption: Institutions and dynamics. *European Journal of Political Economy,* 67(2), article 101952

difficult to write new papers as I was carrying all the previous papers on my back. I could not demonstrate everything once again without self-plagiarizing, and it is bad taste to keep referring to oneself. From now on I will have the great advantage of needing only one self-reference.

Finally, I may as well admit what the reader will soon discover: I am a low-brow empirical economist. I love to spend my days trying to make sense of datasets, and I have done so for half a century. This book is not meant to advance either econometrics or theory-building but to advance our understanding of a key aspect of development in the world – this is more than enough for a project.

A QUICK INTRODUCTION TO VARIABLES, DATA, COUNTRY NAMES

The book uses a limited set of variables, of which six are the most important. They come in various transformations. I have tried to make the notation as simple and consistent as possible, but the reader may still have some trouble keeping track. Tables P.2a and b should help the reader in this endeavor. They list all variables, including transformations, and the key terminology used in the book. I do not expect the reader to learn the tables by heart, but it is useful to look through and to tag the page for easy reference. Table P.2b gives all variables, but the chapters will repeat the relevant part of the table. The six most important variables are described here.

Large datasets of thousands of observations exist for four level variables: y, P, F, and T. They are y, the income, and three institutional indices, namely, P, the Polity2 Index used to measure the political system; F, the Fraser index of economic freedom used to measure the economic system; and T, the Transparency International corruption index. While y has no known bounds, P, F, and T are bounded. The first differences to y, P, and F are growth, g, dP, and dF.

The World Values survey has given two level variables: B and R. Since each poll gives one observation only, they are covered by much smaller datasets: They are B, the ownership index, and R, the religiosity index.

All data used are downloaded from the net, and I give the URLs in Tables 2a and b. These addresses may move, the data may be revised, etc., but they are the ones used. They were all assessed in the fall of 2019, and to make sure everything can be replicated, the data used for the project are all available at the home page: www.martin.paldam.dk/GT-Book-Data. They are in Excel (.xlsx) format.

One of the data-pages is a list of countries and country groups. Though the country groups are based on the World Bank classification, they sometimes change. For example, the group of socialist/post-socialist countries was important from 1960 to 2010, but it is becoming increasingly irrelevant. Country names may change. They sometimes merge or split. I use the shortest and most common name. That is, I use *Bolivia* for the Plurinational State of Bolivia, *Taiwan* for the Republic of China, etc. The two Congos have both changed name several times. They are termed *Congo Br* and *Congo Ki* for the first two letters of their capital cities. I think that *Myanmar* is now established for Burma, but Eswatini is not

TABLE P.2a. *Terminology and variables used in book for easy reference*

Transition terminology: for a level variable $X = y, P, CL, PR, B, F, T$, or R.

Traditional steady state: All countries in 1750 and low-income countries (LICs) until recently.

Modern steady state: High-income countries today (HICs), with the OPEC exception.

Grand Transition: The path that connects a low-level divergence and a high-level convergence.

X_{it}	*Panel* representation of the variable, for country $i = 1, \ldots n$ and time $t = 1, \ldots k$.
X_j	*Unified* representation, j is the order of the data. Divided in *Main* and *OPEC* sample.
$\Pi^X(y_j)$	*Transition* curve, gives the net change in X, necessary for the transition. A transition is termed *beautiful* if the best kernel-estimate has the properties listed in Table 2.2.
λ^X	*Slope* of transition curve, $\lambda^X = \partial \Pi^X / \partial y$. It is either $\leq$ or $\geq$ for the full y-range.
$K^X(y_j, bw)$	*Kernel* estimate of transition, bw is bandwidth. $K^X(y_j, bw) \approx \Pi^X(y_j)$.
dX	*Average* numerical change in X for either all countries, i, or all years, t.
G^X-ratio	*Excess* movements in X. The gross movements in X relative to the net change.

Other terms: Mainly used in Chapters 8 and 9.

Welfare goods are goods with large positive externalities. The *three big ones* are education, healthcare, and social protection. Others are infrastructure, law and order, etc.

A *mixed system* has a large public role in the production of welfare goods, and a small role in the production of other goods. Trade, agriculture, industry, and finance are mainly private.

Data samples for all countries and years are divided into:

Main	Data for countries that have never been an OPEC member.
OPEC	Member, present or past, of the Organization of the Petroleum Exporting Countries.

National accounts variables: Used in all chapters.

Source	Maddison Project: https://www.rug.nl/ggdc/historicaldevelopment/maddison/.
GDP	*Gross Domestic Product*, in fixed PPP, purchasing power parity, prices.
gdp	GDP per capita. The *cgdppc* series. The *rgdpnapc* series is almost equally good.
y	*Income*, the natural logarithm to *gdp*. One lp-point is a *gdp* change of 2.7 times.
g	*Growth* of *gdp*. Π^g-curve is hump-shaped, and is a first difference transition curve.

Political system (1) P-index: Polity (a) Chapters 4, 5, 7, 8, and 13.

Source	Institute for Systemic Peace: https://www.systemicpeace.org/polityproject.html.
P	P-index, integer $[-10, 10]$ from authoritarian to democratic. $P = 0$ for no system. Transition is 12–14 P-points, Π^P-curve is beautiful and $\lambda^P \geq 0$.
dP	Average annual numerical change in P.
zP	Fraction of years with $P = 0$, i.e., anarchy or temporary foreign domination.

Variables and functions derived from P-index: Chapters 2, 4, 5, and 7.

Θ^P	*Tension*, distance from P to transition path, i.e., $\Theta^P = P - \Pi(y)$. The country has *too much* or *too little* P if $\Theta^P > 0$ or $\Theta^P < 0$, respectively.
E	*Event*, binary variable for year t. If P changes, $E = 1$. If P is constant, $E = 0$. *Triggering event*, the change of system to a new system, which is not zero.
J	*Jump* is a change, $P - P_{-1}$. *Large* if $|\Delta P| > 3$. Jumps Model explains larger jumps *Sequences* are P changes in the same direction in consecutive years, incl. zero. *Spells*, periods where P is constant, include a sequence at the start.

Political system (2) CL-index and (3) PR-index: Chapter 4

Source	Freedom House: https://freedomhouse.org/.
CL	*Civil Liberties* index, integer $[7, 1]$, seven for lowest and 1 for highest. Transition is 3.5 CL-points. Π^{CL}-curve is beautiful and $\lambda^{CL} < 0$.
PR	*Political Rights* index, same scale as CL. Transition is 3.5 PR-points. Π^{PR}-curve is beautiful and $\lambda^{PR} < 0$.

---

yet established for *Swaziland*. In none of these cases do I try to make a statement.

The book is mainly empirical – trying to point to main lines in development, and to explain why they occur, but there is no reason to hide that I prefer democracy, honesty, and the modern mixed economy to dictatorship, corruption, and central planning or the laissez faire.

I have tried to make the book accessible to both economists and political scientists, as well as those who are not fully read up. Thus, there are some sections to refresh the reader, which other readers may find trivial. A few paragraphs cover more advanced issues. I have tried to keep such paragraphs together in a section and added a warning in the headline.

TABLE P.2b. *Variables used in book: For easy reference*

Economic System B-index (1): Chapter 8.

Source   World Values Surveys: www.worldvaluessurvey.org/wvs.jsp.

B   Ownership index. Excess preferences for private business in pp,
         percentage points.
         Transition is 18–20 B-pp. Π^B-curve is almost linear, $\lambda^B \geq 0$.

Economic System F-index (2): Chapters 9 and 13.

Source   Fraser Institute: https://www.fraserinstitute.org/studies/economic-
         freedom.

F   F-index (b), [0, 10] two decimals. The Economic Freedom Index
         Transition is 2.8 F-points. Π^F-curve is linear, $\lambda^F \geq 0$.

dF   Average annual numerical change in F.

Corruption T-index: Chapter 10.(d)

Source   Transparency International: https://www.transparency.org/.

T   The T-index [0, 10] for corruption to honesty. It rises when corruption
         falls.

Θ^T The deviation of the T-index from the transition path: $\Theta^T = T - \Pi^T$.
         Transition is 6.5 T-points. Π^T-curve is beautiful and $\lambda^T \geq 0$.

Religiosity R- index: Chapter 11.

Source   World Values Surveys: http://www.worldvaluessurvey.org/wvs.jsp.

R   *Religiosity index* in percentage points. Factor one in factor analysis of
         fourteen religiosity items. The transition is 50 R-points. Π^R-curve is
         almost linear, $\lambda^R \geq 0$.

Religiosity s-proxy (church density): Chapter 11.

Source   Own compilation from several sources; see (8) in Table P.1.

S, s   *Supply* of churches data. The stock of churches and per capita church
         density.

D, d   *Demand* for churches unobserved. Aggregate and demand per capita.

κ *Capacity* utilization, relative to stock: $S_t = D_t(1 + \kappa)$, in equilibrium $S_t{}^* = D_t$.

$d \approx aR$ The relation between the two measures of religiosity, *a* may be
         constant.

Notes: (a) The Polity2 coding is used: Negative values [-10, -1] are authoritarian systems, and positive values [1, 10] are democratic systems. Zero is used for anarchy and for temporary foreign domination/occupation. (b) Index of the freedom to run a private business. It aggregates indicators for small public sector, law and order, stable money, free trade, and few regulations. (d) Chapter 12 discusses two-sector models. Here, T is used for the traditional sector.

Chapters are divided into sections. Thus, Chapter 3.7 is section 7 (s7) of Chapter 3. However, within Chapter 3 references to section (s7) or Table 3.5 are written with one digit. All chapters start with a small introduction that introduces the main content.

PART I

MAIN IDEAS

I

Introduction

This book is about the strong endogenous element in long-run development and especially the development of institutions. The long-run systematic element in a socioeconomic variable is termed a *transition*. Taken together it is the **Grand Transition**. Institutions are of two types. The first involves legal-administrative systems with staff and buildings. Part IIA considers the political system and Part IIB the economic system. The second consists of traditions and beliefs. Part IIC looks at the transitions in corruption and religiosity. All of these institutions change systematically from *LIC*s, low-income countries, to *HIC*s, high-income countries.

The 12 sections of Chapter 1 deal with the theory of transitions, and how they can be analyzed empirically. Section (s1) looks at two

TABLE I.I. *Terminology and variables used in Chapter 1*

National accounts variables

Source	Maddison Project: www.rug.nl/ggdc/historicaldevelopment/maddison/.
GDP	Gross Domestic Product, in 2011 international US$ (i.e., PPP prices).
gdp	GDP per capita. The *cgdppc* series. Preferred to *rgdpnapc* series. (a)
y	Income, the natural logarithm to *gdp*.
g	Growth, annual rate for *gdp*. Thus, it is real and per capita.

Transition terminology

X	The variable having the transition. Table 1.3 lists seven such variables.
Π^X	The transition path, $X = \Pi^X(y)$.

Note: (a) The two *gdp*-series gave similar results, but they are marginally clearer for the *cgdppc series*. One income-point is a change in *gdp* of 2.7 times, equal to 50 years of growth at 2% pa.

well-known transitions. They are **strong but fuzzy** – this introduces transition theory (s2). It predicts that datasets have an underlying common path (s3), which is explained by a set of mechanisms sketched in (s4). The fuzziness means that much data is necessary to see the path. Hence, the study requires that panel data are unified to one string. This relies on the equivalence hypothesis (s5): Wide cross-country samples and long time series tell the same story. The Grand Transition has strong implications for the economic history of the world (s6), which can be interpreted by the good old two-sector model (s7). There are many temporary exceptions, and a large one for the OPEC/MENA countries (s8). The seven institutional indices analyzed in Part II are introduced (s9), and it is shown that they are strongly related to income. All seven give strong but fuzzy relations (s10). A key issue in the book is that the main causal direction is from income to each index, but it is necessary to be modest when analyzing causality (s11). Finally, the empirical strategy is presented (s12).

I.I THE TRANSITION CONCEPT: TWO UNCONTROVERSIAL EXAMPLES

Theoretically, a transition is a change from one *steady state* to another. The *equilibrium* concept in growth theory is the steady state, where the level and growth of production and income are determined by technology. Economic history tells us about two basic steady states. The **traditional** with an almost constant technology, giving low income and very low growth, describes the world until the middle of the eighteenth century, when some countries started to grow. Today, a slowly growing group of countries is in the *modern* steady state with a dynamic international technology that gives a high income and a growth of about 2%.

Most countries were stuck in the traditional steady state until the middle of the twentieth century, and a large gap has developed between the two groups of countries. The change between the steady states is the Grand Transition, which involves transitions in all socioeconomic variables, where the main causal direction is from development to institutional changes.

This section looks at two of the most uncontroversial transitions – neither of which is institutional. They are depicted as the two scatterplots on Figure 1.1. They are strong but fuzzy. Part II of this book shows that institutions have transitions that are equally strong and fuzzy. The new findings in this book are that the transitions of institutions are so strong, and that the main direction of causality is from development to institutions. These findings are controversial, so I have provided much (perhaps too much) evidence.

The proxy for development on the horizontal axis of Figure 1.1 is income, y. It is the (natural) *logarithm* to *gdp*, which is GDP per capita. We know that the economy is roughly log-linear. Thus, income is roughly linear. In principle, Maddison's income data start at year 1 and go to 2016. The data are only sufficiently wide in the cross-country dimension for our purpose since 1950, as seen in Figure 1.2, but most of the series explained by income start later.

The graphs include a *transition curve*, $\Pi(y)$, where y is income. It is estimated by kernel regressions, as explained in Chapter 2. The curves look similar: They are (almost) flat at both ends and have a change with a significant slope in-between. The observations scatter greatly but the Π-curve catches the systematic long-run change, i.e., the transition. The high correlations reported on the figures are due to the large difference between the endpoints.

Figure 1.1a shows the *Agricultural Transition*, Π^s, as the share, s, of agriculture (incl. fishing and forestry) in GDP as a function of income. In LICs the share is about 40% of GDP, and in HICs it is 2–3% of GDP. The same pattern appears in the available long time series, though the share at the low end, when the present HICs were LICs, was about 10 percentage points higher. This suggests that the LICs have already seen some development, and the flat section for the LICs is not perfectly flat. However, the data are thin at the low end.

Figure 1.1b deals with the *Demographic Transition*, Π^f, shown for fertility, f. In LICs the rate is a bit higher than six, and in HICs it is a

(a)

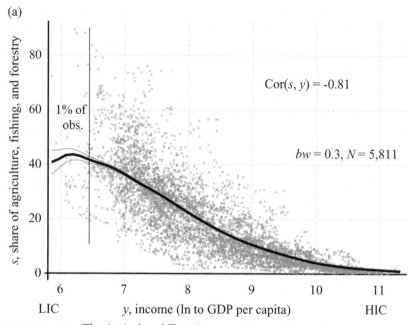

FIGURE 1.1a. The Agricultural Transition

little below two, so it points to a slow fall of the population in the HICs. Until now, it has been offset by an increasing life span. There is a similar transition curve for mortality, but it happens later, so the two parts of the change give a large increase in the size of the population.

A large literature deals with both curves. Causality is uncontroversial as regards the Agricultural Transition. Development causes the fall in the share of agriculture due to both large technical progress in agriculture and limitations in the demand for food. The transition is written $s = \Pi^s(y)$, as the path of the share of agriculture s as a function of income y. Chapter 7 takes the Agricultural Transition for granted.

Causality is less clear as regards fertility. Development reduces the need for children to provide old age support, and at the same time, they become (much) more expensive to educate. However, some causality may also be the other way. The fall in the birth rate increases the growth rate per capita, and it increases the female labor supply.[1] The transition is

---

[1] Clark (2007) has found evidence that demographic changes were causal for the start of the transition in the United Kingdom.

(b)

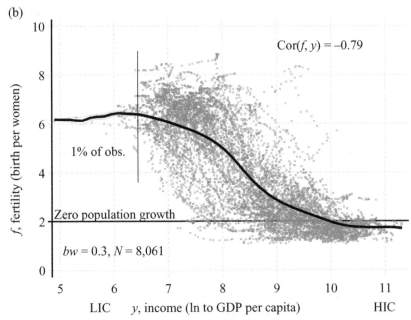

FIGURE 1.1b. The Demographic Transition, the fall in the fertility rate

The bold average curves on Figures 1a and b are a kernel regressions with bandwidth, $bw = 0.3$; see Section 2.2. The data are all N annual observations in the World Development Indicators (references) for which an income observation is available for 1960–2016. The gray lines are 95% confidence intervals for the kernel. Over most of the range, they are invisible as they are too close to the transition curves. Figure 1.1b has 37% more observations than Figure 1.1a. This gives Figure 1.1b a larger range of income at the low end. The thin vertical lines indicate 1% of the smallest observations (for y). The transition curves are fragile to the left of that line. Malthus' mechanism claims that income growth at low levels gives an extra rise in the population, i.e., the slope on Figure 1.1a is positive. There is a weak tendency for this to occur at the very low end in Figure 1.1b, where the data are fragile, but as soon as the data are more than a handful of observations, the weak signs of a rising fertility curve vanish.

written $f = \Pi^f(y)$ for fertility as a function of income y. The relation may need a correction for simultaneity.

The reader will know of other variables that have transitions. Modern production requires much human capital, people move to towns, etc. A key message of this book is that institutions have transitions too – they look much like Figure 1.1. The Π-curves found for institutional indices are often even clearer than the two uncontroversial ones.

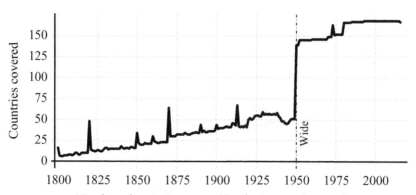

FIGURE 1.2. Number of countries covered by the income data used

The spikes are years where a researcher has assessed the incomes of a set of countries; see Maddison (2002). "Wide" means that there are enough countries at all income levels to allow an estimate of the transition.

1.2 THE TWO BASIC STEADY STATES AND THE GRAND TRANSITION

The two graphs of Figure 1.1 illustrate the argument made on the first page of this chapter: The flat sections on the two curves correspond to the two basic steady states (see Kuznets 1965, Maddison 2001, and Galor 2011), where all ratios are roughly constant. Consequently, technology determines income and growth.

The *traditional steady state* (roughly the LICs) describes all countries before about 1750. As seen from Table 1.2, the average growth per century was in the range of –0.1% to 0.2%. Technologies differed between the continents, but their *gdp*s were rather similar. The populations were also nearly constant, with high fertility and mortality. As countries leave the traditional steady state at different times, *divergence* in countries around this steady state occurs. It is already visible in the last row of the table. The simple fact that the *gdp* of all countries stayed (almost) constant for so many years, as showed in Table 1.2, is a strong indication that the countries were in equilibrium, i.e., in a steady state.

Malthus (1801) presented an equilibrium-upholding mechanism for a country near a subsistence level with a constant technology, where the relation between arable land and the population determined population and *gdp*. In the mechanism, growth caused population growth, reducing farmland per capita. This pulled countries back to the equilibrium. It also worked the other way if disasters, such as war and epidemics, reduced the

TABLE 1.2. *Long historical* gdp *data: the traditional steady state*

Year	Countries	*gdp*	Std	Max	Min	Growth(%)
1	11	1,100	240	1,550	540	–
1000	10	1,100	340	1,840	700	0
1500	15	1,150	375	1,840	430	0.01
1700	12	1,242	600	3,550	430	0.03

The means are rounded to nearest 50. If a country has no observation in the year, but later in the century, the first of these observations is used. The country selection changes somewhat, so the growth rates are crude approximations. Growth is average annual growth. Source: Maddison Project 2018.

population. This gave the surviving farmers more farmland, allowing the population to grow back. This mechanism was the first (gruesome) low-level equilibrium trap, but others have been proposed, making the traditional steady state an equilibrium; see Azariadis and Stachurski (2005). It is a big question whether the traditional steady state persists in a situation where technologies that are more efficient are available from abroad. Chapter 13 looks for such traps, with limited success.

The ***modern steady state*** (HICs) uses a dynamic international technology that gives much higher incomes, which grow at about 2% per year, and the population is once again near constant with low fertility and mortality. The difference between the two steady states grows by about 2% per year, and today it has reached about 60 times (in PPP-prices). Thanks to the international nature of modern technology, countries approaching the modern steady state ***converge***, and once they reach the steady state, the *gdp* of countries differ by less than 50% (0.4 log points). A large literature deals with convergence of modern countries, and how strong it is will be demonstrated; see e.g., Chapters 4 and 12.

The change from one steady state to another is termed a transition; thus, the change from the traditional to the modern steady state is the ***Grand Transition***, where everything in society changes, including its institutions. During this process, countries deviate systematically from either steady state – it is surely misleading to see these deviations as random or noise.

Empirically, an economy is close to a steady state when income fluctuates around a linear path. It makes most "big ratios," such as the rates of saving and consumption, almost constant. The steady state is never perfect: Apart from fluctuations, some ratios, such as mortality, keep falling slowly.

This framework predicts that the growth paths of countries diverge at the low-income levels and converge at high-income levels. Chapter 12 shows that the average country has one peak in between, so that once countries start to grow, they have a fair chance to reach a higher growth than the richer countries, and thus to catch up. However, the transition is a complex process, which is highly variable, and crises often occur on the way. Chapter 13 shows that the transition of institutions adds to the variability and hence harms investments and growth; see also Chapter 3 on the large change out of Soviet socialism.

The traditional political system are variants of hereditary/dynastic kingdoms based on a feudal economic system, while the modern political system is democracy based on a capitalist economic system but with a substantial public sector, as discussed in subsequent chapters.

1.3 PROPERTIES OF THE TRANSITION PATH, Π^X

Figures 1.1a, 1.1b, and many later graphs show the "underlying" path for the variable X diverging from the traditional steady state and converging to the modern steady state, giving a distinct ⌐ shape, as already appeared in Figure 1.1. In first differences, the form becomes a ⌐ shape. These shapes will reappear many times in this book. They are discussed in Section 2.1.

Much of the variation in such large unified data samples is due to the many differences between the countries, but this book concentrates on the general underlying transition path that has a *hypothetical equilibrium property*: If a country could stabilize at income y, all variables with transitions should converge to their $\Pi(y)$-values. This would imply that technology became stable too, so it is not possible. However, it still means that the Π-path must work as an *attractor* for the X variable. Most countries have long periods above or below the path. That is, *too much or too little X* at its level of income. This allows us to pose policy questions differently. Instead of asking if democracy is good for development, one should ask if too much democracy is good for development. That is, if a country has more democracy than other countries at its income level, does it develop faster?

This suggests that it is fruitful to consider the distance to the transition path as a *tension* variable. If the country has too much X, the tension is positive, and the attraction from the transition path should cause X to fall. Vice versa: If the country has too little X, the tension is negative, and the attraction from the path should cause X to rise. The Jumps Model in Chapter 5 finds that the changes of X happen randomly, but when they happen, they are proportional to the tension with a factor of proportionality of about -1.5, which causes X to move much more than necessary. This all adds to the excess movements of X.

A main problem with interpreting institutional variables is that institutions normally have a great deal of inertia. For near continuous institutions such as the economic system, major reforms are rare, and take time to implement, but there are often many small changes in different directions. Institutions that are in the minds and traditions of people, such as corruption and religiosity, change slowly and often have J-curves, so they react differently in the short and long run.

Political system variables are integers with long spells of constancy. This does not only reflect measurement problems but also the reality of *regime consolidation*. Leaders of a political system normally try to consolidate their system, as discussed in Chapter 7. This causes political systems to reach *status quo equilibria*, so that changes are rare, but when they happen, they are often so large that it is clear when they happen. When system variables are in status quo equilibria, they need *triggering events* to change. Later, I find that most triggering events are *unforeseen and have complex explanations that do not generalize*. Such events are termed *practically exogenous*, as discussed in a moment. Once they occur, the Jumps Model claims that they cause changes in the direction suggested by the tensions.

1.4 WHAT DETERMINES TRANSITION PATHS?

Given that transition paths have an equilibrium property, it is important to understand the mechanisms behind the Π-paths.

The different chapters in Part II of the book present a number of such mechanisms. The key factor turning the transitions into long processes is that development itself is a gradual process that normally takes a couple of centuries. In addition, beliefs and traditions have great inertia, so they need the shift between generations to change.

Some examples of the mechanics in the transitions are as follows: Chapter 7 on the Three Pillars Model argues that the agricultural and religious transitions change the power structure in society and thereby the political system. Chapter 10 on corruption argues that modern mass production and large-scale retail trade squeeze the space for corruption. Chapter 11 on the religious transition argues that the knowledge base of society changes from being dominated by religious knowledge controlled by the church, to becoming larger and less controllable with the rapid development of secular scientific and technological knowledge. In addition, Chapter 11 shows that as the education and health sectors grow, the role of churches in these sectors is squeezed, and thus religion gets a smaller role in society, etc.

Thus, there are many reasons why transitions are slow, but very real, processes. As we go along, we will encounter more such reasons. In addition, it is important to recognize that the transitions in the different fields interact. Development is a strongly confluent process, as is shown by the factor analysis of Section 2.2.

1.5 EQUIVALENCE: WIDE CROSS-COUNTRY SAMPLES AND LONG TIME SERIES TELL THE SAME STORY

As transitions normally take a couple of centuries, the study of transitions requires *long* time series. Few time series cover even one century. A *wide* cross-country sample is a sample that contains countries at all stages of development – such datasets exist for the institutional indices studied in this book. They also reflect the transitions as shown in Figure 1.1. Thus, transitions can be studied both in long time series and in wide cross-country samples. The idea that the two dimensions tell roughly the same story is termed the *equivalence hypothesis*.

If possible, the theory that the cross-country pattern found should be confirmed by long time series for each variable analyzed. This has been done for the Democratic Transition, and for the Transition in the Growth Rate, where equivalence is fine approximation. When time series do not exist, I have looked for proxies and surveys of historical narratives, which also seem to confirm equivalence. Thus, we can have some confidence that results reached in one dimension generalize to the other: Equivalence can be taken as the *default*.

Equivalence suggests that panel data can be stacked into one string to give *unified* data samples, such as used for Figure 1.1.[2] Unified samples give large values of N. This makes kernel regressions smooth, with small standard errors, so that the confidence bands of kernels become narrow – often amazingly so. The bands contain both the usual errors due to fluctuations and noise, and the error made by the stacking. If the standard errors are small, the unification errors must be small too, and thus equivalence is a good approximation.

Economic theory gives qualitative predictions that often include the form of the relation. As discussed in Chapter 2, such predictions can be tested by kernel regressions. They allow the researcher to see if the said

---

[2] Unified data samples are alternatives to the much more popular panel-data methods. Both approaches have many advantages. Most of this book explores the advantages of unified samples.

form is possible within the confidence intervals of the kernel. The form-tests become strong when the confidence intervals are narrow.

1.6 ECONOMIC DEVELOPMENT IN A WIDE CROSS-COUNTRY SAMPLE

Figure 1.3 shows economic development in the form of four cross-country graphs. Graph (A) is the situation before the transition started. Here, countries were in the traditional steady state and had roughly the same income and a low growth rate.

Graph (B) shows that a century later a few countries have started to grow, but the traditional steady state still dominates. Graph (C) shows that in 1950 a group of HICs has developed. As the HICs grow faster

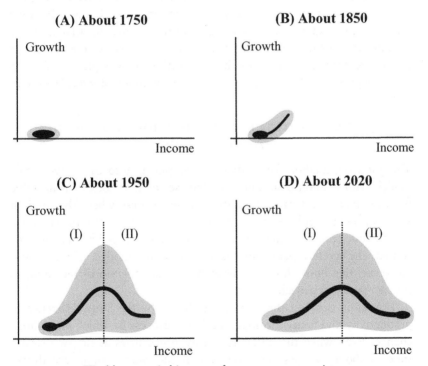

FIGURE 1.3. World economic history as four cross-country pictures

The graphs show the cross-country pattern of development. The gray areas around the bold average curve represent the fuzziness. Countries diverge in sections (I) to the left, and converge in sections (II) to the right. The extreme top curves in the two last graphs are the miracle growth discussed in Section 7. See also Chapter 13.

than the LICs, the gap between the LICs and the HICs grows. The group of LICs was still large, but now many countries were on the way. Therefore, Section (I) had divergence, while Section (II) had convergence. This picture continues in Graph (D), which shows the situation today. The HIC-group has grown larger, while the LIC-group is smaller. In the last three to five decades, the rapid increase in communication between the countries of the world has greatly influenced development. Many modern technologies seep into the traditional sector. Even in the poorest countries, trucks have taken over the transport of goods and people, and mobile phones are everywhere. Consequently, the number of countries at the traditional steady state falls rapidly, and their growth rate is higher. However, the distance from the traditional to the modern steady state keeps growing, so the number of countries in the HIC-group grows more slowly – it has only doubled in the last 50 years.

Consequently, I predict that the number of HIC-countries will grow much faster in the next 50 years. The countries in the area between the two steady states have a higher growth rate on average than at either end, but their growth also has a high variation. A two-sector model can explain the transition curve; see the next section and Chapter 12. The top line on Figures 1.3 (C) and (D) points to the possibility of *miracle growth*.

1.7 THE TWO-SECTOR APPROXIMATION AND THE HIGH POTENTIAL GROWTH

The good old method for studying development is to use a two-sector model, with a traditional and a modern sector that coexist in unstable balance. Here the Grand Transition is the process where the modern sector gradually replaces the traditional. Such models were the standard tool to understand development in the 1970s and 1980s,[3] but as the focus shifted, the models were replaced by one-sector models in the 1990s. However, this book discusses development, so it is worth returning to the two-sector approach.

The shifts between the sectors are driven by the large difference in productivity and hence incomes, and in the process by which institutions change. Even when the difference between countries at the two steady states is about 60 times, the two sectors in the same economy are always somewhat impure – some modern technology seeps into the traditional

---

[3] It goes back to Lewis (1954) and Ranis and Fei (1961). It was updated in Lucas (2009); see Chapter 12.

sector, and modern sectors often have pockets where traditional methods survive. Thus, the difference in productivity between the sectors is typically "only" five to eight times.

Without flows between the two sectors, the theory suggests that a standard one-sector growth model, such as the Solow model, can describe the growth of either sector. Technological growth is rather different in the sectors, as explained previously. However, the core of the two-sector approach is the flows between the sectors. The flows are due to the disequilibrium between the sectors, so they are the nonsteady state part of the model.

The two-sector model predicts that growth has two components. One is the weighted internal growth in the two sectors that follows the average growth of the countries in the two steady states, i.e., it is below 2%. The second is the **growth premium** that happens when resources move from the low-productivity traditional sector to the high-productivity modern sector. The premium is potentially large. Imagine a year where 1% of the labor force moves from the traditional sector to employment in the modern sector. This would give 5–8% extra growth – such growth is known as miracle growth.[4]

Miracles have happened, notably in East Asia, but as implied by the name, they are rare. Chapter 13 discusses why the potential growth is so difficult to reach. A key reason is that the transition causes large changes in institutions, which many people see as instability that harms investment and growth. The changes are often larger than demanded by the transition. Chapter 13 defines the G-ratio (for the gross to net changes) as the sum of the numerical system changes over the changes necessary for the transition. In many countries, the G-ratio is quite large.

1.8 THE OPEC EXCEPTION AND THREE PROBLEMS

Some transitions are driven by windfalls, which in practice happen as a result of the exploitation of large deposits of valuable resources. The exploitation of a resource may lead to a lot of employment with (large) side effects in the rest of the economy. However, this is not always the case.

An oil sector is an extreme case, where the resource sector is an isolated enclave in the economy. It is normally located in a few heavily fenced facilities using imported technology and a few highly skilled workers. The

---

[4] This is an alternative formulation of an old observation. Technology adoption is easier than technology development, and there is a lot of scope for technology adoption in poor countries, so they should be able to grow fast.

main effect is that it provides a large inflow of taxes in foreign currency to the treasury. This flow causes a large increase in public spending and Dutch disease, with a real revaluation that harms the production of tradables; see Paldam (2013). Consequently, OPEC membership is taken as the indicator of a pure windfall, and the data are divided into the **Main** and the **OPEC** sample. It turns out that the OPEC sample is special indeed.

The two-sector model has become a little less relevant over time. Already about 40 countries are modern. They dominate the increasing flow of information and trade in the world today. As a result, bits and pieces of modern technology seep down to the poor countries. As already mentioned, trucks have taken over the transport of goods and people even in the poorest countries; towns grow rapidly; power-lines and roads spread and so do mobile phones, etc. Thus, all countries have left the traditional steady state, though some are still near, as indicated by Graph (4) in Figure 1.3. Only a dozen countries have had no economic growth per capita in the last half century. During the last quarter century, the poorest quarter of countries has had almost the same growth as the richest quarter. This is a new development, and, in addition, populations in the poorest countries are rapidly growing.

Thus, the first problem is that the bottom part of most transition curves for the LICs has turned rather confusing – this was already visible in Figure 1.1, and it will be a recurrent problem. It is important to identify low-level equilibrium traps, and the data at the low end are thin, so it is not clear that the data contain such traps, see Chapter 12. I follow the convention of inserting a thin vertical line where the first 1% of the data reached. It is typically around 6.4 for y, which corresponds to a *gdp* of \$600, which mainly occurs in African countries undergoing civil war.

The second problem is that global warming, pollution, and the scarcity of certain resources may change the world's future growth pattern. As the data are from the past, this is not so relevant, but many believe that we are close to a major break in development. However, the worldwide level of education is rising dramatically and so is the number of people working in research and development. In the past, this would have led to predictions that the growth rate would rise. However, a rising share of the new research is in the area of substituting old CO_2-heavy technologies with new cleaner ones, etc. So perhaps the growth effect of the increasing number of researchers will not be increasing growth, but increasing sustainability.

A third problem is that spatial effects are common in the data, so that events in one country spread quicker to geographical and cultural neighbors than to countries further away. Dealing with spatial effects requires special tools that are complicated to combine with our analysis. In the interest of simplicity, spatial effects are disregarded as a general factor in the analysis, though they are mentioned from time to time. They will appear in the way that countries are grouped in the analysis.

1.9 SEVEN INSTITUTIONAL VARIABLES

Table 1.3 lists the institutional variables analyzed, and gives a brief survey of the results found as regards the relation of the variable to income. Column N reports the number of observations where the institutional variable and the income variable can be paired for the period 1960–2016.

The data in columns (9) and (10) are for the Main sample. *Cor* means correlation. Note that P is scaled to increase with more democracy, while CL and PR decrease with more democracy. Both B and F increase with more capitalism. T decreases with corruption. R increases with more religiosity.

The seven variables are quite different: The two aggregate indices, P and F, represent an ambitious attempt to measure institutional systems – either political or economic – in one dimension by means of an index, which combines a number of indicators. Both indices have been greatly debated conceptually, as regards the indicators chosen and the weights used in the aggregation. The debates suggest that the indices have sizable measurement errors, but for large Ns measurement errors vanish. It is important to note that indicators used for the two indices have a marginal overlap only. Therefore, their correlation, $\text{cor}(P, F) \approx 0.45$, is not by construction.

The main political system index used is Polity, P. It has a one-dimensional scale from authoritarian to democratic, with a range from -10 (North Korea and Saudi Arabia) to $+10$ in most Western democracies. It is often argued that more dimensions are needed. The political systems in North Korea and Saudi Arabia are rather different, and so are the systems in Denmark and Switzerland. Alternative indices with more dimensions do exist, but they only provide marginal additional knowledge as regards the questions analyzed. The two political indices from Freedom House, CL and PR, are used to control the robustness of results, and so are the V-Dem indices.

The economic system index is the Fraser Index of Economic Freedom, F. It measures the freedom to run a business. Low values are given for restrictions on business, high taxes, unstable money, and lack of law and order. The index is carefully compiled in a transparent way, but it is constructed from an ideological standpoint. Consequently, F is supplemented with the B-index measuring preferences for private/public

TABLE I.3. *Institutions considered, indices used, and correlations to income, y*

(1) X	(2) Index	(3) Scale	(4) LIC	(5) HIC	(6) Π-curve	(7) Slope	(8) Simultaneity	(9) N	(10) Cor to y
Political System:									
P	Polity	[-10,10]	-2, -4	9-10	Beautiful	Positive	Not found	7,142	0.55
CL	Civil Liberties	[7,1]	5-6	1-2	Beautiful	Negative	Not found	6,163	-0.66
PR	Political Rights	[7,1]	5-6	1-2	Beautiful	Negative	Not found	6,163	-0.62
Economic system:									
B	Ownership	[-100,100]	0	17	Too linear	Positive	Some	279	0.32
F	Economic Freedom	[0,10]	2-3	6-8	Too linear	Positive	Some	1,965	0.72
Traditions and beliefs									
T	Corruption/honesty	[0, 10]	2-3	8-9	Beautiful	Positive	Not found	2,730	0.78
R	Religiosity	[0, 100]	80%	30%	Too linear	Positive	Not found	332	-0.45

ownership of business, based on the World Values Survey. It is formulated as a politically neutral question. Fortunately, the two indices give a similar transition pattern, even when the indices have a correlation of 0.20 only.

The two remaining indices are for institutions that exist in people's minds as traditions and beliefs: Transparency International's Corruption Index, T, reports perceptions of corruption on a ten-point scale, which rises when corruption falls. It is possible to see corruption/honesty as an aspect of both political and economic institutions. However, it does not enter directly in the underlying indicators of either the P or the F-index.

Religion is an important institution that, on the face of it, has little to do with development. Whether or not people belong to a religion is a binary variable that rarely changes. However, religiosity means the importance of religion for the individual – irrespective of their religion. The World Values Survey has a set of variables measuring aspects of the religiosity of respondents. This allows us to develop a robust religiosity index, R, which can be measured for 111 countries and six waves of the World Values Survey. It changes systematically with development.

1.10 DEVELOPMENT AND INSTITUTIONS: STRONG BUT FUZZY RELATIONS

All correlations in column (10) of Table 1.3 are substantial, and as significant as anyone could wish. Thus, they suggest strong relations. It is important to recognize that the relations are fuzzy. We all want to find clear and direct relations, such as the relation between prices and quantities on a market. However, as soon as one starts to think about the relation between development and any of the four institutions listed in Table 1.3, it is obvious that we are dealing with relations of a different nature.

Income is a fine proxy for development, but development is a complex process, with many dimensions. However, measures trying to catch these dimensions are strongly correlated, so development is a fuzzy band around income. In addition, it is arguable that development both causes and requires changes in all fields, and many of these changes are intermediaries in the relation between income, y, and the institutional index. When the relation between y and a system variable such as P is written as $P = P(y)$, it is a *reduced form of a fuzzy relation*. Institutions are measured by crude indices such as P or F. These indices have much inertia – most years they change very little or, in the case of P, not at all. In addition, causality is known to be controversial between income and all four institutions.

Causality is even less direct with variables such as T and R, for perceived corruption and polled religiosity, which reflect peoples' beliefs and traditions as well as their perceptions about society. They do not react in a direct way to changes of income, but they are deeply influenced by changes in society brought about by development. Thus, once again, a relation such as $T = T(y)$ is a reduced form of a strong but fuzzy relation.

The realization that we are looking for fuzzy relations is important for the choice of statistical technique. Economists consider regression techniques as the main tool, and it is a fine tool for estimating clear and direct relations. However, it is a poor tool for dealing with relations that are strong in the long run, and which work through a complex of other variables. Fortunately, there are other tools in our box, as discussed in Section 2.4.

1.11 MODEST CAUSALITY: LOOKING FOR THE MAIN CAUSAL DIRECTION AND PRACTICAL EXOGENEITY

The key idea in this book is that transitions – including transitions in institutions – are caused by development. This claim is not trivial. An alternative claim is that institutions are causal to development, as proclaimed by the *PoI*, the Primacy of Institutions school of Daron Acemoglu and associates (see their survey from 2005). Both theories start from the observation that income and institutions are correlated, as already demonstrated.

When two macro-variables such as y and X are correlated, it may be because of the causal links listed in Table 1.4. Like everybody else, I would like to find clean causal directions, but macro variables include many phenomena, so some modesty is necessary. I can only hope to find the **main causal direction**.

TABLE 1.4. *Possible causal links between income, y, and an institutional index, X*

	Causal link	Formal	Possible problem
1	Clean link from y to X	$y \Rightarrow X$	Some simultaneity, to be tested
2	Clean link from X to y	$X \Rightarrow y$	Some simultaneity, to be tested
3	Simultaneity between y and X	$y \Leftrightarrow X$	An identifying assumption is needed
4	Spuriousness, due to Z	$Z \Rightarrow y$ and $Z \Rightarrow X$	Z might be a vector
5	Intermediate variable Q	$y \Rightarrow Q \Rightarrow X$	Q might be a vector

As many variables, including the seven institutional variables, have transitions, this means that they all contain similar long-run paths, so they are confluent; see Section 2.2. I have found that the best variable to pick up this confluence is income, y, which is, of course, an aggregate of many other variables. As each institutional variable, X, has some production/income consequences, they contribute to GDP. Thus, there is inevitably some causality from X to income. It should give a simultaneity effect in the causal relation between income and the institutional variable, but the size of the effect is typically so small that it is hard to detect.

When it is found that income causes X, i.e., $y \Rightarrow X$, a problem immediately emerges. It is obvious that income is not a "truly" exogenous variable. Thus, this finding is merely one part of a larger story. It is quite possible that X is causal to variables Z and Q, which ultimately explain y. Thus, the relation $y \Rightarrow X$ should be seen as a building block in a larger model. However, it is still good to have one solid block.

When we look at another variable, Q, and find that $Q \Rightarrow X$, the story stops at Q in two cases, as follows: The ideal case is that Q is *truly exogenous*. A common example is the effect on a small country of events abroad. This brings us to the second modest concept: Q may be *practically exogenous* when Q is due to *unforeseeable events* that involve *complex* factors, which do *not generalize*. This is typically the case for larger historical events. It turns out that many triggering events setting changes into motion are of this nature; see Chapter 6.

The classical case is the First World War, which caused long-term changes in both the economic and political systems of many countries. The war broke out approximately one century ago, and a library has been written about the reasons why it happened. The triggering event was the murder of Archduke Franz Ferdinand of Austria in Sarajevo on June 28, 1914 by a Serbian nationalist. However, it is not easy to explain why this led to a war between France, the United Kingdom, Russia, and Germany just one month later. A whole set of complex factors and misconceptions came into play.[5] Historians still discuss the relative importance of these factors. It is clear that there had been tensions between the aforementioned countries for a long time, but even two weeks after the murder in Sarajevo few observers predicted that a world war would result.

Chapter 3 is a short discussion of the largest historical event in the last 50 years: The collapse of Soviet socialism, which led to many changes in

---

[5] A widespread misconception on the eve of the First World War was that wars had become less bloody.

institutions throughout the world. The triggering event happened in Moscow, where it was unforeseen, complex, and did not generalize, so it is characterized as practically exogenous. In the other countries of the Eastern Bloc, the Russian collapse was the triggering event, and hence it was truly exogenous.

Sometimes, cliometric methods may find strong evidence about historical events. Aidt and Franck (2015) is a fine example, with many tests that cover the three years leading to the 1832 democratic reforms in the United Kingdom. For our purpose, it is important that the analysis tells an unforeseen, complex story that fails to generalize to other democratic reforms.

The modesty necessary in the study of causality is part of a larger problem. We know from Arrow that a perfect aggregation of preferences is impossible, so all political systems are imperfect. Parallel proofs exist for the price index, so that a perfect aggregation of prices is impossible. It follows that the real product is imperfect too. Economics requires some modesty.

1.12 MY EMPIRICAL STRATEGY: REPLICABILITY AND ROBUSTNESS

The reader will know that a wave of recent papers discuss the related crises of **lack of replicability and publication bias** in economics – and science in general.[6]

I am undertaking a parallel project in meta-analysis of economic papers and the sociology of economic research, and I can confirm that there are indeed problems.[7] This has taught me a sobering lesson about the flexibility of the standard tools of economics. Published estimates normally have fine t-ratios above two – embarrassingly often just above two! Nevertheless, estimates from sets of studies that pertain to be of the same effect normally have amazingly wide distributions, and it is easy to pick estimates that differ significantly.

In addition, the distribution of estimates of the same effect often has interesting asymmetries pointing to publication biases. Research requires choices, and choices are affected by preferences. If one preference is

---

[6] As of now, Google Scholar has about 4 million hits on *replication* and even more hits on *publication bias*, so it is a major research question.

[7] See Doucouliagos and Paldam (2009) and Paldam (2018) and the cited literature therein.

common, it gives biases. A large literature finds and analyzes such biases. Various preferences are important. (i) One is *sponsor preferences*, where researchers with a sponsor find results that are more often in line with the sponsor's interests than other results.[8] (ii) Another bias is *theory preferences*. When theory predicts a sign on a coefficient, this causes many researchers to suppress results with the wrong sign. Thus, the average result is exaggerated in the direction of the theoretical prediction – my own rule of thumb is to expect an exaggeration by a factor of two. (iii) A *goodness preference* occurs when one sign on the coefficient is morally/politically better than others, etc.[9]

Most of the choices that create publication bias are related to the selection of control variables. Think of the panel regression, where t is time and i is county:

$$y_{it} = a_{(it)} + b x_{it} + [c_1 z_{1it} + c_2 z_{2it} + \ldots + c_n z_{nit} + \varepsilon_{it}] \tag{1.1}$$

Here b is the parameter of interest, and $a_{(it)}$ is the constant that may be broken into FE, fixed effects, for time and countries. Thus, the first two terms in Equation (1.1) require four choices (no FEs, FE for t, FE for i, both FEs). The []-brackets contain n controls. The controls belong to the Z-set of m acceptable controls, where $m > n$. The n controls can be chosen in m over n ways. This is normally a large number. If m is large, for example 50, and n is limited to 8, it yields about 5.4×10^8 estimates of b. In total, it is 2×10^9 possibilities. Each of these estimates differ. Why one is preferred over another is often difficult to know.[10] The estimates in a literature are likely to have substantial variation. The distribution of the bs is shown as replaced by the funnel that is the (b, p)-scatter, where p is the precision of the estimate. The central limit theorem suggests that the funnel is symmetric around a peak for the most precise estimates. This is precisely as found in simulation experiments of the effect of random model variation. However, parts of the funnel are often missing, and we

---

[8] If there are many competing sponsors with different preferences, the problem vanishes, but in some fields one sponsor dominates – this is often the case when a large public program finances most research in a certain field.

[9] In the following chapters, it would be good to find that good governance – in the form of democracy and low corruption – causes faster economic development. Thus, the literature may find this result too often.

[10] When lecturing, I have often written the control variables used in the preferred regression of an author on the blackboard and asked my students why these controls are chosen. This question often gives rise to a great deal of discussion, as it is rare that the controls are the only possible ones, and then there are the instruments used in TSIV regressions – often they just appear in a footnote to the key table.

can often explain why. This allows the analysis to find a meta-average that is closer to the true value than the mean.

My work with these problems has given me a strong *preference for replicability and robustness*. I trust that everything in this book is easy to replicate and very robust. I use only data everybody can download, and I use the convention that all variables are used as they came from the provider.[11] However, data are sometimes revised, or replaced by new data. Consequently, the data used are available at http://martin.paldam .dk/GT-book-data.

In addition, I have tried to be parsimonious with control variables. That is, I only use controls that are strongly justified by the theory discussed. Hence, I trust that the *t*-ratios are believable. If the *t*-ratio is larger than two, the estimate is bolded.

All calculations are made with Stata. In the few cases where more advanced statistics are used, the Stata add-on code is available from the author (at least for some years). It is important to stress that this book is problem-driven, rather than driven by econometric technique. This reflects the common finding in meta-analysis that little of the great variability of estimates is due to estimators, except in rare cases.

---

[11] When you work with indices with thousands of observations, you normally find some you do not believe. For the Polity index, I find it hard to understand why Singapore is 6 P-points below Russia (2010–17). For the Fraser index, I do not believe that Romania in 1985 had more economic freedom than South Korea. Even in such cases, I have not changed the value.

2

Some Technical Points

The nine sections of Chapter 2 introduce the techniques used in this book (Table 2.1). First, the *five properties* of an ideal transition curve are listed (s1). A factor analysis of the four main variables gives one and only one strong common factor – it is the joint transition.

The literature shows that the usual regression tools often fail to find transitions. It is argued that the tools are wrong for the problem (s3). A more appropriate tool is *kernel regressions* on unified data samples using income as the organizing variable. The logic of this tool is explained (s4), and it is demonstrated that kernel regressions effectively scramble the panel structure, so that only the income variable matters for the form of the kernel (s5). The kernels found have most or all of the five properties within narrow confidence intervals. Thus, kernel

TABLE 2.1. *Terminology used in Chapter 2*

Transition terminology for the institutional index X (a)

Traditional steady state. All countries in 1750 and low-income countries (LICs) until recently.

Modern steady state. High-income countries today (HICs), with the OPEC exception.

Grand transition. The path that connects a low-level divergence and a high-level convergence.

X_{it}	*Panel* representation of the variable, where i is the country and t is time (a).
X_j	*Unified* representation, where j is the order of the data. Divided into *Main* and *OPEC* samples.
$\Pi^X(y_j)$	*Transition* curve. X_j is sorted by y_j. Gives the net change in X, necessary for the transition.
λ^X	*Slope* of transition curve, $\lambda^X = \partial\Pi^X/\partial y$. It has the same sign, either $\leq$ or $\geq$, for full y-range.
$K^X(y_j, bw)$	*Kernel* estimate of $\Pi^X(y_j)$, with bandwidth bw. Thus, $K^X(y_j bw) \approx \Pi^X(y_j)$.
Θ	*Tension* variable, $\Theta = X(y)-\Pi^X(y)$. If $\Theta > 0$, the country has too much X, and vice versa.
G^X-*ratio*	*Excess* movements in X. The gross movements in X relative to the net change.

Note (a): In this chapter, X is one of the bounded indices for the level of institutions P, F, or T; see Table 1.2. These four variables are all scaled to increase with y as in graph (B) in Figure 2.1.

curves are fine estimates of transition curves. This allows (s6) the interpretation of the curves as *equilibrium* paths, so that they are attractors for changes in the indices.

Three causality tests are used. (s7) The beauty test compares two reverse kernels – one explaining the index by income and the other explaining income by the index. It is often easy to see which explanation is closest to its theory. Correlograms for income and each index are used to show whether either variable can predict the other. The DP-test is a formal TSIV-test (two-stage instrument variable) using the development potential of countries as instruments for income (s8). Finally, whether transition curves may be artifacts is discussed (s9).

2.1 VARIANTS OF THE TRANSITION CURVE, $\Pi^X(y_j)$

The variable of interest is termed X. Table 2.2 shows the characteristics of a Π^X-curve – if it has all these characteristics, it is termed beautiful. Figure 2.1 shows how such curves should look.

TABLE 2.2. *Six characteristics of a beautiful transition curve for the variable* X

No	Characteristic of the transition path for a variable with a bounded range
1	Traditional (low-end) steady state level, X^T. Countries diverge from this level.
2	Modern (high-end) steady state level, X^M. Countries converge to this level.
3	X^T and X^M are rather different.
4	Average path is smooth between the two levels – the slope has the same sign.
5	Explanatory power is substantial, but the transition does not explain everything.
6	The transition is a causal relation from y to X, though it may have a simultaneity bias.

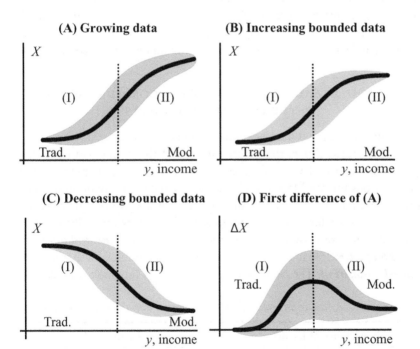

FIGURE 2.1. Transition curves, $X = \Pi(y)$

"Trad." and "Mod." are short for the traditional steady state and the modern steady state. The vertical dotted line is where the transition is fastest. The area (I) to the left of the line has divergence, and the area (II) to the right of the line has convergence. Graph (D) is graphs (C) and (D) from Figure 1.2. The curves on figure (A) to (C) are for *level* variables, while (D) is for a *first difference* variable. The gray areas point to the fuzziness around the transition curve. It is particularly large on graph (D) for the first difference data.

Graph (A) considers a growing variable, such as a GDP component. It is constant at the traditional level, but it grows faster than GDP during the transitions, and it ends by growing parallel with GDP in the modern steady state. The transitions for bounded indices are flat at the two ends, so they look like graph (B) or (C), depending on the scaling of the data.

As the slope of the transition curve for a *level* variable has the same sign (either $\geq$ or $\leq$), the changes along the curve are net changes adding up to the transition, where the G^X-ratio is one. In practice, most countries go through more changes, for any X-variable, giving a G^X-ratio that is well above one, as discussed in Chapter 1.

Chapter 12 analyzes the growth rate of GDP. It looks like graph (D) in Figure 2.1. The "corresponding" graph in (log) levels (A) makes no sense, as it has the same variable at both axes. This reflects that the GDP is the aggregate of all sectors, so that when some increase (relatively), others have to fall (relatively). In this case, graph (D) is the interesting one. It is **hump-shaped**, as it is the first difference of many graphs looking like (B) and (D). However, by going to the first difference, the variation around the curve becomes larger.

2.2 THE GRAND TRANSITION AS THE COMMON FACTOR IN THE FOUR MAIN DATASETS

The four main annual datasets used in the book are (i) y, income, (ii) P, the Polity index, (iii) F, the Fraser index, and (iv) T, the Transparency corruption index. The four variables have 1,965 overlapping annual observations for the Main sample. Table 2.3 reports a factor analysis of the four variables. Factor1 has an eigenvalue of 2.4, while higher factors have eigenvalues far below the acceptable level that is normally set at 1. Thus, the analysis shows that these four variables have **one and only one common factor**. It loads strongly to all four variables. I claim that it is the **Grand Transition**. The claim will be supported as the book proceeds.

TABLE 2.3. *A factor analysis of the four annual variables T, y, F, and P*

Importance of factors				Factor loadings		
Factor	Eigenvalue	Cumulative		Variable	Factor1	Factor2
Factor1	2.416	1.098		T-index	0.856	−0.048
Factor2	0.018	1.106		y, income	0.850	−0.055
Factor3	−0.114	1.054		F-index	0.827	0.040
Factor4	−0.120	1.000		P-index	0.526	0.103

Run for $N = 1,965$ overlapping observations. Gray shading indicates results that are of no consequence.

2.3 PROBLEMATIC REGRESSION TECHNIQUES

The toolkit of economists is full of regression techniques. For the study of transitions, they have four problems: (a) Transitions are slow, so the data have a lot of inertia; (b) they occur in many variables, creating confluence; (c) they are nonlinear; and (d) they are fuzzy. The present section concentrates on problem (a).

The (X, y)-scatter often looks like one of the graphs in Figure 1.1, where the two variables are highly correlated. Typically, the data are short in time (e.g., two to three decades) and wide in countries (e.g., 150). If we try to estimate the effect of income with models (1) and (2):

$$X_{it} = \alpha + \beta_1 y_{it} + u_{1it} \qquad \text{is a cross-country country}$$
$$\text{long-run relation, with residuals } u. \quad (2.1)$$

$$X_{it} = \alpha + \gamma X_{it-1} + \beta_2 y_{it} + u_{1it} \qquad \text{is the corresponding short-run}$$
$$\text{adjustment model.} \qquad (2.2)$$

Regression (2.1) will typically get a positive coefficient, with a high t-ratio such as 20, so all looks well. If the short-run relation is clear and direct and the data are plentiful, (2.2) may also hold rather well, and it can be solved for the steady state.[1] It gives credibility if (2.1) and (2.2) give consistent estimates of the steady state slope β^*:

$$\beta^* \approx \beta_1 \approx \beta_2/(1 - \gamma) \qquad (2.3)$$

Provided the equivalence hypothesis is valid, β^* is an estimate of the slope of the transition curve, and the kernel curve discussed in the next section will have this slope. If X_{it} has too much inertia, γ may be so close to the unit root of one that (2.2) becomes shaky, and (2.3) breaks down.

The standard way to concentrate on the short run is to clean the relation for country differences and common time trends, which is done by breaking the constant into fixed effects α_i and α_t for countries and years, respectively:

$$X_{it} = \alpha_i + \alpha_t + \beta y_{it} + u_{2it} \qquad \text{by adding the short-run}$$
$$\text{adjustments, it becomes} \qquad (2.4)$$

$$X_{it} = \gamma X_{it-1} + \alpha_i + \alpha_t + \beta y_{it} + u_{2it} \qquad \text{L2FE-estimate}$$
$$\text{(Lagged } X, 2 \text{ fixed effects)} \quad (2.5)[2]$$

If X_{it} has a lot of inertia, α_i and X_{it-1} will be collinear, and hence the estimates of the fixed effects, notably α_i, may come to reduce the effect of

---

[1] The steady state solution to (2.2) is reached by setting $X_{it-1} = X_{ti}$, and solving for X_{it}.
[2] In the econometric literature, it is often termed a GDPM regression, standing for generic dynamic panel model.

X_{it-1}, making the estimate of γ too small, so that (2.3) does not hold any more. This is surely the case when institutions are stable most years and only change by occasional jumps, as in the case of the *P*-index (Polity). In such cases, (2.5) is the wrong tool; see the second part of Chapter 5.

Acemoglu et al. (2008) used model (2.5) to show that income has no effect on democracy, i.e., the *P*-index. Gundlach and Paldam (2010) replicate their result and show that in addition, it makes the Agricultural Transition and the Demographic Transition (from Figure 1.1) and several other transitions go away. This suggests that the L2FE-estimation model is the wrong tool for a strong and fuzzy relation with a lot of inertia. As we are close to a unit root, anything can happen; see Section 5.5.

Transitions often have larger movements than necessary, i.e., the *G*-ratio is larger than 1. Thus, the variable fluctuates around the transition path. If it is below the path, an income shock will move it upward, but if it is above the path, it may move it downward. Hence, it is no wonder that the L2FE-estimate tends to find very little – even when there is a lot to be found.

2.4 ESTIMATING THE TRANSITION CURVE, Π: FROM SCATTERS TO KERNELS

The best method I have found for estimating transitions is to use kernel regressions on unified datasets organized by income. Such datasets easily become large, and the kernel shows the transition curve rather neatly.

The scatter-plot (X, y) of the data is a wide swarm of points that cover countries with a lot of heterogeneity, but the raw scatter normally suggests a nonlinear underlying curve as seen in Figure 1.1, and thus it averages into a neat curve by means of a kernel regression. If the curve has (most of) the properties listed in Table 2.2, it is interpreted as a transition curve:

$$X = \Pi(y) + u, \qquad \text{where } u \text{ is the noise term.}$$
$$\text{(6) is estimated by the kernel} \qquad (2.6)$$

$$X = K^X(y, bw) \approx \Pi(y), \qquad \text{where } bw \text{ is the band width} \qquad (2.7)$$

A kernel regression is a smoothed MA-process with a fixed bandwidth, bw. This book always estimates kernels by means of the Stata command *lpoly*. The program (and presumably all other kernel-programs) has a number of options. Two defaults are always used: The smoothing formula is Epanechnikov's kernel. The results are amazingly robust to variation of this choice. The degree of polynomial smooth is kept at zero. In addition, the following options are used: *nos*catter suppresses the scatter, *ci* provides 95% confidence *i*ntervals, and *gen*erate outputs the kernel curves as a data series.

Economic theory often predicts the qualitative form of a relation, as, for example, the predictions in Table 2.2. The confidence intervals allow us to test if a curve of the predicted form is possible within the intervals estimated. Large unified datasets normally yield amazingly narrow *ci*s, so the 'form test' is strong.

The robustness of the kernel is always analyzed by means of a set of experiments: Kernels are calculated for separate decades, and for different groups of countries. Systematic experiments are always made with the bandwidth, *bw*. Too short bandwidths give a wobbly curve, where some unexplainable stochastic fluctuations remain. As the bandwidth increases, the curve becomes smoother but also gradually more linear, and, in the end, it converges to a horizontal line at the average. In my experience, there is always a broad *bw*-range where the curve has the same form. The "central" estimate is the curve with the clearest form. Deviations of 25% or even 50% in the *bw*, from the central estimate, are barely visible on the curve. Stata calculates a rule-of-thumb bandwidth, which is a fine starting point, but the weighting formula favors narrow *ci*'s that catch too many random fluctuations of the curve. I prefer interpretability, so a slightly larger bandwidth is preferred.

The great advantage of kernel regression is that it is a nonparametric technique, which does not presume a functional form. Thus, if the variable has a transition, the kernel will find a nice, and often even a beautiful, curve looking like Figure 2.1, with most or even all of the characteristics listed in Table 2.2. More advanced statistical methods exist – and this also applies to nonparametric techniques.[3] However, I am looking for the big pattern in the data, and I do not try to explain everything.

---

[3] One of the papers received a referee report that concentrated on this point and recommended a handful of papers using frontline nonparametric statistics. These papers were indeed advanced, but the statistical techniques had managed to squeeze out all economics, and they reached results that neither the authors nor we could interpret. It is important that new methods are developed but also that development only happens when they become useful.

2.5 SCRAMBLING TESTS IN THE DATA OF THE MAIN SAMPLE
FOR THE AVERAGE KERNEL

Kernel regression $X = K^X(y, bw)$ starts by sorting all (X, y)-observations by income, y. The kernel is a useful analytical tool if the sorting randomizes the panel structure. This means that the countries and years do not cluster within the bandwidth. To examine if this is the case, two *scrambling tests* are run. Scrambling is also important to break the complex processes in the residuals, as further discussed in Chapter 8. All kernels presented use (subsets of) the 7,142 income observations in the Main sample. The sample spans 140 countries and 57 years from 1960 to 2016. The average kernel uses approximately 250–400 sorted observations from this dataset. When it is divided by 325, it yields 22 non-overlapping subsets, which corresponds to the number of observations within the bandwidth of the average kernel.

Scrambling test 1: In the average subset, an observation, y_{it}, is followed by an observation for the same country, y_i, in 4.3% of cases, and by an observation for the following year, y_{t+1}, in 3.5% of cases. In 0.7% of cases, y_{it} is followed by an observation for the same country and the following year, y_{it+1}. The scrambling is least complete in the first and last of the 22 subsets. The three numbers listed fall to 2.9%, 3.2%, and 0.5%, respectively, if the two outermost subsets are disregarded. I consider these results satisfactory.

Scrambling test 2: This test calculates the country and time range in the average sample. The average number of countries within each subset is 52, or 37% of the 140 countries. Nearly all samples contain observations that spans the full 57 years. It is only the last two subsamples that have a shorter time-range. Once again, this is rather satisfactory.

2.6 THE ATTRACTION MECHANICS, THE TENSION VARIABLE,
Θ, AND THE EXCESS MOVEMENT

Section 1.3 discussed how transition curves should be understood. It suggested some mechanics: If the kernel $X = K^X(y, bw)$ shows a nice $\Pi^X(y)$-curve, it is the hypothetical equilibrium path during the transition. There are many reasons for the big variation around the Π^X-curve, but there must be a pull from the curve. It means that the Π^X-curve is an *attractor* for X. All kinds of disturbances occur to push X into (random?) walks around the Π^X-path, but X is also pulled toward the Π^X-curve. I propose that the pull from the attractor $\Pi^X(y)$ is proportional to the distance Θ (theta) from the transition curve:

$$\Theta = X - \Pi^X(y) \tag{2.8a}$$

and

$$\Delta X = -\alpha \Theta \tag{2.8b}$$

Θ is termed the **tension** variable (for X). If Θ is positive, the country has too much X at its level of income, and I predict that the country will come to see a fall in X. If Θ is negative, the country has too little X at its level of income, and I predict that the country will come to see an increase in X. Thus, Θ and ΔX should be negatively correlated.

If X is on the equilibrium path, i.e., $X = \Pi^X(y)$, $\Theta = 0$. However, when income increases from y_0 to y_1, while X is constant, X moves a little away from equilibrium, which can be seen as a change in the tension. The change is $\Delta \Pi^1 = \Pi(y_1) - \Pi(y_0)$, so the tension changes from Θ^0 to $\Theta^1 = \Theta^0 + \Delta \Pi^1$.

Think of the Democratic Transition. If a country has too much democracy (Θ^0 is positive), economic growth will reduce the tension. Vice versa, if a country has too little democracy (Θ^0 is negative), economic growth will increase the tension. If X is not on the Π-path, we expect an adjustment of X toward $\Pi(y)$ as a movement in n steps of Θ from the original value Θ^0. Step 1 reduces Θ from Θ^0 to Θ^1.[4]

Step 1 : $\Theta^1 = (1 - \alpha)\Theta^0$ during step 1 income grows, so Π changes by $\Delta \Pi^1$

Step 2 : $\Theta^2 = (1 - \alpha)^2(\Theta^0 + \Delta \Pi^1)$ this continues

Step n : $\Theta^n = (1 - \alpha)^n(\Theta^0 + \Delta \Pi^{n-1})$ where $\Delta \Pi^{n-1}$ is the change in Π since the start $\tag{2.9}$

Equation (2.9) makes sense only if α is in the interval from 0 to 2 [0, 2], so that numerically the tension falls if $\Delta \Pi$ is small (as it surely is). If the steps are small, for example, a year, $\Delta \Pi$ is negligible, but (as shown in Chapter 7) the steps might be long, perhaps a decade apart. Thus, $\Delta \Pi$ might not be negligible. Consider a situation where X is on the Π-path. Now one disturbance occurs that pushes X to Θ^0 – no further disturbances occur. As the number of adjustments n rises, the numerical value $|\Theta^n| \rightarrow 0$. Thus, X converges to the Π-curve, as shown in Figure 2.2.

---

[4] Chapters 5 and 6 show that while the adjustments are as predicted, it is very difficult to predict when they occur.

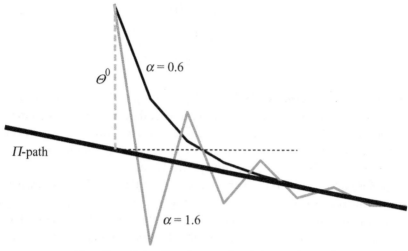

FIGURE 2.2. The effect of the disturbance Θ° and the resulting adjustments
Π-path for $\alpha = 0.6$ is the black declining transition path in the figure. The eight first steps
of the adjustment process are visible. For $\alpha = 1.6$, it gives the gray adjustment path,
where every step overshoots the Π-path. The horizontal dotted line shows when the
adjustment has reached the old value of X, but in the meantime, Π has moved due to the
growth of income.

If α is in the interval $[0, 1]$, the adjustments sum to Θ°, and the number
of steps necessary to go back to the Π-path is larger, the smaller α is. If
$\alpha = 1$, X goes to the path in one step. The total amount of numerical
change in X due to the disturbance is thus $2\Theta^\circ$.

If α is in the interval $[1, 2]$, the signs on Θ'' change from step to step in
the process, as shown with the gray zigzag curve in Figure 2.2. This means
the X *overshoots* the Π-path, so that the convergence to the Π-path takes
the form of damped oscillations around the path. Hence, the sum of the
numerical steps is larger than the original disturbance.

Figure 2.3 suggests the size of the total variation caused by a random
disturbance of 1 unit. If $\alpha = 1.5$ (as found in Chapter 5), the total change
becomes 4. A disturbance of one P-point leads to three extra P-points of
changes in due time. This is all part of the excess amount of institutional
change leading to the large G-ratios found in Chapter 14. While the
mechanism of the adjustment to the path is simple, the timing of the steps
is a more difficult question, which will be a recurrent theme in Part II of
the book.

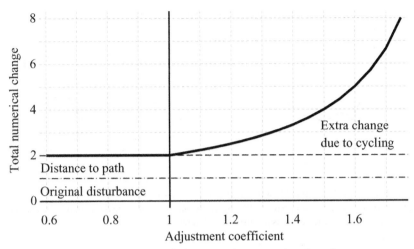

FIGURE 2.3. The total numerical change as function of α, the adjustment coefficient

To the left of the vertical line (at $\alpha = 1$), X returns to the equilibrium path by steps that add to 1. Thus, the total change is $2\Theta°$. The size of α determines the adjustment speed. To the right of the vertical line, the adjustments are damped cycles, giving extra numerical changes. More cycles are needed if α is large.

2.7 THREE WAYS TO ESTABLISH THE MAIN CAUSAL DIRECTION

I now turn to methods for distinguishing between two causal directions: $y \Rightarrow X$ and $X \Rightarrow y$. This section discusses three methods, while Section 2.8 discusses a fourth.

Method one. An economic model is a causal explanation. If it fits the data, this is causal evidence; see in particular Chapter 5 on the Jumps Model. In addition, I use three statistical tools to get an empirical handle on causality.

Method two. Causality in the long run. The **beauty test** for kernels (see Paldam 2019a). Transition theory proposes that $y \Rightarrow X$, and that $X = \Pi^X(y)$ has the form described in Table 2.2. Thus, the kernel $X = K^X(y)$ should have the said form. If an alternative Λ-theory proposes that $X \Rightarrow y$, and that $y = \Lambda(X)$ has a particular form, it can be estimated by $y = K^y(X)$. Hence, we compare the two kernel estimates that correspond to two theories:

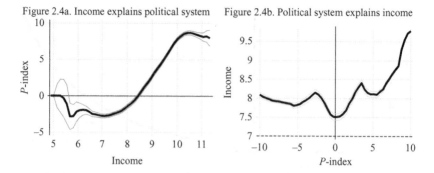

Figure 2.4a. Income explains political system Figure 2.4b. Political system explains income

FIGURE 2.4. Example of two reverse causal theories
Both curves use the default bandwidth chosen by Stata. The income data are thin below 6.4.
The economics of the curves is discussed in Chapter 4.

$$X = K^X(y, bw) \approx \Pi(y) \quad \text{which tells us if the } \Pi\text{-theory can explain the data}$$
$$(2.10)$$

$$y = K^y(X, bw) \approx \Lambda(X) \quad \text{which tells us if the } \Lambda\text{-theory can explain the data}$$
$$(2.11)$$

In (2.10) the dataset is sorted by y, and the average (over bw) is calculated around each y. In (11) the dataset is sorted by X, and the average (over bw) is calculated around each X. These calculations are quite different, so it is no wonder that the reverse kernels often look strikingly different. Furthermore, normally only one looks as it should according to its theory. This is causal evidence in favor of the winning theory. The two graphs in Figure 2.4 show the Democratic Transition from Chapter 4 and the reverse curve. The transition curve looks beautiful, while the reverse makes little sense. Thus, Figure 2.4 (strongly) suggests that the main direction is from income to the P-index. The Democratic Transition (shown) and the Transition of Corruption analyzed in Chapters 4 and 10, respectively, both lead to beautiful curves, while the reverse kernels do not look as they should according to any theory.

Method three. Causality in the short run. Most chapters use a Granger-like causality test in the form of correlograms based on time-series of n_1 years for n_2 countries. For country i the correlogram is:

$$\text{cor}\left(X_{it}, y_{it+j}\right), \text{ where } j = -q, \ldots, +q, \quad \text{where } q \text{ is a number such}$$
$$\text{as 5 or larger} \quad (2.12)$$

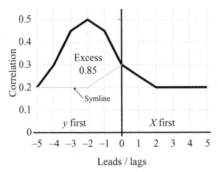

FIGURE 2.5. Hypothetical example of correlogram test

Each point drawn as the bold black curve is the average of the

$$n_2 \text{ country-correlations} \qquad (2.13)$$

Figure 2.5 is a hypothetical illustration of the average correlogram. Long-run confluence appears as a level of the correlogram. In the figure, the underlying level is 0.2. Correlograms often have a hump that goes above or below that level. If the hump is for X before y, which means that X is a predictor of y. If the hump is for y before X, then y is a predictor of X, as in the example. This indicates that y predicts X, and is taken as an indication of the causal direction. To see the hump as clearly as possible, the gray *symline* is drawn. This gives the half of the correlogram that has the lowest correlations drawn symmetrically around the vertical axis.

If the two variables correlated are simultaneous, the correlogram is symmetric around a peak at zero, drawn as the vertical axis. Asymmetry suggests causality. It is indicated as the *excess* area on the figure. It is also given as a sum of the excess for each lead. The example is "unusually" neat. The symline and the correlogram will normally start at different points, the two curves may intersect more than once, and the underlying level may have a clear trend, etc.

Each average correlation indicated as a kink-point for the correlogram is calculated for n_1 years. This allows a test of significance for (Ho: cor $= 0$). The two-sided 5% level of significance for the correlation for $n_1 = 50$ is cor$^* = 0.27$. Most of the correlograms are averages of such correlograms for n_2 countries. If the country observations were independent, the aggregate level of significance should be cor$^*/\sqrt{n_2}$. If n_2 is 100, this reduces cor* by a factor $1/10$. However, the country observations are dependent, so the reduction is not so large. In the next section, I use a crude rule of thumb whereby the correlations in the correlograms are significant if they are numerically larger than 0.09. In some cases, the correlograms are rather different across countries, and then it is better to calculate the standard error of the correlation with the same lag (see Figure 6.11 in Chapter 6).

2.8 THE FOURTH METHOD: DP-TESTS – USING THE DEVELOPMENT POTENTIAL BEFORE IT HAPPENED

Method four to establish long-run causality is the **DP-*test*,** which uses variables for the *d*evelopment *p*otential of countries as instruments.[5] These variables measure the nature-given development potential long before modern development started – they are reported at the end of the section. While they predict the development of countries fairly well, it appears unlikely that they can predict the institutions of countries. As the DP-variables are time-invariant, the test works only on cross-country samples. Table 2.4 shows the mechanics of the TSIV-test.

Equations (15a) to (15c) in Table 2.4 use the instrument D to calculate whether y causes X. However, first a set of tests has to be performed to ascertain whether the instrument D is strong and valid. If the tests are accepted, and the estimate of β_2 is significantly different from zero, a causal link from y to X has been established. Furthermore, if β_1 from equation (14) and β_2 from equation (15c) are the same, we can draw the strong conclusion that the causal relation from y to X is the only relation between y and X.

The strong conclusion should mean that reverse relations (17a) and (17c) detect no causality. This is often discovered already when the tests show that D is not a strong and valid instrument for X. However, a couple of cases are found where (weaker) reverse causality is detected. In this case, the (y, X)-relation has simultaneity.

As the test deals with the long run, the DP-tests run use averages from the period 2005–10 if the data are annual.[6] These data are unlikely to be

---

[5] The DP-test comes from Gundlach and Paldam (2009). It is used in Chapters 4, 8, 9, 10, and 11.

[6] The period includes both four very good years and two crisis years, so they are about average.

TABLE 2.4. *The equation of the standard TSIV-test*

Transition causality	Reverse causality	Comment
(14) $X_i = \alpha_1 + \beta_1 y_i + u_{1i}$	(16) $y_i = \alpha_3 + \beta_3 X_i + u_{4i}$,	Simple regression of X and y
(15a) $y_i = \gamma_2 + \lambda_2 D_i + u_{2i}$	(17a) $X_i = \gamma_2 + \lambda_2 D_i + u_{5i}$	D is the instrument
(15b) $y_i^D = \gamma_2 + \lambda_2 D_i$	(17b) $X_i^D = \gamma_2 + \lambda_2 D_i$	Calculate the instrumented variable
(15c) $X_i = \alpha_2 + \beta_2 y_i^D + u_{3i}$	(17c) $y_i = \alpha_4 + \beta_4 X_i^D + u_{6i}$	The TSIV estimate

The six u-variables are the residual terms.

revised, so the test should replicate nicely. The regressions (14) and (15) are run for one year, but cross-country samples exist for about 40 years, so the regressions can be run every year, and the 40 sets of coefficient estimates can be used to test the robustness of the results. The DP-test is run for all seven institutional variables listed in Table 1.3. All TSIV regressions report four tests, as follows:

The **Cragg–Donald** (CD) test for instrument strength. If we see a value below the critical value (10 percent maximal size), the instruments are weak. The critical value is between 20 and 22. Thus, if the CD-value reported exceeds the critical value, I say that the instruments are strong, and the test values are bolded.

The **Sargan** test for overidentification rejects the joint null hypothesis that the instruments are valid and correctly excluded from the estimate. Here the p-value is reported; it should show that the test is not rejected, i.e., the p-values are above 0.05, preferably above 0.15.

The **Hausman** test for parameter consistency of OLS and IV estimates, i.e., does β_1 differ significantly from β_2. Once again, the test tries to reject homogeneity, so the p-values should be above 0.05, preferably above 0.15.

The last section in the tables reporting the DP-tests is a test for the detection of reverse causality. It runs equations (16) and (17) from Table 2.4, explaining y by X. Here I just report the Cragg–Donald test, which in all cases shows that the instruments are weaker in this case, but sometimes they are acceptable, indicating some simultaneity.

The DP-variables are given in Table 2.5. The idea of the DP-variables and most of the effort to put the variables together came from D. A. Hibbs and O. Olsson. They use the suggestions of Jared Diamond (from Diamond 1997). The variables represent facts that predict development before it happened. As development has long roots, the variables

TABLE 2.5 *The DP-variables*

Biological variables

Animals   Number of domesticable big mammals, weighing more than 45 kilos, which are believed to have been present in various regions of the world in prehistory.

Plants   Number of arable wild grasses known to have existed in various regions of the world in prehistory, with a mean kernel weight exceeding 10 mg.

Bioavg   Average of plants and animals, where each variable was first normalized by dividing by its maximum value.

Biofpc.   The first principal component of plants and animals.

Maleco   Measure of malaria ecology. It combines climatic factors and biological properties of the regionally dominant malaria vector into an index of the stability of malaria transmission (malaria ecology). The index is an average for each country of highly disaggregated sub-national data. Source: Kiszewski et al. (2004).

Geographic variables

Axis   Relative east–west orientation of a country, measured as east–west distance (longitudinal degrees) divided by north–south distance (latitudinal degrees).

Climate   A ranking of climates according to how favorable they are to agriculture, based on the Köppen classification.

Coast   Proportion of land area within 100 km of the coast. Source: McArthur and Sachs (2001).

Frost   Proportion of a country's land receiving five or more frost days in that country's winter, defined as December through February in the Northern hemisphere, and June through August in the Southern hemisphere. Source: Masters and McMillan (2001).

Geoav   Average of climate, lat, and axis, where each variable was first normalized by dividing by its maximum value.

Geofpc   The first principal component of climate, *lat*, *axis*, and *size*.

Lat   Distance from the equator as measured by the absolute value of country-specific latitude in degrees divided by 90 to place it on a [0,1] scale. Source: Hall and Jones (1999).

Size   The size of the landmass to which the country belongs, in millions of square kilometers (a country may belong to Eurasia or it may be an island).

Variables reported without source are from Hibbs and Olsson (2004) and Olsson and Hibbs (2005). To include Ethiopia in the 1995 sample, the 1993 observation for *polity* is used. Belize, Cap Verde, Hong Kong, Iceland, Luxembourg, Maldives, Malta, and Samoa are not included in the Polity IV database. Fiji, Papua New Guinea, and the Solomon Islands are not included in the Maddison database. The estimation results are not statistically significicantly affected by the additional observation on Ethiopia.

should come from before these roots developed. The variables are biological and geographical. Hibbs and Olsson have compiled the variables reported without source. The biogeography data include 112 country observations. If income data or institutional index data are missing for 1995 (or another of the selected cross section years), the next observation within a time interval of +/–10 years is used.

In regressions explaining present day income, these variables work rather well. The four overseas western countries (Australia, Canada, New Zealand, and the United States) were established in areas with rather low values as regards *animals* and *plants*. The largest domesticable animal in North America was the turkey, and there were no such animals in Australia and New Zealand. However, the European immigrants quickly brought animals and plants over from their countries of origin. Thus, the four overseas Western countries may be treated as part of Europe.

2.9 CAN TRANSITION CURVES BE STATISTICAL ARTIFACTS?

The following section does not come naturally anywhere in the book. It discusses an argument I have sometimes encountered. Maybe Π-curves are an artefact due to the definition of the institutional indices as integers in a closed interval. The argument exists in two versions exemplified by the Polity index P, which is defined in $[-10, +10]$.

The first version is the *truncation argument*, which claims that a true index measuring the political system would use a larger scale; thus, the bends at the top and the bottom have been created by limiting the possibilities to the closed set of integers. The problem is small at the bottom, as the flat part of the curves is some distance from the end of the interval, but the Π-curve does converge to the top of the interval. This may be an artefact.

My assessment is that it is no artefact, but a fact. There is little evidence that mass democracy can be more democratic than it is in the typical developed Western country – proposals for more democracy are either marginal or utopian. The author has participated in a study comparing Denmark and Switzerland. The two countries both had top scores on all three indices (P, CL, and PR), and in the World Values Survey, a large part of the respondents in both countries answered that the country had full democracy. However, the two countries have rather different political institutions and traditions; see Chapter 6 in Christoffersen et al. 2014. It is possible that the best institutions of the two countries could be combined into a more democratic system, but it is more likely that a combined system would be too complex to operate. Thus, I think that the upper bound is real.

The other argument is that the transition path can be modeled as a *random walk in a closed interval.* A pure random walk does not generate a Π-curve. It will inevitably be trendless around the center of the interval (which is zero for P). However, if a drift toward the Π-curve is added, then it can be made to work, but then we have reached a version of the Jumps Model that is discussed in Chapter 5.

3

The Largest Historical Event

The End of Soviet Socialism

An economic system of public ownership of the means of production is Socialism. In combination with central planning, it is Soviet Socialism. It was the economic system in 15 countries before 1988.[1] The system collapsed between 1988 and 1991 in ten of these countries, and, as shown in Table 3.1, 28–29 countries emerged from the former Soviet Bloc and Yugoslavia. This is by far the biggest event in the period since 1960, and it has influenced many other countries. In the perspective of the book, Soviet Socialism is the story of a large detour from the path of the Grand Transition that ended as a result of a set of exogenous triggering events, which caused the ten countries, their successors, and many others to move toward the transition path.[2] The chapter concentrates on this story.

---

[1] A large literature describes Soviet Socialism – in particular, see Nove (1977). Another large literature discusses the change out of Socialism; see Gross and Steinherr (2009) and Paldam (2002b), which runs to 319 pages. This effort should permit me to be dogmatically short at present.

[2] In the literature on the change from Socialism, it is often termed a transition. This is not how the term is used in this book, as there is no steady state at either end of the changes in the countries involved.

TABLE 3.1. *The ten countries with Soviet Socialism until 1989/90*
and the 28–29 successor states

Socialist	Post-socialist	Socialist	Post-socialist
Soviet Union/new countries		Soviet Bloc/mostly old countries	
USSR	1. Armenia	Bulgaria	Bulgaria
	2. Azerbaijan	Czechoslovakia	1. Czech R.
	3. Belarus	breaks up 1992	2. Slovak R.
	4. Estonia	East Germany	Part of Germany
	5. Georgia	Poland	Poland
	6. Kazakhstan	Hungary	Hungary
	7. Kyrgyzstan	Mongolia	Mongolia
	8. Latvia	Romania	Romania
	9. Lithuania	Other socialist/mostly new countries	
	10. Moldova	Albania	Albania
	11. Russia	Yugoslavia	1. Bosnia
	12. Tajikistan		2. Croatia
	13. Turkmenistan		3. Macedonia
	14. Ukraine		4. Montenegro
	15. Uzbekistan		5. Serbia
	Seven areas with		6. Slovenia
	unclear status (a)		7. Kosovo (b)

Notes: (a) Abkhazia, Nagorno-Karabakh, South Ossetia, Transnistria, Donetsk, Luhansk, and Crimea. (b) Kosovo is an independent country, but it is not recognized by all countries. It has weak data. The 28–29 countries included in Figures 3.1 and 3.2 are all the post-socialist countries except Kosovo. The 28 countries are for 1990–91, but Czechoslovakia broke into two in 1992, which gives 29 countries. Serbia included Montenegro until 2006. Wars between Serbia, Croatia, Bosnia, and Kosovo started in 1991 and continued to 1995–99.

The five sections of Chapter 3 give an overview of the events and explain why they are exogenous. The first section (s1) describes the amazing difference in the performance of the Soviet and Western systems. Next follows a brief survey (s2) of the change in economic and political systems, where six Muslim countries followed a different path (s3). The events in Russia were complex, unexpected, and unique, and hence practically exogenous. The changes were an external shock to the rest of the Soviet Bloc (s4) and in many other countries (s5).

3.1 SOVIET SOCIALISM: IT DID MATTER

Table 3.1 lists the ten countries within the Soviet system, at the start of our data, in which the system collapsed. This collapse resulted in 29 successor states. Cuba and North Korea still have Soviet-style Socialism, while China and Vietnam and perhaps Laos have moved out of

Socialism by taking a more gradual route. The crucial trait in the Soviet Socialism model was that it only relied on markets in marginal ways. Instead, it used central planning and administrative allocation of staple goods. This required a totalitarian dictatorship, which is a large cost of the system. This empirical fact has a number of explanations going back to Schumpeter and Hayek.[3]

That the Soviet model was very inefficient is illustrated by the twin-test of Table 3.2. It covers a number of cases where two parts of an old country, or two similar neighboring countries, have operated different systems. The degree of similarity falls from the start until the end of the table. The data have many measurement problems, so only crude assessments are reported, but the differences are large in any case.

The capitalist twin has always done much better, both in the economic and political dimension (with one exception). In addition, the rates of accumulation as a fraction of GDP were about twice as high in the Socialist twin as in the capitalist one, but still they came to lag more and more behind. Obviously, Soviet Socialism is an economic system with much lower efficiency.

I think that this inefficiency evidence offers the strongest support for the Primacy of Institutions theory; see Section 1.11. The inefficiency of the Soviet economic system seems to have been a result of the economic system – not the totalitarian political system.

In a wider perspective, many have tried to compare Russia with the United States and Western Europe in the years 1913 and 1990. The index problem is large, but as far as the data goes, the difference has been fairly constant – the USSR did not manage to reduce the gap with the West, while a number of other countries have closed most of the gap.

Finland was part of the Russian empire from 1809 to 1918. In 1918, when Finland became independent, the *gdp* of Russia was a little higher than that of Finland. The USSR reported higher growth than Finland nearly every year from 1920 to 1990, but in 1990 Finland had a *gdp* that was much like other Western countries, while the *gdp* of Russia was about one-third of Finland's. In addition, the costs in human suffering in Russia were much larger than the social costs of development under capitalism.

---

[3] All political systems need to take popular and unpopular decisions. In a market economy, the political system takes most of the popular decisions, while most unpopular ones are left to the market. In a socialist system, the political system takes all decisions, hence public debates and interest groups have to be controlled. Political parties often promise too much before elections. Think of a situation where all decisions are political.

TABLE 3.2. *Twins with different economic systems*

Capitalist twin	Socialist twin		Initial values		Duration	Resulting difference	
Name	Name	Established	gdp (a)	Polity (b)	Years	gdp (a)	Polity (b)
South Korea	North Korea	1946	1.0	same (c)	60	0.1	-17 (2015)
West Germany	East Germany	1946	0.9	same (c)	44	0.3	-19 (1988)
Finland	Estonia (d)	1939/44	1.2	-10 (1940)	46	0.3	-16 (1988)
Austria	Czechoslovakia (e)	1946	0.8	-1 (1932)	44	0.3	-17 (1988)
Austria	Hungary (e)	1946	0.7	-9 (1932)	44	0.3	-12 (1988)
Chinese Tigers (f)	China	1948	0.6	differ	58	0.2	-12 (2003)
Finland	Russian SR	1918	1.1	-9 (1918)	72	0.3	-15 (1988)
Costa Rica	Nicaragua	1979	0.8	-18 (1978)	10	0.3	-11 (1990)
Dominican Rep.	Cuba	1960	1.2	0 (1959)	45	0.3	-15 (2015)

Notes: (a) The relative gdp of the socialist twin at the start and the end, measured as gdp-ratio of socialist twin to capitalist twin. (b) The Polity point difference measures how far behind in democracy the socialist twin was at the end. (c) Before foreign occupation. (d) Finland and Estonia have almost the same language and history from 1800 to 1939, when Estonia was forced to rejoin the USSR. (e) Austria, Hungary and Czechoslovakia were the central countries in the Habsburg Monarchy until 1918. (f) The Chinese Tigers are Taiwan, Hong Kong, and Singapore. The first pair of twins is used as a smoking gun test in Acemoglu et al. (2005).

46

3.2 THE CHANGE FROM THE SOVIET MODEL – BIG COSTS
AND A LONG LAG

The change from Socialism in the ten countries listed in Table 3.1 happened from 1988 to 1993. The change occurred in both the economic and political systems, and greatly influenced economic development and all institutions.

Figure 3.1 shows that the change caused an economic crisis in this country group that, at its lowest point after 2–5 years, reached a fall in *gdp* of about 40%. It led to a rebuilding boom, and most post-socialist countries are now wealthier than they would have been without the change. Thus, there have been *short-run costs* and *long-run benefits*. This is a common result in studies of institutional reforms, but it was certainly large in the case at hand.

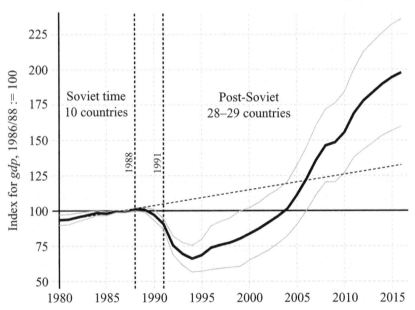

FIGURE 3.1. The average path of *gdp* in the countries listed in Table 3.1
The bold curve is the average of the gdp indices calculated so that the average for the three years 1986–88 is set to 100. The gray lines are confidence intervals (gray lines) at two standard errors. The downturn caused by the system change bottomed out at a gdp-loss of 40%. The path reached 100 once again in 2004. It overtook the old path (dashed line) two years later. The loss suffered (the sum of the losses below the dashed line) will be recovered (as a similar sum of gains above the line) in 2020/22.

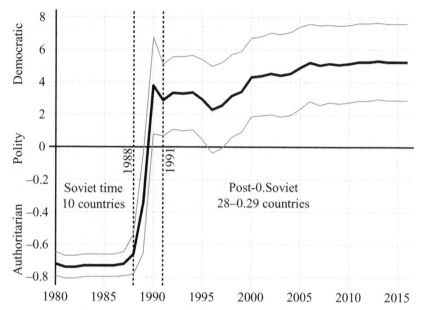

FIGURE 3.2. The average path of the Polity index in the countries listed in
Table 3.1

Some countries have no observations in some of the years between 1988 and 1991. The large
rise in *P* during the change from Socialism did cause some cyclicality, but not as much as
is normal.

The story of collapse and reforms leading to new development differ
from one country to the next. Things went fastest in countries that were
closest to the West, and managed to create national unity around a fast
reform process – known as shock therapy.

Figure 3.2 shows the same average curve for the Polity index.
Here a big jump occurred toward democracy. The size of the jump is
10 *P*-points, which after a small cycle and a decade has consolidated at
12 *P*-points.

The pattern found becomes even clearer when the incomes of the
countries are adjusted for. The richest countries – which are also the
countries closest to the West – moved to full democracy. The reader
will know that several of the new countries – which have few democratic
traditions (such as Hungary and Poland) – have found it difficult to
consolidate the new institutions, and recently there has been
some backlash.

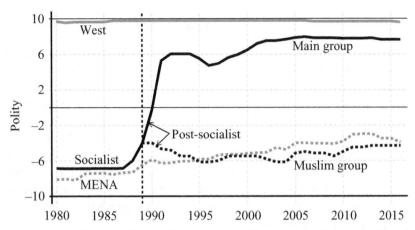

FIGURE 3.3. The path of the Polity index from Figure 3.2 divided into main and Muslim groups

The Muslim post-socialist sample consists of Azerbaijan, Kazakhstan, Kirgizstan, Tajikistan, Turkmenistan, and Uzbekistan. I have included Albania in the main group due to the evidence of low religiosity in the country. Here the main group consists of the remaining 23 post-socialist countries. The West also comprises 23 countries.

3.3 THE EXCEPTION OF THE MUSLIM/MENA COUNTRIES

Throughout the book a main exception is the OPEC/MENA countries.[4] Six of the 28/29 new countries of the block belong in the MENA group in the cultural sense, although only one is an oil country. However, the five central Asian countries are also relatively poor. Figure 3.3 shows that they are indeed an exception.

While the main group of post-socialist countries is approaching the West, this is not the case for the six Muslim post-socialist countries. They rapidly moved to become typical MENA countries. Figure 3.3 seems to argue that it is Islam more than oil that causes the OPEC exception. However, in other work I have found that both Islam and oil count (see Borooah and Paldam 2007). The rest of the book does speak of the OPEC exception, as it is the easiest to explain; see Sections 1.8 and 4.8.

---

[4] MENA means Middle East and North Africa. Thus, it covers all Arab countries, Turkey, and Iran. I exclude Israel from the group. Today Israel is a typical Western country.

3.4 CAUSALITY

It is easy to argue that the collapse was *a ketchup effect*, which is a visual illustration of the Jumps Model in Chapter 5 – although the shakes of the bottle happen with lags of a random length. The economic and political systems of the Soviet bloc were doing badly compared with countries at the same level of development, and this created tensions. Gradually, tensions grew, and finally the system broke in a big way. However, it might have happened 15 years before or 15 years after, and it might have been a gradual process, as in China and Vietnam. Chapter 6 tests the effect and demonstrates that increasing tension does not explain why systems break at a particular time, but it does explain what happens when the triggering event occurs.

What happened in Russia was a large version of a story that will return in subsequent chapters: First, a triggering event occurred, and then the country went toward the transition path, both as regards the economic and political systems. The triggering events are as follows,

(i)   A set of complex, unexpected, and unique events in the center, i.e., Moscow.

(ii) It caused the Russian grip on the rest of the Socialist bloc to weaken, so that the change could spread through the bloc, and further to other Socialist countries.

(iii) It also caused a large wave of changes in perceptions and beliefs – which involve the mysterious concept: *zeitgeist*. Socialism went out of fashion in a big way.

A large literature exists about (i) the historical events in Moscow (Google has 14.3 million hits on the "collapse of Soviet Socialism"). Factors to consider were the failed coup of the old guard, and the resulting weakening of the position of Gorbachev relative to his main rival Yeltsin,[5] etc. Once the process of collapse started, the Communist Party crumbled, and the whole structure of the regime came tumbling down. Thus, the triggering event was a set of rather random political events. Section 1.11 termed such events *practically exogenous*.

Compare this with events in Romania: The collapse of the USSR made a big impression on the Romanians, causing fears of the strongman Ceaușescu to vanish. In early December 1989, he suddenly faced large

---

[5] During the coup attempt, Gorbachev was isolated in his vacation home in the Crimea, while Yeltsin was a main actor resisting the coup.

hostile demonstrations, and he then discovered that he could not command his troops to shoot at the demonstrators. This caused a rapid disintegration of the regime, and at the end of the month, the strongman was executed. Thus, the triggering event was an external one that had the character of an exogenous shock. Events in the remaining 26 countries are causally similar to the events in Romania, in the sense that they would not have happened without the events in Russia and the resulting wave of changes in perceptions and beliefs. While the trigger was the same, the process of changes it caused differed between countries, but a few years later the outcome was much the same. The events were greatly influenced by the difficulties of privatization that led to periods of unclear property rights, allowing large-scale rent-grabs, where a small number of bold entrepreneurs suddenly became oligarchs.

As regards changes in the zeitgeist, history has seen a number of large swings in opinions and beliefs that happened internationally. It is hard to provide rational explanations for such swings. The revolutionary years 1830, 1848, and 1918 were rather international. Often the ideas spread from students to trade unions but in small towns far from universities, they may appear as a small ripple. However, they do influence politics.

Our period since 1960 experienced a wave of utopian Socialism in the West in the late 1960s and for the next 3–5 years. It was probably inspired by the Cultural Revolution in China in 1966, and started at the universities in California and Paris in 1968, and then rapidly spread. With a few years' delay, it was one of the factors driving Socialism in the LDC-world. It also led to a wave of extremism that caused the formation of terrorist movements in several Western countries and in countries far away. It peaked in China after 6–8 years of the Cultural Revolution, and it became even more extreme in Cambodia, where the government tried to exterminate the ideas and beliefs of the old system using mass murder between 1975 and 1978.

In the late 1980s, an opposite wave against Socialism and for privatization and other market reforms took place, as already mentioned. Though it is often possible to find an initial reason for these movements, it is also clear that they have an inner dynamics that may make them much larger than the initial reason justifies. Moreover, they do have a large international element and come in cycles.

3.5 EFFECTS ON THE REST OF THE WORLD

In addition to all the countries in the Soviet Bloc, the wave of changes hit Albania and Yugoslavia, which were Socialist countries outside the Bloc.

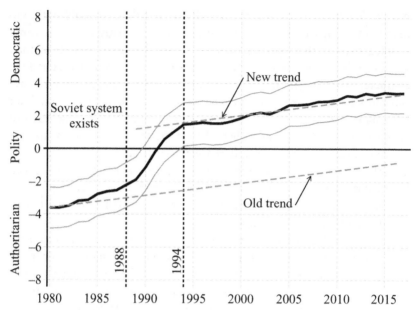

FIGURE 3.4. The effect of the collapse of the Soviet model on 94 other countries
Average of all countries with complete data that are not post-socialist, Western, or OPEC.

Figure 3.4 looks at the average for the 94 countries that are not post-socialist, Western, or OPEC countries, for which data are available for all years from 1985 to 2016. It is drawn on the same scale as Figure 3.2 for easy comparison. There is more of a trend in these data than in Figure 3.2, but it is clear that there is a shift in the trend of about four *P*-points, which is one-third of the change in the post-socialist countries in Figure 3.2. In addition, the change shown in Figure 3.4 takes twice as long.

In some countries, the change was quite dramatic: An example is Congo Br, formerly the Democratic People's Republic of the Congo, which was ruled by the Marxist-Leninist party. In 1990, the ideology and many policies changed quickly. Other political parties were allowed, and a free election took place in 1991. A similar story happened in Nicaragua, which was a one-party socialist state ruled by the Sandinista party. It allowed free elections in 1990, which the Sandinistas lost to a democratic coalition.

PART II

THE TRANSITIONS OF INSTITUTIONS

PART IIA

THE DEMOCRATIC TRANSITION

The next four chapters deal with

Note three points: (i) Chapters 4–6 are based on the wide dataset 1960–2016, while Chapter 7 uses the long time-series from 1800. (ii) The transition differs in the Main and the OPEC sample: (iii) When democracy rises, so does the P-index, while the CL and PR indices decrease.

TABLE IIA.I. *New variables and concepts used in Chapters 4–7*

Political system index (1), P-index

Source   Institute for Systemic Peace: www.systemicpeace.org/polityproject .html.

P_{it}, P_j *Polity index*, integer $[-10, 10]$ from authoritarian to democratic.(a)

$\Pi^P(y_j)$ Transition curve. Transition is 12–14 P-points, Π^P-curve is beautiful, slope $\lambda^P > 0$.

Θ^P_{it} *Tension*, distance from P to the transition path, i.e., $\Theta^P = P - \Pi(y)$. The country has *too much* or *too little* P if $\Theta^P > 0$ or $\Theta^P < 0$, respectively.

E_{it} *Event*, binary variable for the year when P changes ($E = 1$) or stays constant ($E = 0$).

(continued)

TABLE IIA.I. *(continued)*

	Triggering event, causes a change to a new system, which is not anarchy (where $P = 0$).
J_{it}	*Jump* is change, $P - P_{-1}$. Termed *large* if $|J| > 3$. Most jumps are *discrete*, but some are *Sequences* of changes in the same direction in consecutive years, may include zero.
	Spells, periods where P is constant, include a sequence at the start.
G^P	*Excess movements of P*. The gross/net ratio for change in P.

Political system indices (2) CL-index and (3) PR-index

Source	Freedom House: https://freedomhouse.org/.
CL	*Civil Liberties* index, integer scale from 7 to 1, seven for lowest and one for highest.
$\Pi^{CL}(y_j)$	Transition curve. Transition is 3.7 CL-points, Π^{CL}-curve is beautiful, slope $\lambda^{CL} \leq 0$.
PR	*Political Rights* index, integer scale from 7 to 1, seven for lowest and one for highest.
$\Pi^{PR}(y_j)$	Transition curve. Transition is 3.7 PR-points, Π^{PR}-curve is beautiful, slope $\lambda^{PR} \leq 0$.

Notes: (a) The Polity2 coding is used: Negative values $[-10, -1]$ for authoritarian systems. Positive values $[1, 10]$ for democratic ones. Zero is for anarchy and (contrary to Polity2) for temporary foreign domination.

4

Literature, Data, Transition Path, and Causality

The *Democratic Transition*, $\Pi(y)$, is complex. Kernel regressions show a long-run "underlying" path, Π, which has all the properties (from Table 2.2) of a beautiful transition curve. The curve generalizes to the main political indices: *Polity*, the two indices from Freedom house *CL* and *PR*, and the five main *V-Dem* indices. However, political systems consolidate in status quo equilibria, so they are *constant* in most years. The status quo is sometimes broken by a random *triggering event* that causes a *system jump*. The transition path is an *attractor* for these jumps.

The four chapters of Part IIA analyze this complex. The chapters present two theoretical models. The long-run ***Three Pillars Model*** shows how the Grand Transition changes the political system from autocracy to

TABLE 4.1. *What is in the four chapters on the political system?*

Chapter 4. Literature, transition curve, Π, and causality. The tension is the distance Θ^P from P to the Π-curve.

Chapter 5. The short run Jumps Model explains jumps of P by the tensions. Jumps happen due to triggering events. The Π-curve acts as an attractor for the jumps. Sequences are more positive than discrete jumps. The grievance asymmetry is strong for system jumps. Regression models between P and y do not work.

Chapter 6. System consolidation results in status quo equilibria appearing as spells of constancy for the P-index. Triggering occurs randomly: (i) Neither development nor the tension explains why they occur at a certain time. (ii) Articles in *the Economist* show what contemporary observers thought were the triggering events. They are very different.

Chapter 7. The long run Three Pillars Model behind the Π-curve: Traditional political systems have three pillars: A royal dynasty, a feudal class, and the national Church. Transition undermines two of the pillars. Equivalence is confirmed by the long time-series. The spells of constant political systems are analyzed.

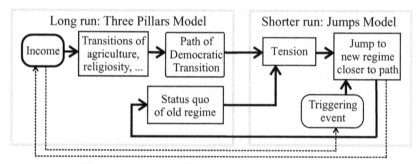

FIGURE 4.1. The main structure of the transition model

The tension is, $\Theta^P = P - \Pi(y)$. The main direction of causality is from income to the political system, as the two dashed arrows are weak. They are not part of the two models.

democracy – it is a strong but fuzzy relation. The short-run *Jumps Model* sets out the attractor properties of the transition path. Figure 4.1 shows how the models work together, while Table 4.1 shows where the different parts of the analysis are found.

The 12 sections of Chapter 4 start with a survey of the literature (s1), and present the three indices, P (Polity), CL (Civil Liberties), and PR (Political Rights) and a set of descriptive statistics (s2–s4). The transition curve, Π, follows for the three indices, which are shown to be very similar and quite robust (s5–s8) – the *V-Dem* indices are covered in (s6). The system tension $\Theta^P = P - \Pi(y)$ follows from Π. The Muslim/OPEC countries are an exception (s9). The system variability vanishes in the modern steady state (s10). The causality analysis (s11) finds that the main causal direction is from income to the political system, and this causality result is very robust over time (s12).

4.1 THE LITERATURE EXPLAINING THE HIGH CORRELATION BETWEEN INCOME AND THE POLITICAL SYSTEM

Transition theory claims that political systems are stable in the two steady states. Traditional political systems were normally stable for a handful of centuries before transition began. In most of the oldest modern countries of the West, the political system – democracy – has already been stable for more than a century. In between, many systems, such as military or one-party rule, often occur. Many theories attempt to explain the relationship between political change and development. The main ones are classified by the causal direction and are listed here:

From income to democracy. This is the tradition started by Lipset (1959), see also his 1994.[1] I see this as the theory of the Democratic Transition. As already indicated, the Three Pillars Model in Chapter 7 explains the long run, while the Jumps Model in Chapter 5 explains how the long run comes about. The transition equation is:

$$P_{it} = \Pi^P(y_{it}) + u_{it}, \qquad \text{where } u_{it} \text{ are the (large) residuals} \qquad (4.1)$$

The residual term u_{it} catches the large random element in the variation of the political system and the strong autocorrelation caused by long spells of stability. Thus, u_{it} contains rather complex processes. One of the reasons for studying the transition by means of kernel regressions is that they scramble the observations (see Section 2.5), so the residual processes are randomized.

From the political system to development. The theory of economic growth sees the economy as a production function, where income is produced by the factors of labor, capital, human capital, and technology, so that growth is the result of the dynamics of the production function brought about by technological progress and by the transfer of resources from the traditional to the modern sector. In standard surveys of the theory, such as Jones and Vollrath (2013), labor grows exogenously, capital is accumulated from past production, and human capital is connected to production in a similar way. Technology was for a long time taken to be exogenous, but in endogenous growth models, it is produced by labor and human capital.

Maybe the political system has some minor indirect role in these processes, but it is not obvious how it contributes. It is not even mentioned in

---

[1] Versions of the theory are often known as Modernization Theory, which is covered by a large literature; Google Scholar shows 1.1 million hits to "Modernization Theory."

Jones and Vollrath (2013). In the massive four volume *Handbook of Economic Growth* (Aghion and Durlauf 2005, 2014), the political system plays a modest role, although it is discussed in Chapter 5 by Acemoglu et al. (2005). In addition, there is a largely verbal literature on the effect of good governance on development.[2] The causal relation is written:

$$y_{it} = \Lambda(P_{it}) + v_{it}, \qquad \text{where } v_{it} \text{ are the residuals} \qquad (4.2)$$

Thus, the theory of economic growth predicts that the connection between the political system and development is weak and indirect. However, in view of the political importance of this theory, a literature of about 200 papers analyzes the relation between political systems and growth. It is often formulated as the question, Does democracy cause growth? It is a literature with modest findings. All 84 primary studies until about 2005 are covered by a meta-study (Doucouliagos and Ulubaşoğlu 2008) that shows a wide range of results, with a dubious average. If corrected for publication bias, the connection disappears.[3] Some later studies, such as Gründler and Krieger (2016) and Acemoglu et al. (2019), find a small positive effect. A new meta-study that covers 188 papers (Colagrossi et al. 2019) confirms the small positive effect.

The main mechanisms in this literature are that democracies may promote three factors of production: education, public health, and administrative quality. If a new democracy wants to increase enrolment rates in primary education, it will take, e.g., five years to increase enrolment by 10 percentage points more than it would have under the previous regime. It takes another ten years before the extra children enrolled emerge from the system, and their increased human capital will only affect production gradually. Thus, lags of two to three decades are needed to generate an effect.[4] Chapter 10 examines the effect of the political system on corruption, which is a major aspect of administrative quality. It is shown that a reduction in corruption only increases growth with a long lag, and the Transition of Corruption happens later than the Democratic Transition.

A second literature analyzes the connection between political instability and growth. This connection is discussed in Chapter 13. It finds that the Grand Transition causes instability in the political and economic system. It reduces growth, slowing down the transition speed.

---

[2] Good governance is a soft term chosen so that nobody can be opposed to it. It covers democracy, low corruption, and administrative quality. Obviously, it is good in itself, but it is less obvious whether it is good for development.

[3] The standard test for publication bias is not reported, but I have asked one of the authors what the test result was.

[4] The lags are shorter for secondary education, but they are still one to two decades.

Thus, both causal directions (1) $y \Rightarrow P$ and (2) $P \Rightarrow y$ have been shown to matter, but from the arguments so far and the findings in this chapter, I claim that (1) is by far the strongest. Most of the book disregards the two dashed arrows in Figure 4.1, so that the arrow from the political system to income is treated as a reduced form relation that may give a (small) simultaneity bias, but Chapter 6 demonstrates that most triggering events are exogenous.

4.2 THE DATA: THREE POLITICAL INDICES *P*, *CL*, AND *PR*

Table 4.2 provides some counts of the *P*-index. It is an integer in the interval [−10, +10], where a perfect autocracy like Saudi Arabia scores −10, while most Western countries score +10. The score zero is used when countries have no political system in place.

To study whether the results are robust, the two Freedom House indices (reported from 1972) are used: They are the *CL*-index for civil liberties and the *PR* index for political rights. They use a more compressed scale [7, 1] that runs in the opposite direction (of the *P*-index), so that democracy increases when the two indices fall. The three indices are constant in most years.

The three indices use integers, as they are judgmental, and limits exist to the precision of judgment. Small regime adjustments may escape registration by the indices, especially in autarchies, but larger changes are unlikely to go unnoticed.

Table 4.3 shows the available number of observations that can be paired with an income observation and how the indices correlate with income. The signs on the correlations differ as a result of the scaling of the political variables. The political data are divided into the Main and the OPEC sample. These samples give correlations to income with reverse signs. While democracy increases with wealth in the Main sample, it decreases in the OPEC countries. The *t*-tests in the table confirm that OPEC countries have less democracy than other countries.

4.3 THE PATH OF THE P-INDEX OVER TIME

Figure 4.2 shows the path of the *P*-index since 1960. Apart from the reverse scaling, the *CL*- and *PR*-indices have much the same path. The data contain two major historical events,

(i)   Decolonization from 1960 created about 40 new countries. The new countries often started with democratic systems, but in the first decade after independence, they often changed to systems that were more in line with their historical roots. That is, instead of authoritarian colonial rule, they got authoritarian native rule.

TABLE 4.2. *Some counts of the Polity data, 1960–2015. Divided into small and larger jumps*

Number of Countries	Observations			Small jumps ≤3			Larger jumps >3		All Jumps
	Available	Missing	Zeroes	Discrete	Sequence	Discrete	Sequence	
170	7,992	1,305	223	358	17	179	83	637

The data cover 170 countries, and the time span is the 56 years from 1960 to 2015, so ideally there should be $170 \times 56 = 9,520 = 7,992 + 1,305 + 223$ observations, of which $179 + 83 = 262$ are larger jumps. There are 199 in the Main sample and they can be paired with income data. Missing observations are from dependent countries. Zeroes are for periods with anarchy and for temporary foreign dependency.

TABLE 4.3. *Descriptive statistics for Polity, P, civil liberties, CL, and political rights, PR*

		P	CL	PR
Main	N	7,174	6,163	6,163
	Correlation to income, y	0.55	−0.66	−0.62
	Mean	2.04	3.79	3.80
	Std, standard deviation	7.24	1.91	2.22
OPEC	N	818	692	692
	Correlation to income, y	−0.30	0.08	0.09
	Mean	−3.94	5.26	5.47
	Std, standard deviation	6.02	1.35	1.58
Comparison	*t*-tests, all reject	20.9	−19.6	−19.1

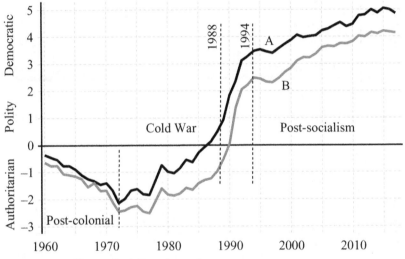

FIGURE 4.2. The path of the Polity index 1960–2016

The black A-curve is for the 110 countries with data for all years, while the gray B-curve is for all countries. The two curves are very similar. See Figures 3.2 and 3.3 in Chapter 3, analyzing the period 1988–94.

(ii) The collapse of the Soviet system between 1988 and 1992 created almost 20 countries and caused a big shift in the *P*-level. As it is the largest historical event in our data, it was discussed in Chapter 3. It influenced many more countries than those of the Soviet bloc, and it continued until 1994.

4.4 EVENTS, TRIGGERING EVENTS, JUMPS, AND SEQUENCES

An **event** occurs when *P* changes. It is a **triggering event** if it leads to a new system, and not to/from zero (anarchy). This change is termed a **jump**. If it is numerically greater than 3, it is termed a **larger jump**. Changes to the same side in consecutive years are a sequence – most sequences are larger jumps. This is coded as the sum of the changes anchored in the first year. A sequence may continue for up to four years.

Figure 4.3a shows that triggering events are evenly distributed over the years, except for the big post-socialist peak. Figure 4.3b is the sum of the

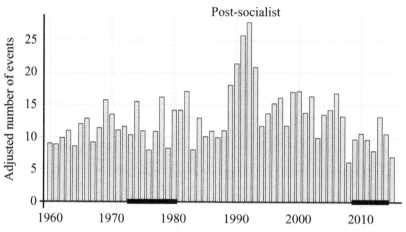

FIGURE 4.3a. The number of triggering events per year, adjusted, 1960–2015

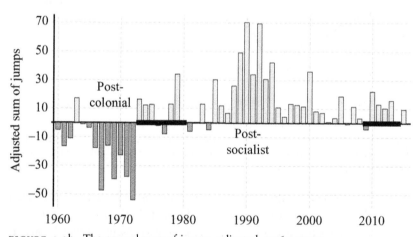

FIGURE 4.3b. The annual sum of jumps, adjusted, 1960–2015

The adjustment is to impute the number of countries to the average of 142.7 countries for all years. The bold segments on the horizontal axis indicate the periods of the Oil Crisis and the Bank Crisis.

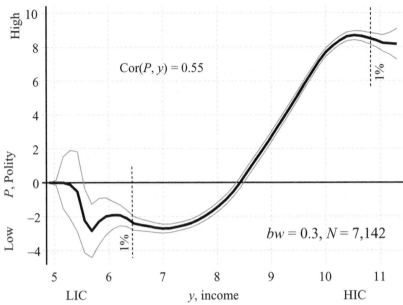

FIGURE 4.4a. The transition curve for *P*, Polity, Main sample

For y < 6.40, the gdp < US$ 600, so it is low indeed. The interval from 4.9 to 6.4 is 23.4% of the range, and holds 1% of the observations, so it is no wonder the curves are wobbly and have wide confidence intervals. The small bend toward less democracy at the HIC end in Figures 4.4a and 4.4c is caused by three outliers, Bahrain, Oman, and Singapore – if they are omitted the curve looks even better, see Paldam (2020b). The bandwidth 0.3 is close to the rule-of-thumb bandwidth calculated by Stata. The same applies to Figures 4.4b and 4.4c.

changes, so that the sign of the changes matters. It shows that the post-colonial peak is negative, while the post-socialist peak is positive. The two international economic crises, indicated by the bolded sections of the time axis, have no effect on either Figure 4.3a or Figure 4.3b. The jumps took place in 113 countries, while 57 countries have no jumps. The group of stable countries includes almost all developed nations.

4.5 THE TRANSITION CURVE FOR THE *P*, *CL*, AND *PR* INDICES

Figure 4.4 shows the kernels (from Section 2.4) of the Democratic Transition on the Polity index *P*, the Civil Liberties index *CL*, and the Political Rights index *PR*. The curve for *P* rises, but the reverse scaling causes the curves for *CL* and *PR* to fall. The 1% smallest and largest observations are indicated. The interval for the 1% smallest is wide – here

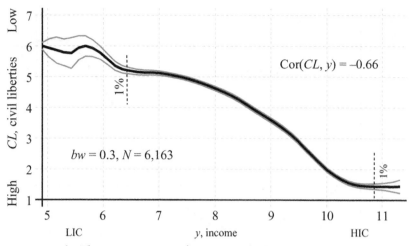

FIGURE 4.4b. The transition curve for, *CL*, Civil Liberties, Main sample

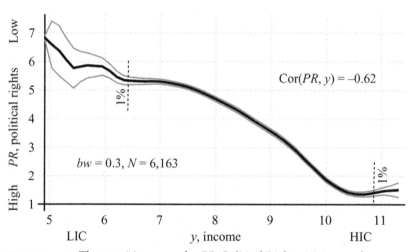

FIGURE 4.4c. The transition curve for *PR*, Political Rights, Main sample

the curves are wobbly and the confidence intervals wide. However, for 98% of the data the curves are perfect.

Figure 4.4a for Polity starts at $P = 0$, as most of the very poorest countries had civil wars. While the *P*-kernel is a straight line from 7.5 to

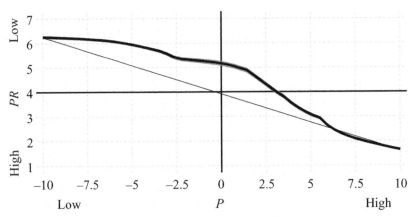

FIGURE 4.5. Explaining the *PR*-index using the *P*-index
Estimated for *bw* = 2. The graph where L is explained by *P* looks much the same, but is slightly less concave. The confidence intervals are so close to the kernel-curve that they are hard to see.

10, the *CL* and *PR* curves are concave. Thus, the intermediate countries are systematically scored slightly differently by the indices.

The most beautiful curve occurs for *P*, which suggests that the scaling of the *P*-index is better. The system **tension** $\Theta^P = P - \Pi(y)$ is the difference between the transition curve on Figure 4.4a and *P*, as explained in Chapter 2. The tension is a key variable in Chapters 5 and 6.

Figure 4.5 explains the *PR*-index by means of the *P*-index. The curve is concave, but the 95% confidence intervals are so narrow that it is clear that the two indices tell the same story.

4.6 THE VARIETIES OF DEMOCRACY FAMILY OF INDICES

The newest large-scale attempt to measure democracy in the world is the V-Dem project, which was set up to account for the varieties of democracy. It has presented a whole family of democracy indices: The *Polyarchy* index for electoral democracy, the *Liberal Democracy* index, the *Participatory Democracy* index, the *Deliberative Democracy* index, and the *Egalitarian Democracy* index. Paldam (2021) studies how these indices fit into the transition story, and finds that they fit very well. All these indices are reported for nearly all countries and years in the Main sample (the overlap is *N* = 6,852), and they all give a beautiful transition curve that looks strikingly like the curve for *Polity* shown in Figure 4.4a. From a factor analysis, it appears that all five V-Dem indices and the *Polity* index contain one common factor only, which obtains very high factor loadings. It is the one and only Transition of Democracy.

The *Polyarchy* index encompasses the other V-Dem indices, and it seems that it tries to measure the same things as the *Polity* index. From the detailed manuals it is clear that they differ somewhat in construction.[5] *Polyarchy* and *Polity* have a correlation of 0.90 in the Main sample, but the conversion relation is not linear; however, in the interest of transparency, a linear approximation that fixes the two steady state levels to the same value is used to convert *Polyarchy* to *PolP*, which has the *Polity* scale.

It is used to calculate a $Dif = Polity - PolP$. For the overlapping observations in the Main sample the mean of *Dif* is small, but the average numerical value is about three polity points. This is interpreted as an estimate of the inevitable measurement uncertainty.

Given that *perfect* democracy is an ideal, which Arrow (1963) has demonstrated does not exist, it should be noted that a range of good institutions do exist, giving a fairly narrow range of imperfect compromises. It follows that the degree of democracy can be measured only up to a point.[6] Thus, it is important that when two independent groups of competent and diligent researchers spend years of work trying to measure the degree of democracy in the world, their assessments differ by 3 points on a 20-point scale. This is 15%, which seems to be rather precise, but still substantial.

Chapter 5 shows that larger system jumps are explained rather well by the distance of the pre-jump political system from the transition path. The Jumps Model cannot explain smaller jumps. The important point is that larger jumps are found to be jumps with a value greater than three. So measurement uncertainty will reappear in the next chapter.

4.7 THE ROBUSTNESS OF THE TRANSITION CURVE

Figures 4.6, 4.7, and 4.8 give three robustness tests for the Main sample of the *P*-index. The corresponding analysis for the *CL*- and *PR*-indices is found in Paldam and Gundlach (2012).

---

[5] The Polity manual is Marshall et al. (2018), and the V-Dem manual is Coppedge (2020), which compares the V-Dem indices with the Polity index on pp. 332–34.

[6] The reader will know that perfect aggregation is rarely possible. A highly technical literature exists that demonstrates that the perfect aggregation of preferences by a decision process is impossible, and the perfect aggregation of prices by a price index is impossible, etc.

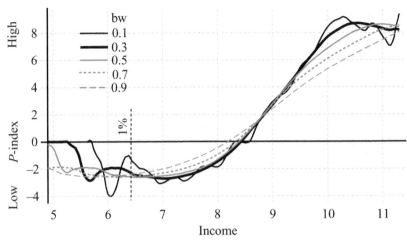

FIGURE 4.6. Transition curves with five bandwidths, Main sample

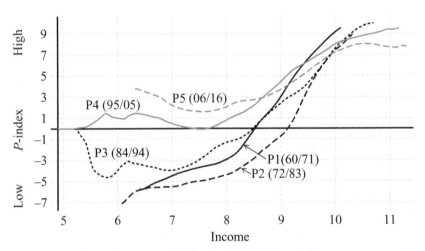

FIGURE 4.7. Transition curves for five periods, Main sample

Figure 4.6 analyzes the robustness of the transition for $bw = 0.1, 0.3, 0.5, 0.7$, and 0.9. It is obvious that the curve is rather robust to the wide range of bandwidths tried. The experiments show once again that the section below $y = 6.4$ is rather fragile. However, the bend and the democratization are robust.

Figure 4.7 looks at the kernel for five periods, P1 (1960/71), P2 (1972/83), P3 (1984/94), P4 (1995/2005), and P5 (2006/16). The key

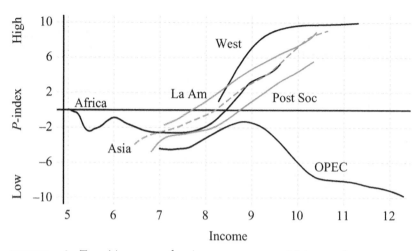

FIGURE 4.8. Transition curves for six country groups, Main sample
The file "countries" in the data appendix defines the groups. The MENA-countries outside OPEC have a curve like the OPEC curve – it is excluded, as it is a small group.

observation is that the curves have the same form. At the top (for HICs), all five curves are similar, but at the bottom (for LICs), the curves are higher after the end of Soviet Socialism, as suggested by Figure 4.2.

Figure 4.8 reports transition curves for six groups of countries. The West has been democratic for a long period, and thus democracy is strongly consolidated. The post-socialist group emerged from a totalitarian system around 1990, so they started low and are delayed in the Democratic Transition. The confidence intervals of the curves for Sub-Saharan Africa, Asia, and Latin America are overlapping. The big exception is the OPEC sample, as expected. The great variation at the low end (the LICs) with income y < 6.4 appears to apply to Africa only and to the period from 1984–2005 only. This is the period when the "African Growth Tragedy" ended, new growth started, and the African countries started to diverge.[7]

My reading of the evidence is that the Transition is much the same over time and across country groups except for the OPEC group. This gives support to the equivalence hypothesis that time-series and cross-country

---

[7] Average growth in the 44 Sub-Saharan African countries was negative from 1972 to 1994. Then it turned positive, and since 1994 the growth rate has been much as in the West. However, while σ-convergence (the coefficient of variation std/avr) for the 44 countries was trendless until 1988, it has risen since then; see Paldam (2017a).

data tell roughly the same story. The curve for the West shows an early and large bend, indicating that the Western countries had an early transition.

4.8 THE OPEC/MUSLIM EXCEPTION

Both Table 4.2 and Figure 4.8 show that OPEC/Muslim countries are less democratic than other countries. It also appears that these countries become less democratic the richer they become. It is much debated whether this is because of Islam or oil.

It is well known that extreme Muslims (Islamists/Salafists/Jihadists) reject Democracy as a political system. Maybe the argument is that the ideal political system is the one in Mecca at the time of the Prophet.[8] Today, the traditional Arab countries are kingdoms, where the elders within the royal family appoint the king (for life). The political indices score such systems as fully authoritarian. In Iran a compromise has been made, so that a Guardian Council of religious leaders headed by the Supreme Leader supervises a roughly normal democratic system. The Supreme Leader appoints the Council, and the council appoints the Supreme Leader. The political indices disagree about the degree of democracy in this system. Most Muslim countries are, of course, less extreme, but democracy is still rare. Today, Indonesia, Malaysia, Tunisia, and decreasingly Turkey have democracy, although it is still poorly consolidated in these countries.

The OPEC argument is simpler. As argued in Section 1.8, an oil sector is an enclave that produces a large flow of income to the ruler. Section 6.1 deals with regime consolidation and mentions some of the methods used to secure future stability. These methods become easier to implement if the ruler has great wealth.

4.9 SYSTEM VARIABILITY VANISHES

The variability of the Polity-score over the transition is analyzed by the income-sorted and stacked (P_j, y_j)-data of the Main sample. Treating these data as if they represented an ordered sequence of observations, a running standard deviation of the Polity-score, $Sdt(P, 51)$, is calculated for a moving sequence of $k = 51$ Polity-scores. Each $Std(P, 51)$ is placed

---

[8] The most extreme Islamist states or movements have been headed by a charismatic and self-proclaimed Khalif or Mahdi. Such leaders punish any critique severely as blasphemous.

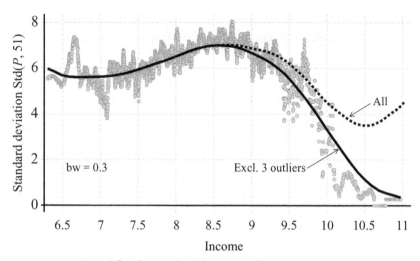

FIGURE 4.9. Kernel for the standard deviation of the Main sample
The bandwidth $bw = 0.25$. The three outliers are Bahrain, Oman, and Singapore.

next to the mid observation of income in the interval to give the $(Std(P, 51)_j, y_j)$-dataset shown as the gray scatter. These data are analyzed by kernel regressions as before, giving Figure 4.9.

This procedure is a double "averaging," first over the k-sequence, and then over the kernel. This causes very narrow confidence intervals for the kernel curve (they are not shown). The robustness of the kernel on Figure 4.9 has been analyzed by varying the bandwidth and k, the size of the moving sequence of Polity-scores. The result proves to be stable to a wide range of both parameters. The figure is drawn with and without three outliers.

The key result is that the Polity-scores have a rather high and growing standard deviation for countries in the transition, which points to a high degree of political regime volatility from low to medium income levels.[9] When income converges toward the modern steady state, a substantial decrease in political regime volatility occurs, from a standard deviation of the Polity-score of over seven to well below one. It appears that when countries reach the modern steady state, they become stable democracies, as is also found in Chapter 7. This is in line with the end-of-history hypothesis advanced by Fukuyama (1992).

---

[9] In Section 4.7 it appears that traditional systems were rather stable, so the instability at the low level on Figure 4.9 shows that the transition has started in most LICs.

4.10 CAUSALITY 1: THE BEAUTY TEST AND THE
CORRELOGRAM TEST

The perennial causality problem is tackled in four ways: (1) The beauty test of Figure 4.10; (2) the correlogram test of Figure 4.11; (3) the TSIV (two-stage instrument variables) test in Section 4.11; or (4) the jumps model of Chapter 5, which has a clear causality structure.

Figure 4.10 shows the transition curve from Figure 4.4a and adds the reverse kernel where P explains y, as explained in Section 2.7. For L and R, the graphs look the same. It is clear that the $y = K^y(P, 1)$-*kernel* explains little of the variance in income. Income is largely the same for P, rising from -10 to 8. Then there is a small rise, but it is likely to be a weak reflection of the $P = K^P(y, 0.3)$-*kernel*. Thus, the P, CL, and PR

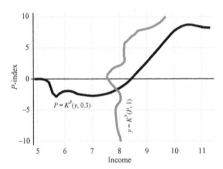

FIGURE 4.10. Reverse kernel for beauty test

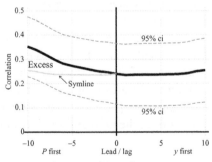

FIGURE 4.11. Average correlogram of P and y

The correlogram in Figure 4.11 is calculated (independently) for the 77 countries with full data and non-constant P's, 1960 to 2016. The graph is the average of the 77 correlograms. The confidence interval is $\pm$ 2 standard errors. It is consistent with no slope at all, but there is a significantly positive correlation throughout.

series do a poor job of explaining income, while income does a fine job explaining the three indices for the political system.

Figure 4.11 is the correlogram between P and y with 21 leads/lags.[10] It is the average of the correlograms calculated independently for all 77 countries, where P is non-constant and data are complete. The 77 correlograms vary considerably, so the 95% confidence intervals are rather wide and consistent with a straight horizontal line. The only strong finding is that the underlying correlation for all 21 leads/lags is significant, as the level is about 0.23. It is also important that the average curve is rather smooth. There is nothing that a regression may grab on to! Finally, we note that the weak tendency of P leading y is insignificant.

4.11 CAUSALITY 2: THE DP-TEST (FROM SECTION 2.6)

Table 4.4 is the first example of the TSIV (two-stage instrument variable) causality test using the development potential DP-variables. All specifications in the table refer to a single cross-country regression on average data for 2005–10. These regressions include no control variables. The top section of the table presents the OLS results. The five estimates in row (5) use different instruments for robustness. The adjusted (centered) R^2 of the OLS regression indicates that 20% of the cross-country variation in the degree of democracy in 1995 is associated with the cross-country variation in income.

The statistical properties of the TSIV estimates are analyzed in rows (6) to (9). The first indication that the instruments are statistically satisfactory is row (5), showing that the first stage regression has a partial R^2 of about 0.5. More formally, the Cragg–Donald test statistic shows that the instruments are *strong* in all five columns of Table 4.4, because it is always greater than the stated critical values. In addition, most Sargan tests for overidentifying restrictions are fairly satisfactory. The instrumented measure of income has a large and statistically significant effect on the degree of democracy in all regressions presented. The estimated coefficient on income is about 2, using both the OLS and the IV estimator.[11]

---

[10] The correlogram also looks for causality, but it detects nothing!

[11] What this means can be illustrated by an example: Ghana is close to the 25th percentile of the income measure in our sample (7.05), and Thailand is close to the 75th percentile (8.79). The income difference between Thailand and Ghana predicts a $(8.79-7.05) \cdot 2.8 \approx$ 4.9 Polity-point difference between the countries. The actual difference in 1995 is 10

TABLE 4.4. *The DP-test for long-run causality from income to the P-index,*
2005–10

Dependent variable: *P*	Main model	Robustness of model to instrument variation			
Estimate	(1)	(2)	(3)	(4)	(5)
No. of countries	101	106	101	101	142
	OLS estimates				
(1) Income, *y*	1.99	2.07	1.99	1.99	1.41
t-ratio	(5.2)	(5.8)	(5.2)	(5.2)	(3.5)
(2) Centered R^2	0.21	0.24	0.21	0.21	0.08
	IV estimates: *y* is instrumented				
(3) Income, *y*	1.63	2.52	1.37	2.45	2.18
t-ratio	(2.8)	(5.0)	(2.4)	(4.5)	(3.7)
(4) Instruments	*biofpc, geofpc*	*bioavg, geoavg*	*animals, plants*	*axis, size, climate*	*coast, frost maleco*
(5) First stage partial R^2	0.44	0.52	0.44	0.50	0.47
(6) CD F-statistic	39.03	55.05	39.05	32.06	40.95
CD critical value	19.93	19.93	19.93	22.30	22.30
(7) Sargan test	2.97	10.03	0.78	8.20	3.37
p-value	0.08	0.00	0.38	0.02	0.19
	Hausman test for parameter consistency of OLS and IV estimates (none rejected)				
(8) C-statistic	0.74	1.70	2.12	1.42	3.26
p-value	0.39	0.19	0.15	0.23	0.07
	Check for reverse causality (none works)				
(9) CD F-statistic	4.62	17.86	2.64	9.40	5.87

See Section 2.6. All observations for averages of 2005–10. All estimates include a constant (not reported).

Row (3) in the table shows that income causes democracy (the *P*-index). The estimate of the *main model* is given in column (1). It uses the first principal components of four measures of geographic conditions and two measures of biological conditions. This model is used in further

Polity points, so the estimate explains half of the observed *P*-difference of the two countries.

analysis, as the most parsimonious set of variables catches the largest amount of variation in the measures of biogeography. Columns (2) to (5) show that the result in (1) is robust to variations in the instruments. The instruments in columns (3) and (4) refer either to biology or to geography, and the instruments in column (5) provide only a limited amount of biological variation.[12]

When the OLS and IV estimates are compared in row (8), it appears that they do not differ. Thus, no causality from democracy to income is detected. The same result appears in the reverse causality estimate of row (9). Hence, whatever the institutional history of the sample countries and irrespective of the critical junctions passed on the way, the long-run outcome is essentially the same, and it is explained fairly well by income.

4.12 STABILITY OF THE MAIN CROSS-COUNTRY ESTIMATE OVER TIME: 1820–2016

The analysis deals with a long-run effect, and the results should hold for a great many years.

Figure 4.12 analyzes the stability of the main result for each of the 197 years from 1820 to 2016. The figure shows the OLS- and the IV-estimates of the income coefficient, surrounded by 95% confidence intervals (*ci*) for all these years. To catch the transition, the country sample must be wide. This is only the case after 1960. Consequently, the time-period 1820–2016 is separated into Figures 4.12a and b.

Figure 4.12a starts in 1960. For every year after 1960, the CD-F statistic is greater than 22, so the instruments are strong. Both the OLS- and the IV-estimates have a fairly stable average as in Table 4.4. It is interesting that the result is higher before 1990 than after the demise of Soviet Socialism. The confidence intervals of the two estimates have considerable overlap all year, so the two estimates do not differ. Thus, the results for the 57 years where the instruments are strong remain like the ones reported in Table 4.4.

Figure 4.12b goes back an additional 140 years to 1820. The cross-country sample concentrates on two and then one dozen of today's rich

---

[12] Column (2) includes the four overseas Western countries as having European biogeography. Since the inclusion of the recoded data would potentially bias the results in favor of the hypothesis of a Democratic Transition, we use the original observations of *bioavg* in column (2), but do not find different results relative to the other columns.

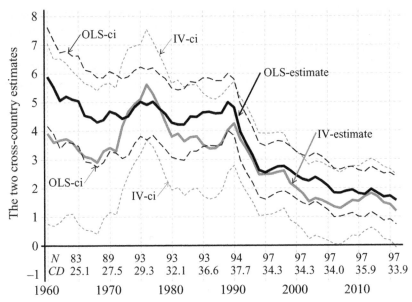

FIGURE 4.12a. The OLS and IV estimates of the income coefficient, 1960–2016

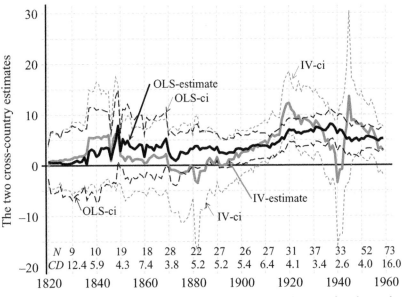

FIGURE 4.12b. The same estimates, 1820–1960. Note change of scale on the vertical axis

countries. The Cragg–Donald test statistic (CD) shows that this weakens the instruments. Thus, the results are unreliable, and they do vary much more than the reliable results of Figure 4.12a. However, for most years the OLS and the TSIV instrument estimates of the income effect are still within the confidence intervals of each other. So, as far as it goes, the main result is confirmed.

5

The Jumps Model for the Short Run

Changes of the P-index are known as jumps. The Main sample contains 515 jumps, of which 199 are larger, i.e. greater than 3 P-points. Section (s1) explains the 515 jumps by the tensions, and shows that the explanation only works for the larger jumps (s2). Some of the jumps are sequences that may be planned changes – they are more positive than discrete jumps (s3). A grievance asymmetry means that the political effect of a negative shock is stronger than the effect of a positive shock – the asymmetry is large for system jumps (s4). Finally, a range of regression estimators are used to show that they give random results (s5), and an explanation for this is provided (s6).

5.1 EXPLAINING JUMPS

Table 5.1 tries to explain the jumps by means of the following four variables: Initial tension, $\Theta^P_{(-)}$,[1] initial income, $y_{(-)}$, annual growth rate, g;

---

[1] Recall that the tension is the difference $\Theta^P = P - \Pi(y)$ between the actual P and transition path from Figure 4.4a.

TABLE 5.1. *OLS regressions explaining the jumps, J, in the Main sample*

N = 515	(1)	(2)	(3)	(4)	(5)
Initial tension, $\Theta^P_{(-)}$	0.583 (14.6)	0.849 (17.4)	0.965 (19.2)		0.579 (14.6)
Initial income, $y_{(-)}$	-0.070 (-0.2)	0.512 (0.7)	-3.053 (-3.5)	0.487 (1.4)	
Growth, g	0.021 (0.6)	0.008 (0.2)	0.028 (-0.6)	-0.015 (-0.3)	
Growth 5 years, $g5$	-0.079 (-1.1)	-0.129 (-1.6)	-0.014 (-0.2)	-0.071 (-0.9)	
Constant	1.573 (0.7)	-3.221 (-0.4)	26.665 (3.2.4)	-2.497 (-1.0)	0.995 (4.1)
FE for countries	No	Yes (121)	Yes (121)	No	No
FE for years	No	No	Yes (49)	No	No
R^2 net of FE	0.297	0.297	0.297	0.005	0.295
R^2 of FE		0.214	0.254		

See also the parallel Tables 3 and 6.1. The effect of the fixed effect is reached by running the regression in the column without the other variables. The fixed effects, has some collinearity to income and the tension. Thus, 0.75 as the best estimate of the effect of the tension. The number of fixed effects are added in brackets after the 'yes'.

and average growth rate over the preceding five years, g_5. In addition, fixed effects for countries and years are included in some of the regressions. These variables are taken to measure the transition and development. Only one of the four explanatory variables works. It is the tension, Θ^P, as seen from regressions (1) to (3) and (5). When it is excluded in regression (4), the R^2-score drops to 0.005. The tension variable is a function of Polity, $P(y)$, hence Θ^P has some covariance with y; but income is statistically insignificant when Θ^P is omitted in column (4). The two growth variables have no effect.

See also the parallel Tables 5.3 and 6.1. The effect of the fixed effect is reached by running the regression in the column without the other variables. The fixed effects, has some collinearity to income and the tension. Thus, 0.75 is the best estimate of the effect of the tension. The number of fixed effects is added in brackets after the "yes."

The estimated effects of the tension are all positive and highly significant with a size of about 0.75. When Table 5.3 looks at the larger jumps only, it finds an effect that is twice as large. Both tables find that the average change is toward the Π-curve, and getting to the curve normally requires several jumps. A main result is that the inclusion of both fixed effects in column (3) generates a large negative income effect, but the effect of the tension does not fall –rather, it rises.

Chapter 6 compares the explanation of the jumps in Table 5.1 with the parallel Table 6.1 explaining the events. The important point is that the same variables do not explain the events. The tension is the key variable in Table 5.1, but it explains nothing in Table 6.1. The jumps happen close to randomly.

This is the core of the Jumps Model. It does not explain why the system changes at a particular time, but once it does, it moves toward the transition path. Thus, the transition path is an attractor for the jumps that happen randomly. The randomness evidence follows in Chapter 6.

5.2 THE IMPORTANCE OF THE SIZE OF THE JUMP

The next step is to analyze the direction of the jumps as a function of their size. Table 5.2 counts the number of jumps that move toward and away from the Π-curve, so the *right* jumps are in the direction predicted by the tension, and the *wrong* jumps are in the opposite direction.

Row (1) of the table reports 187 jumps of a numerical size of 1, where 91 move in the *right* direction, while 96 move in the *wrong* direction. The test in column (6) reports that this is random. Row (2) shows that jumps of 2 and 3 move slightly more often in the right direction, but the difference is not statistically significant at the 5% level. However, jumps with larger sizes in rows (3) to (6) are significantly more likely to be in the

TABLE 5.2. *The size of the numerical jump and its direction relative to Π*

	(1)	(2)	(3)	(4)	(5)	(6)
	Jump size	Direction relative to tension			Fraction	Binominal tests in %
		Both	Right	Wrong	Right	
(1)	1	187	91	96	0.487	66.95
(2)	2–3	129	74	55	0.574	5.63
(3)	4–6	50	36	14	0.720	0.13
(4)	7–9	43	32	11	0.744	0.10
(5)	10–12	50	49	1	0.980	0.00
(6)	12 up	56	56	0	1.000	0.00
	All jumps	515	338	177	0.656	0.00

Table explained in text. The test is a one-sided binominal test for Ho: The number of right jumps is random with the probability 0.5. All bolded test results reject randomness. The sum of the larger jumps in rows (3) to (6) is 199.

right direction; jumps with a numerical size of 12 and up all move in the right direction. Part of this is an artefact, as the Polity index is limited to the interval [−10, 10]. While this barely limits jumps in the right direction at low levels of income, it does limit jumps in the wrong direction at high income levels.

The two top rows show that small jumps −4 < J < 4 are random, with 165 jumps toward the transition curve, Π, and 151 jumps away from it. However, the 199 larger jumps have 173 right and only 26 wrong. This suggests that small jumps may be considered as *regime adjustments* – and they are within the gray zone of measurement uncertainty – that can go either way, while *larger jumps* are system changes that mostly go in the direction of the Π-curve. The correlation between the jumps and the initial tension is 0.54, but the correlation between the jumps and the resulting tension (i.e., after the jump) is −0.34. This suggests that large jumps overshoot the Π-curve. Figure 5.1 and Table 5.3 confirm this.

Figure 5.1 shows a (J, T)-scatter plot of the jumps and the tensions reported in Table 5.2. The hollow circles represent 316 small jumps where −4 < J < 4, showing regime adjustments. The 199 larger jumps represent genuine regime changes. They are of three types: 26 are in the wrong direction (gray diamonds); 18 undershoot the Π-curve (gray squares). No less than 155 jumps are larger than the tension (black circles), so they overshoot the Π-curve. They are the points within the two symmetrical wedges. Wedge 1 holds the (J, Θ^P)-points, where $J > \Theta^P > 0$. The positive tension means that countries have too little democracy relative to their

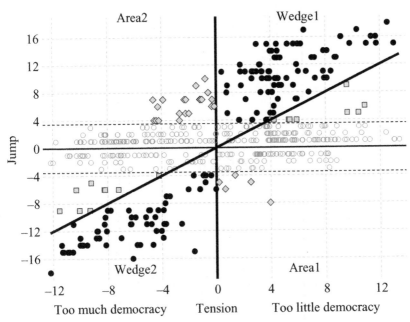

FIGURE 5.1. Scatter of jumps over tensions
Explained in text. Overshooting is represented by the black circles in the two symmetrical wedges. They are the areas between the 45-degree line ($J = T$) and the vertical line through (0, 0). Area1 and Area2 show cases of undershooting. The hollow grey circles show small system adjustments, which may not be real, see Section 4.6.

income level. They jump toward more democracy by more than Θ^P, so they overshoot the Π-curve. Conversely, in the negative Wedge2, where $J < \Theta^P < 0$, countries have too much democracy relative to their income level and overshoot the Π-curve to get too little democracy.

The many cases of under- and especially overshooting explain why full convergence to the Π-curve tends to be slow, even if income would stay constant. Table 5.3 employs the regression specification used in Table 5.1 for the sample of the larger jumps. The results have a fine fit and an average overshooting of about 50% of the initial tension. Thus, it rises to (damped) cyclical movements of the P-index as discussed in Chapter 2.

5.3 THE DIFFERENCE BETWEEN DISCRETE JUMPS AND SEQUENCES

Table 5.4 compares the discrete jumps and the sequences. The sample includes all 262 larger jumps. While the standard deviations are roughly similar, the means are significantly different, as shown by a *t*-test.

TABLE 5.3. Explaining the 199 larger jumps

$N = 199$	(1)	(2)	(3)	(4)	(5)
Initial tension $\Theta^P_{(-)}\,\Theta_{(-)}$	1.567 (26.2)	1.737 (25.5)	1.786 (22.8)		1.427 (23.5)
Initial income, $y_{(-)}$	-2.721 (-5.8)	-1.470 (-1.0)	-2.818 (-1.4)	1.896 (2.0)	
Growth, g	0.027 (0.5)	0.006 (0.1)	0.018 (0.2)	-0.007 (-0.1)	
Growth 5 years, $g5$	-0.068 (-0.7)	-0.297 (-2.0)	-0.306 (-1.6)	-0.270 (-1.2)	
Constant	21.832 (6.3)	15.567 (1.3)	22.967 (1.3)	-11.773 (1.7)	
FE for countries	No	Yes (87)	Yes (87)	No	No
FE for years	No	No	Yes (47)	No	No
R² net of FE	0.785	0.785	0.785	0.023	
R² of FE		0.112	0.180		0.738

See also the two parallel tables, Tables 5.1 and 6.1. There is some multicollinearity between the fixed effects, income, and the tension. Thus, I take 1.5 as the best estimate of the effect of the tension.

TABLE 5.4. *A comparison of jumps: discrete versus sequences*

Size of jump	Discrete		Sequences	
	Negative	Positive	Negative	Positive
4–5	16	25	8	8
6–7	11	12	1	11
8–9	15	17	3	9
10–11	13	21	1	13
12–13	12	10	1	6
14 up	14	13	5	17
Sum	81	98	19	64
Average		0.65		5.88
Std		9.83		8.87

t-test = 4.13 for equal means, rejects for p < 0.005%

Numbers in the gray cells are in ΔP-points, while the remaining numbers are counts of cases.

Jumps toward a more authoritarian regime are normally fast. A military coup typically takes one day, and the preparations are secret, for good reasons. Most coups are rather peaceful, and *The Economist* often reports that people first note that a coup has taken place when they wake up in the morning and see tanks in the streets.

Jumps toward democracy normally require a sequential process, which often contains four steps, as follows: (i) A government of national conciliation is appointed; (ii) it proposes a new constitution; (iii) it is approved by a referendum; and finally (iv) a general election takes place. The process normally takes two years, but it may take as many as four years.

5.4 THE GRIEVANCE ASYMMETRY FOR SYSTEM CHANGES

The literature on vote and popularity often finds a grievance asymmetry: A negative event causes a loss of government popularity that is about twice the gain the government experiences from a positive event of the same size (see Nannestad and Paldam 1994, 1997).

Table 5.5 shows that the grievance-hypothesis generalizes to regime jumps. It shows the number of events at each of eight intervals for the growth rate, with one lag. The gray area, in rows (r4) and (r5), represents normal growth. The top panel, in rows (r1) to (r3), shows the effect of below-average growth. There, countries have too many events, as they would if the regime is held responsible for poor growth performance. In all cells, excess instability is significantly positive, but it sums only to

TABLE 5.5. *Number of events at different growth rates*

		(c1)	(c2)	(c3)	(c4)	(c5)	(c6)	(c7)	(c8)
		Growth rates		Observations		Fraction	Binominal test (%)		Excess
		From	To	Events	All	(c3)/(c4)	$(c5) \geq x$	$(c5) \leq x$	events
Low	(r1)	$-\infty$	-6	61	343	0.178	0		31.9
	(r2)	-6	-2	81	565	0.143	0		33.0
	(r3)	-2	0	97	702	0.138	0		37.3
Avr	(r4)	0	2	107	1259	0.085	51.1	52.5	0.0
	(r5)	2	4	119	1404	0.085	52.6	51.1	−0.3
High	(r6)	4	6	80	905	0.088		67.0	3.1
	(r7)	6	8	29	424	0.068		12.6	−7.0
	(r8)	8	∞	40	514	0.078		31.3	−3.7

The gray cells are used to calculate the normal frequencies of events. It is $(107 + 119)/(1,259 + 1,404) = 0.085$. Columns (c6) and (c7) report one-sided binominal tests for $x = 0.085$. Significant test results are bolded. The excess events are calculated as (c3) − x(c4). The zeros in (c6) are p-values below 0.005%.

102.2 $(= 31.9 + 33.0 + 37.3)$ over $1,610$ $(= 343 + 565 + 702)$ observations. That is 6.3%, so the effect is moderate.

The bottom panel, in rows (r6) to (r8), displays the effect of above-average growth. More than half are negative, as they would be if the regime is rewarded for good growth performance, but the "excess" stability sums only to -7.6 $(= 3.1 - 7.0 - 3.7)$ for $N = 1,843$ $(= 905 + 424 + 514)$, which is -0.4%. The positive effect of high growth is small, and insignificant. The grievance asymmetry is larger for system stability than for government popularity.

5.5 REGRESSION MODELS (FOR THE ECONOMETRICIAN)

The most important counter-argument to the analysis in the previous section is presented in Acemoglu et al. (2008), who used the L2FE panel regression (also known as a GDPM):

$P_{it} = a_{1i} + a_{2t} + b_1 P_{i,t-1} + b_2 y_{i,t-1} + u_{it}$, where the a's are fixed effects for countries and time, and u is the residuals. The steady state income effect is $b^* = b_2/(1 - b_1)$. It should be equal to the income effect in Table 1. (5.1)

The surprising result in estimates of (5.1) is that b_2 became small and insignificant, which of course carries over to b^*. Thus, there is a contradiction. I interpret Equation (5.1) as representing the Granger-causality idea, as it analyzes whether income adds anything when P is explained by fixed effects and P lagged. Thanks to the long spells of constant Ps, it is not surprising that Equation (5.1) finds that y explained nothing. Next, this result is replicated, and in addition it is shown that a whole spectrum of 11 regression models gives rather fickle results.

These results are reported in Table 5.6. The regression results are based on *pooled* and *heterogeneous* parameter models. A common feature of the pooled models is that the within-effects of the explanatory variable *income* and the effects of common shocks are restricted to be the same for all countries in the sample. By contrast, the heterogeneous models allow for country-specific income effects and for country-specific effects of common shocks. A dynamic specification of the Democratic Transition across countries i, over time t, with Polity, P_{it}, and income, y_{it}, can be written as:

$$P_{it} = b_{1i} P_{i,t-1} + b_{2i} y_{i,t-1} + u_{it} \quad \text{with} \quad u_{it} = \mu_i + \lambda_i f_t + \varepsilon_{it}, \quad (5.2)$$

where $b_{2i}/(1 - b_{1i})$ is the country-specific (heterogeneous) long-run parameter of interest, and u_{it} is an error term that includes an unobserved

TABLE 5.6. *Regressions using a range of estimators*

	(1)	(2)	(3)	(4)	(5)
			Part A. Pooled parameter models		
	POLS-T	2FE	AB	BB	CCEP
Income	3.21	−2.90	−10.52	1.88	−0.30
[z-statistic]	[7.8]	[3.0]	[1.5]	[2.3]	[−0.3]
Observations	5,688	5,688	5,568	5,688	4,905
Countries	118	118	118	118	118
RMSE	1.73	1.70	1.66	1.81	1.57
Non-stat. residuals (CIPS *p*-val.)	0.00	0.00	0.00	0.00	0.00
Weak cross-sec. dependence (CD *p*-val.)	0.00	0.00	0.00	0.00	0.00
Instrument count			58	67	
AR1-*p*			0.00	0.00	
AR2-*p*			0.19	0.18	
Hansen test of overid. restrictions (*p*-val.)			0.29	0.04	
Diff.-in-Hansen test of IV subset (*p*-val.)				0.05	

Part B: Heterogeneous parameter models

	(6) PMG	(7) MG	(8) CD-MG	(9) CCEMG	(10) AMG-D	(11) AMG-S
Income	-0.56	0.46	-3.60	0.77	-1.45	-1.27
[z-statistic]	[-1.7]	[0.5]	[-2.3]	[0.4]	[-1.7]	[-1.2]
Common dynamic process					0.41	0.96
[z-statistic]					[6.0]	[7.3]
Observations	5,568	5,568	5,568	4,905	4,120	4,120
Countries	118	118	118	118	103	103
RMSE	1.55	1.68	1.64	1.44	1.48	2.18
Nonstationary residuals (CIPS p-val.)	0.00	0.00	0.00	0.00	0.00	0.99
Weak cross-sec. dependence (CSD p-val.)	0.01	0.00	0.00	0.82	0.58	0.04

Cross-country time series data, 1960–2010. OPEC members and countries with less than 21 consecutive time series observations excluded. All estimates based on dynamic model, except AMG-S. Reported coefficients are long-run income effects. Bolded coefficients are statistically significant at the 5% level.

The regressions are: POLS-T: Pooled OLS with time-fixed effects. 2FE: Two-way Fixed Effects. AB: Difference-GMM (Arellano-Bond) with restricted instrument count. BB: System-GMM (Blundell-Bond) with restricted instrument count. CCEP: Common Correlated Effects Pooled including year fixed effects and three lags of the cross-section averaged variables. PMG: Pooled Mean Group using four lags of cross-section averaged variables. MG: Mean Group. CD-MG: Cross-sectionally Demeaned Mean Group. CCEMG: Common Correlated Effects Mean Group. AMG-D/S: Augmented Mean Group; dynamic model/static model. CIPS: Correlated-Im-Pesaran-Shin panel unit root test for non-stationarity of residuals. CSD: Test for weak cross-sectional dependence of the residuals.

country-specific effect, μ_i, and an unobserved common factor, f_t, with country-specific (heterogeneous) factor loadings, λ_i.

The most popular panel estimators in the empirical growth literature (POLS, 2FE, Difference-GMM, System-GMM) impose the restriction of common within effects ($b_{ji} = b_j$) and identify μ_i and f_t with country and year dummies (or first-differencing and cross-sectional demeaning).

Common shocks may have different effects across countries, and some variables may be nonstationary, leading to potentially biased pooled parameter estimates. More flexible *mean group* panel estimators have been developed by Pesaran and Smith (1995), Pesaran et al. (1999), Pesaran (2006), and Bond and Eberhardt (2013).

A broad range of both types of estimators is used. *Part A: Pooled parameter models*: The estimates reported in the first and second columns of Part A of Table 5.6 should reveal a reasonable range of the effect of income on the degree of democracy. Due to the inclusion of the lagged endogenous variable, pooled OLS (POLS) and two-way fixed effects (2FE) are known to produce biased results, though in different directions. This suggests that the true income effect is expected to be somewhere within the range given by the two reported estimates – which is of little help in the present case because the range includes zero. Similarly, the AB (Arellano-Bond) and the BB (Blundell-Bond) estimators give results with different signs, while the CCEP (Common Correlated Effects Pooled) estimator gives a statistically insignificant coefficient close to zero. Thus, the results for the pooled parameter models do not provide convincing empirical evidence for a positive effect of income on democracy, in line with results in the recent literature.

The residual diagnostics for all pooled estimators suggest that the null hypothesis of nonstationary residuals is rejected, which allows for the possibility of a cointegrating equilibrium relation between the degree of democracy and per capita income.[2] However, the null hypothesis of weak cross-sectional dependence of the residuals is rejected for all estimators, which implies that there is strong cross-sectional dependence in the residuals, thereby violating the conditions for unbiased estimates.

Part B: Heterogeneous parameter models: Part B of Table 5.6 reports the results for estimates of the Democratic Transition using heterogeneous

---

[2] The Correlated-Im-Pesaran-Shin (CIPS) unit root test for non-stationarity is done with the Stata module pescadf (Lewandowski 2007). The CSD test for weak cross-sectional dependence (Pesaran 2015) is done with the Stata module xtcd2 (Ditzen 2016).

parameter models. All estimators run country-specific regressions to allow for individual income effects (which are reported as unweighted cross-country averages), but differ with respect to the modeling of common shocks and weak cross-sectional dependence of the residuals. Four variants are considered.

The Pooled Mean Group (PMG) estimator (Pesaran et al. 1999) allows for short-run country-specific effects, but imposes the restriction that the long-run effects are the same for all countries. Like the PMG estimator, the mean group (MG) estimator (Pesaran and Smith 1995) does not control for cross-sectional correlation with a year dummy, but when it is estimated on cross-sectionally demeaned data (CD-MG), it implies that a common shock has the same effect in each country (like the pooled estimators that include a year dummy). The Common Correlated Effects Mean Group (CCEMG) estimator (Pesaran 2006) augments the country-specific regressions with panel cross-section averages of the dependent and independent variables to allow for unobserved country-specific effects of common shocks, but treats the implicit estimates as nuisance parameters that cannot be interpreted.

The Augmented Common Correlated Effects Mean Group (AMG) estimator (Bond and Eberhardt 2013) goes a step further by explicitly identifying a common dynamic process (CDP) that is caused by otherwise unobservable variables.[3] The idea is to run a first-stage regression of (3) in first differences and to collect the estimated coefficients on the (first-differenced) year dummies (f_t), which are held to capture the common evolution of unobservables in the level of P across countries and over time. This common dynamic process is plugged back into equation (3) as an additional covariate and yields, in the second-stage regression, an explicit estimate of the mean effect of unobservables on the degree of democracy.

Part B of Table 5.6 studies country-specific effects in combination with more sophisticated modeling of the error term. This does not help to find statistically significant positive effects of income on the degree of democracy. The only exception is the CD-MG estimator, where a negative income effect comes with a rejection of the null of weak cross-sectional dependence of the residuals. For all other heterogeneous models, the coefficient on income is statistically insignificant with favorable residual

---

[3] PMG, MG, and CCEMG are implemented with the Stata module xtdcce2 (Ditzen 2016); AMG is implemented with the Stata module xtmg (Eberhardt 2012).

diagnostics in the sense that the null of nonstationary residuals is rejected, which is required for a possible cointegration between income and democracy. However, only CCEMG and the dynamic version of AMG (AMG-D) do not reject the null of weak cross-sectional dependence of the residuals. Hence, even the two statistically preferred estimators do not identify a robust direct effect of income on the degree of democracy.

The main positive result of part B is that the two AMG estimators confirm the presence of a common dynamic process as a statistically significant driver of the transition from an authoritarian to a democratic regime. It appears that the kernel regression and the common dynamic process identified by the AMG estimator both point to the existence of a long-run pattern in the degree of democracy.

The kernel regressions in Section 5.4 show a clear link between income and democracy, but they cannot control for omitted variables. The panel regressions in Table 5.6 do not show a comparable link between income and democracy for a broad range of pooled and heterogeneous estimators. The introduction claimed that the statistical properties of the two variables income, y, and Polity, P, are so different that it is unlikely that y can explain P within a standard regression model. Nevertheless, it is evident that rich countries are more democratic than poor countries.

5.6 CONCLUDING REMARKS ON THE PROBLEMATIC REGRESSION ESTIMATES

When the whole set of 11 regression estimates of the income effect is considered, it is clear that something strange is going on. Normally, a sequence of regressions that increasingly adjust for more and more potential problems should show an improvement in the results, indicating a convergence to the true result. Thus, the coefficient estimate should move in a predictable way and the t- or z-ratios should increase. This is not the case in Table 5.6. The income effect jumps up and down in a seemingly random way.

My interpretation is that this shows that *the regression tools of the profession are inappropriate for the problem at hand*. The main statistical problem appears to be that the Polity-variable is a bounded step-wise stable variable, where infrequent jumps of variable size interrupt substantial periods of stability, while income is an almost linear variable (i.e., *gdp* is almost log-linear). In addition, the kernel estimates reveal that there are nonlinearities involved at both ends of the range. Maybe some sort of a hazard model could be developed for the problem, but linear regression models are the wrong tool, even if they contain many refinements.

Another way to understand why short-run panel models are likely to fail is to look back to Figure 4.11. There are no signs that any lags/leads between the two variables have a peak giving a choice. While a rise in income will cause a rise in the P-index, it cannot be predicted exactly when it will happen within (at least) a ten-year period. However, the average correlation is significantly positive throughout – we are clearly dealing with a long-run connection. Though the relation is strong in the long run, it is fuzzy in the short run.

6

Events Are Practically Random

To study the spells of constant regimes empirically requires long time series, so this research is covered in Chapter 7, which shows that the average spell is about 15 years, and much longer at the ends of the P-range. Even in the middle of the transition, most regimes are constant for greater than ten years. Thus, political regimes have a great deal of stability.

Chapter 6 argues that stability is a result of the efforts of regimes to consolidate, which means that regimes develop status quo equilibria (s1). To break such equilibria requires a *triggering event*. Two sections of the chapter show the two ways in which such events happen (almost) randomly: (i) It is demonstrated that economic development variables, income and growth, cannot explain the events, and neither can the tension variable, Θ^P (s2). System changes do not happen when Θ^P reaches a certain size. Thus, the explanation of the particular time at which it happens is different from the explanation of what happens (s3). The rest of the chapter (s4–9) tries to identify the triggers by searching the historical archive of *The Economist*. This research shows what well-informed contemporary observers thought were the triggering events for all 262 larger jumps. The triggering events are found to be very diverse and most are unconnected to development.

6.1 REGIME CONSOLIDATION: MAKING A STATUS QUO EQUILIBRIUM

Any political regime wants to survive, so as soon as it is established, a regime starts a consolidation process. Regimes use three main methods, as follows,

(i) As much as possible, the regime reorganizes its administration by discharging staff loyal to the old regime and appointing new loyalists in their place. This is particularly important as regards the control apparatus, including police and security personnel.[1] It is made clear to the public that it is dangerous to join an opposition movement.

(ii) The regime strives to establish legitimacy – often by holding some kind of election, by creating a new constitution, by obtaining the blessing of the Church, or by disseminating propaganda stressing the national-historical roots of the regime, etc. The regime may also undertake conspicuous public works.

(iii) The regime creates a class of loyal clients by means of mechanisms distributing rents. It is important that the recipients of the rents understand that the rents are "unreasonable," so that they are likely to be abolished by the next regime.

These methods require that the ruler has adequate funds, but the population will certainly resent taxes spent for regime consolidation. Thus, the methods are much easier to apply in oil-rich countries, where the ruler has no need for taxes, as mentioned in Section 4.7.

6.2 DOES DEVELOPMENT AND THE TENSION EXPLAIN EVENTS?

Table 6.1 explains events by using the same variables as Table 4.1: initial income, $y_{(-)}$; initial tension, $\Theta^P_{(-)}$; the annual growth rate, g; and the average growth rate over the preceding five years, g_5. In addition, fixed effects

---

[1] Less democratic regimes often create an especially dangerous security force that is under the control of the leader of the regime only.

TABLE 6.1. *OLS regressions explaining the 675 events, E*

N = 6,211	(1)	(2)	(3)	(4)	(5)
Initial tension, $\Theta^P_{(-)}$	0.000 (-0.1)	0.000 (0.1)	0.002 (2.1)		0.000 (0.4)
Initial income, $y_{(-)}$	-0.032 (-9.2)	-0.025 (-2.3)	-0.081 (-5.3)	-0.032 (-9.3)	
Growth, g	-0.002 (-3.5)	-0.003 (-3.7)	-0.003 (-3.7)	-0.002 (-3.5)	
Growth 5 years, g5	-0.004 (-3.7)	-0.004 (-3.6)	-0.003 (-2.1)	-0.004 (-3.7)	
Constant	0.371 (13.3)	0.206 (1.1)	0.544 (1.5)	0.370 (13.4)	0.099 (26.2)
FE for countries	No	Yes	Yes	No	No
FE for years	No	No	Yes	No	No
R² net of FE	0.024	0.006	0.009	0.024	0.000
R² of FE		0.060	0.073	0.000	0.000
N	6,211	6,208	6,208	6,211	6,211

See Table 5.1. The difference between the R² of 0.024 in columns (1) and (4) and the R2's in columns (2) and (3) is a measure of the collinearity of the four variables, $T_{(-)}$, $y_{(-)}$, g, and g5 and the dummies. Stata deletes some degrees of freedom when all the dummies are included.

for countries and years are included in some of the regressions. The table reports OLS regression results. The corresponding probit regressions give similar results. With $N = 6,211$, "everything" is normally statistically significant. This is also the case in Table 6.1, but the key finding is that the regressions explain a small fraction of the variation only. The country and year dummies provide about 85% of the explanatory power – such as it is.

The most important observation from Table 6.1 is that the tension variable, which played a key role in the Jumps Model of Chapter 5, turns out to explain none of the variation in the events. Hence, the probability of an event does not depend on the distance of the *Polity*-score from its equilibrium value on the transition curve.

The coefficients on both growth variables are negative and statistically significant, but they are tiny. Consider the averaged estimated coefficient of growth g of 0.0025 in the regressions (1) to (4). Imagine a boom where the economy grows 3 percentage points faster than it usually does. Such a boom would reduce the chance of a political regime change by no more than $3 \times 0.0025\% \approx 0.0075$ (percentage points). For the averaged 5-year growth rate, g_5, the estimated effect is a bit larger, but still small.

Governments and regimes that are successful in generating high economic growth may become popular and hence more stable, so that the coefficients on growth should be negative, but Section 5.2 showed that the effect is small. In addition, high economic growth is disruptive for old political structures; see Chapter 13. Thus, it is not surprising that the negative effect of growth is close to zero.

6.3 THE BIG DIFFERENCE BETWEEN THE EXPLANATION OF EVENTS AND JUMPS

Table 6.2 compares Table 6.1, explaining events, to the parallel Table 4.1, explaining jumps, and Table 4.3, explaining the larger jumps. The explanations are strikingly different. Column (3) compares the fit, and columns (4) to (7) compare the marginal R^2 of the four explanatory variables. The key difference is column (4) for the Θ^P-variable: It gives no contribution in Table 6.1, but it is the key variable in Tables 5.1 and 5.3. Thus, the comparison demonstrates that events happen randomly, while the tensions explain the size of the jumps.

The reader may think that this comparison is "unfair," as Table 6.2 is calculated for all 6,211 observations, while Table 4.1 uses data for the 515 jumps only. However, Table 4.1 has also been recalculated using all 6,211 observations, including jumps of size zero, as shown in the last row of the table. This reduces the difference between the results, but there is still a large difference in the explanatory power of the tension.

TABLE 6.2. *A comparison of the fit of estimates in Tables 6.2, 5.1, and 5.3*

Columns	(1)	(2)	(3)	(4)	(5)	(6)	(7)
			R^2		Marginal R^2 from Model (3)		
			Model (1)	Tension, Θ^P	Income, y	Growth, g	Growth, $g5$
Explaining	Table	N					
Events, E	6.1	6,211	0.024	0.001	0.004	0.003	0.006
All jumps	5.1	514	0.297	0.363	0.012	0.000	0.000
Larger jumps	5.3	199	0.785	1.567	0.011	0.000	0.002
Jumps, incl. $J = 0$	Not included	6,211	0.026	0.068	0.011	0.000	0.000

The marginal R^2 is calculated in each column from model (3) in the tables by comparing the full estimate with the estimate when the variable in the column is deleted. Both the tension and the income are the initial values. Column (3) reports the R^2-values net of fixed effects. The regression 5.1 has 137 fixed effects.

TABLE 6.3. *The number of jumps in six equally large intervals of the data sorted by income*

Interval of 1/6	Counts		Frequency of jumps	Binominal tests of fall [a]			Income interval	
	N	Jumps		1-step	2-step	3-step	from	to
First (lowest)	1,035	120	0.116	n.a.	n.a.	n.a.	5.319	6.748
Second	1,035	112	0.108	23.3	n.a.	n.a.	6.749	7.261
Third	1,035	102	0.098	15.1	3.3	n.a.	7.261	7.952
Fourth	1,035	98	0.095	38.5	9	1.6	7.952	8.517
Fifth	1,035	71	0.069	0.3	0	0	8.517	9.215
Last (highest)	1,036	12	0.012	0	0	0	9.217	10.363
All	6,211	515						

Main sample. (a) The test is the probability that n or less of 1,035 draws with the frequency of the preceding 1, 2, or 3 cells occurs by chance. The tests show a significant downward trend, as in Figures 4.7 and 4.8.

Table 6.3 studies the effect of income in another way. It considers *triggering* events that actually lead to regime change: The 675 events discussed in Chapter 4 gave only 515 jumps. The table finds that the number of jumps falls with a rising income level. In the beginning, the fall is small, but then it becomes substantial, as expected from Chapter 4. At high income levels, the countries are already democracies and the populations want no further regime change. The expected stability (absence of events) of political regimes at low income levels is not confirmed, but then there are only a few, if any, countries left in the traditional steady state where modern development has not (yet) started. The result in Table 6.3 reflects that many LDCs have political regimes built around a single person. When an event triggers a change away from that person, there is often a regime jump. This is not the case in developed countries, where widely respected institutions secure the idea that rulers can change without a system change.

6.4 THE TRIGGERING EVENT IN THE HISTORICAL ARCHIVE OF *THE ECONOMIST*

The second way to study whether events are random is to find out what close contemporary observers thought were the triggering events for all the 262 larger jumps. One or more articles in *The Economist* cover each jump. The triggering events for the jumps are all classified in two dimensions. One is domestic/external (D/X), and the other is political/economic (P/E). Thus, in Table 6.6, all triggering events are placed into four cells: (DP), (DE), (XP), and (XE).

This section provides a few well-known examples that fit into the four cells of the (2×2) table. The short stories in Sections 6.4–6.6 are parts of the systematic analysis in Section 6.5. The articles in *The Economist* may be one-paragraph notes or articles of up to two pages. The latter describe some of the process leading to change. If more than one month elapses between the trigger and the eventual change, as is often the case, the story may be quite complex, which makes it difficult to pinpoint the crucial event starting the process, and I have frequently coded more than one event. This is particularly true when there is a lull in the process.

A strong impression that emerges when reading approximately 270 articles is that they deal mostly with *domestic politics*. This may be in order to tell newsworthy stories. Even when the magazine is called *The Economist*, it is obvious that the (anonymous) journalists writing the articles are concentrating on the stories, rarely discussing whether the economy mattered. Maybe it did not, as suggested by the negative finding reported at the end of Section 2.3, but it could also be a reporting bias. Therefore, all cases in which the economy or external events are mentioned have been coded.[2]

The journalists normally try to identify the triggering event. For reasons of space, the process leading to the change is merely sketched, but one or two important events in the process are often stated. The process is conditional on background factors such as the strength of the regime, but such factors are not included systematically. In some cases, several similar events that did not lead to a jump occurred well before the triggering event. That a particular event became the trigger may be because something went wrong in the process, or background events weakened the incumbent regime.

A well-organized political regime can absorb even large popular demonstrations and riots. In France, P stayed constant during the large wave of demonstrations and strikes of 1968,[3] and French voters reelected President de Gaulle after the demonstrations were over. One year later, however, he lost a constitutional reform referendum and resigned. In the same way, the military dictatorship of Chilean President Pinochet absorbed the large wave of popular unrest in connection with the breakdown of the fixed exchange rate policy in 1982–83.[4] He resigned peacefully in 1988, after narrowly losing a plebiscite on the extension of his rule.

Some of the crises that caused a system jump have a complex history of economic and political interaction – here the choice of the triggering event is difficult.

In the two decades from 1965 to 1985, Argentina experienced four large regime changes.[5] The country has a long history of unrealistic economic policies fueled by populism. In the two decades mentioned, the country experienced the return and subsequent death of Juan Peron, the so-called Dirty (civil) War, repeated waves of high inflation, several military coups, and it started and lost the Falklands War to the United Kingdom. It later defaulted on the national debt; see Tanzi (2018) for a fine survey. Those

---

[2] I have made a check of the coding of the countries, using Wikipedia, which devotes one or two pages to the modern history of each country. A few coding errors were found. However, I am glad to say that the sources agree surprisingly well, both with respect to the timing of larger changes and their explanations.

[3] The events of 1968 in France are examples of large-scale demonstrations/riots that were caused by a wave of utopian beliefs that came and went for no concrete reason; see Chapter 3.

[4] The fixing of the peso to the US dollar tried to eradicate the residual inflation left after high inflation in 1972–75, which was stopped by standard monetary means. The fixed-peso policy had large costs, but inflation did decline.

[5] As usual, the large jumps were of a cyclical nature: –8 (1966), +15 (1973), –15 (1976), and +16 (1983).

events did follow from one another, but it is impossible to claim that everything was endogenous, so that the tragic path of events was inevitable given the country's state in 1965. *The Economist* does identify triggering events for all four jumps – it is actually quite easy in three of the four cases.

6.5 THE (DP) DOMESTIC POLITICAL CELL: FOUR CASES OF COUNTRIES JOINING THE WEST

Portugal, Spain, Taiwan, and South Korea are countries that first witnessed strong economic development and then experienced a system jump after the death of the old dictator. Figure 6.1 shows where the triggering events happened relative to economic development. The deaths of leaders caused a process to start, during which popular pressures emerged. In those four cases, the jump seems to be unconnected to short-run economic perform-ance. Therefore, the triggering events are classified as domestic and political.

When the jumps occurred, the countries had reached an income level of $y \approx 9.5 \pm 0.5$. The four countries all had large positive tensions, with

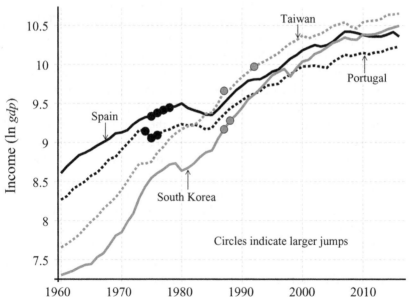

FIGURE 6.1. Four cases of countries that have joined the group of wealthy countries

The increases in P-points are: (i) 1974–76 in Portugal (18 points); (ii) 1975–78 in Spain (16 points); (iii) 1987–88 in South Korea (11 points); and (iv) 1987 and 1992 in Taiwan (14 points), which is treated as two jumps.

P-scores well below the transition curve. Thus, the jumps reduced the tension. In Portugal and Spain, the jump overshot the curve, which made the countries *too* democratic for a while until income caught up.[6]

6.6 THE (XP) EXTERNAL POLITICAL CELL: THE POST-SOCIALIST WAVE FROM CHAPTER 3

The dataset includes ten old socialist countries that left Soviet Socialism to become 28 countries. Table 6.4 shows a condensed version of the process for their regime jump.

A great many articles in *The Economist* cover the collapse of Socialism, and it is also covered by a large literature (e.g., Paldam 2002b). The key event was that the Communist Party of the USSR "imploded" during 1988–89 owing to domestic political events. With a large reduction in central power, a process started that spread throughout the Socialist world, both in the countries under Soviet patronage as well as in Yugoslavia and Albania, which were outside the Soviet sphere. The transitions involved large popular demonstrations in most countries, and a few years later they caused serious economic setbacks.

The initial triggering event for all the large jumps listed in Table 6.4 thus is a political shock that originated in the center and spread throughout the Socialist world. Only a few East Asian Communist countries and Cuba managed to protect their regimes against the political wave. All European (or near-European) countries saw large jumps toward democracy, and only a few jumped back later on, while the five poor central Asian countries and Azerbaijan, listed at the end of the new Ex-USSR group, remained authoritarian. The events are classified as external political shocks, except in Russia, where the jump was a domestic political shock.

What happened in the cases covered by Table 6.4 is reasonably clear, but it is less clear what went on in the countries that were distant from the USSR. Two such cases are Nicaragua and Congo Br, mentioned in the last paragraph of Chapter 3. *The Economist*'s article describes the new parties in Congo (Br) and the peacefulness of the process from the regime change to the election, but it does not mention the collapse of the

---

[6] The changes in South Korea and Taiwan happened in overlapping years, and so did the changes in Portugal and Spain. This suggests a common background factor. Andersen and Jensen (2019) provide evidence that the change of Catholic doctrine as regards democracy is such a factor. *The Economist* does not mention this factor.

TABLE 6.4. *The jumps in 1988–92 in the 28/29 post-socialist countries*

Country	Jump/sequence	Country	Jump/sequence	Country	Jump/sequence
USSR, 1989, $P = -4$		Kazakhstan	1, stable	Countries created (long) before 1988	
Lithuania	14, stable	Kirgizstan	1, fairly stable	Hungary	17, stable
Latvia	12, stable	Tajikistan	2, unstable	Mongolia	16, stable
Armenia	11, unstable	Turkmenistan	−4, stable	Bulgaria	15, stable
Belarus	11, unstable	Uzbekistan	−5, stable	Poland	15, fairly stable
Estonia	10, fairly stable	Yugoslavia, 1988, $P = -5$		Czechoslovakia	15, stable
Ukraine	10, fairly unstable	Slovenia	15, stable	Czech Republic	Stable since 1993
Moldova	9, fairly stable	Macedonia	11, fairly stable	Slovak Republic	Stable since 1993
Russia	9, unstable	Croatia	2, unstable	Albania	14, fairly stable
Georgia	8, fairly stable	Serbia	0, unstable	Romania	13, fairly stable
Azerbaijan	1, unstable and back	Montenegro	Stable since 2006		

See Table 2.1. In 1993, Czechoslovakia broke into two countries. The two big countries of Ex-Yugoslavia, Croatia and Serbia, went through democratization in 1999–2000 after the wars between Serbia and Croatia and in Bosnia and Kosovo were finally over. Montenegro broke with Serbia in 2006. Armenia exhibits a major zigzag in 1995–98. Azerbaijan has gradually turned more authoritarian. $P = 0$ in 1990 for USSR as that was a rather chaotic year. Finally, the DDR (East Germany) joined West Germany.

Socialist world.[7] Even more puzzling is the article about Nicaragua, where the Sandinista government allowed a free election in 1990. The article mentions economic chaos (with hyperinflation and a debt burden of ten times GDP) and stresses US pressure, but makes only a brief remark about the collapse of the USSR in the last paragraph of the article.

6.7 THE (DE) DOMESTIC ECONOMIC CELL: REACTIONS TO ECONOMIC MISMANAGEMENT

The coup in Chile in 1973 produced a jump in the Polity index of −13 points. Much has been written about the coup, and since it had a strong Left–Right dimension, rather different explanations have been given involving various conspiracies. Salvador Allende's Unidad Popular government had created both high hopes and a severe crisis because of its utopian economic policies:[8] Real GDP was falling, and the inflation rate was fast approaching hyperinflation, producing major waves of demonstrations and counter-demonstrations organized by the parties of the ruling bloc.

The coup-makers were the heads of the army, navy, and air force, and its stated purpose was to save the nation from economic chaos. There is no reason to believe that the coup-makers did not mean what they said, so the triggering event was economic mismanagement by the democratically elected government, well in accordance with the coverage in *The Economist*. Thus, it is classified as a domestic economic trigger.[9]

From our reading of the case articles, it appears that external economic events have caused no regime changes, so the (XE) cell has remained empty. This corresponds to the observation from Figures 4.11 and 4.12, showing the distribution over time of the triggering events and the jumps.

6.8 THE 262 TRIGGERING EVENTS

Table 6.5 shows the coding of the events reported to be "causal" for the 262 jumps. On average, 2.5 such events are listed for each jump. They are amazingly diverse.

---

[7] Here, I could not resist deviating from the source and make the jump external political.

[8] Chile is home to many fine economists, but none of them were associated with the Allende government, which disliked economic theory in general and what it called "neoclassical theory" in particular.

[9] When Chile reverted to democracy in 1988–89 in a two-year sequence of two upward jumps of +5 and +9 polity-points, the change was caused by domestic political events.

TABLE 6.5. *Types of events mentioned as important for the 262 jumps*

	Countries	113
	Jumps	262
	Of which sequences	83
Domestic political	Demonstrations/riots	69
	Fight within government	16
	Ruler takes steps toward democracy	93
	Ruler takes steps toward autocracy	46
	New constitution	41
	Collapse of policy	17
	Election unfree	51
	Election free	108
	Coup non violent	63
	Coup violent	19
	Natural death of ruler	11
	Murder of ruler	8
	Civil war won	10
	Civil war lost	3
	Peace accord ending civil war	8
Domestic economic	Negative growth	10
	High inflation	9
	Other	4
External political	Collapse of USSR and Yugoslavia	24
	Pressure incl. military from abroad	28
	War won	1
	War lost	7
External economic	International economic crisis	0
	Changes in commodity prices	0
Number of events	Average per jump 2.5	646

The format of *The Economist* demands that articles are of moderate size. The journalists always look for two types of events that they think (i) will start and (ii) are important for the story. I interpret the journalists' missions as attempts to identify events with an element of exogeneity, but, of course, the journalists do not try to say how salient such elements are.

Some of the events are (almost) fully exogenous in the context of specific countries, such as the wave of post-communist transitions beyond the borders of the Russian Soviet Republic. Almost 100 large changes happened during 1989–92 in connection with the collapse of the USSR. In some of those cases, the USSR (or Yugoslavia) was the protector of the government that collapsed when protection was withdrawn. In other cases, the USSR was a distant supporter, but the government of the country decided that it had to adapt to the new world order. Thus, the 1988–92 period saw a widespread diffusion of ideas and beliefs: Socialism went out of fashion.

Other such waves have happened, such as the revolutionary year of 1848,[10] the youth revolution of 1968, and the (failed) Arab Spring of 2010. They are difficult to handle in a systematic way, as the mysterious concept of *zeitgeist* is an important part of the story. Other demonstrations/riots might have more limited elements of exogeneity.

Sometimes a government decides to take a (major) step toward or away from democracy. Some reasons must underlie such transitions, but the inside stories typically are not well known, so in our perspective they are exogenous.

The sample contains seven cases of successful foreign military interventions for the explicit purpose of changing a country's political system without modifying its borders. In those cases, the intervention was caused by domestic circumstances, notably human rights violations, but once again, in none of the cases did the system change come immediately after a sudden deterioration in human rights.[11] Vietnam's invasion of Cambodia did oust the regime of the Khmer Rouge that had killed over 20% of the population, but the Vietnamese "excuse" for the invasion was border incidents.

Most coup-makers issue a proclamation after they have occupied the national broadcasting center. Such proclamations may reflect what the coup-makers think, but normally they are a great deal loftier than the actual goals of the men seizing power. No one ever admits that the coup-makers have exploited an opportunity to hijack the gravy train. The articles in *The Economist* often report the coup's announced motives and speculate about the true intentions when a gap seems obvious. The most common declared motive is to stop the wheeling and dealing of corrupt

---

[10] A large literature discusses the revolutionary wave of 1848. It proposes various explanations. Berger and Spoerer (2001) survey the literature and claim that the wave resulted from a sudden international economic crisis, contrary to our findings for the period after 1960. Aidt and Jensen (2014) propose that democratization in 1848 was the result of an international wave of revolutionary zeal, which is a nice example of an external political trigger.

[11] France (2), Tanzania (1), the United States (3), and Vietnam (1) led the foreign military interventions. In addition, some foreign interference took place in three to four cases when it is unclear that the intervention was crucial. Finally, foreign mercenaries were involved in another three to four cases. The mercenaries may have worked for or with a state agency in their country of origin (see https://en.wikipedia.org/wiki/Bob_Denard).

politicians. It is part of the military ethos that officers are upright and honest. Such declarations are domestic/political in nature. However, if the motive is declared to be an economic crisis and the country does have a crisis, the jump has an economic trigger.

Often, *The Economist* mentions that the triggering events happened because of an unsatisfactory economic development, but by then things typically had been bad for a long time. Many observers have argued that the gradual slowing down of the USSR's growth may have had a causal relation to the big collapse of the late 1980s and early 1990s, but the country's poor economic performance had been going on for 20 years or more; the implosion of the regimes took only a couple of years.

None of the stories claim that external economic events are important for precipitating jumps. They are mentioned only rarely, both in 1973–80 when commodity prices exhibited dramatic swings, and in 2009–14 during the international banking/debt crisis. The copper price drop after the Vietnam War did affect economic developments in Zambia and Chile, but it appears to have had no influence on the two countries' regimes.

The key observation from Table 6.5 is the diversity of the triggering events found. It is easy to further subdivide the list – triggering events are very diverse.

6.9 THE SUMMARY TABLE

Table 6.6 reports the final counts in the four cells (DP), (DE), (XP), and (XE) of our 2 × 2 matrix. If the chain of events from the triggering event to the jump is within the political sphere, as is often the case, there is no doubt that the triggering event is domestic (cell DP).

As mentioned, I started my quest from the theory of the democratic transition, notably from the Jumps Model, and looked for economic factors in the political transition. The model claimed that triggering events are (almost) random. Tables 6.4 and 6.6 provide strong additional evidence of the unpredictability of such events. The vast majority of the

TABLE 6.6. *The 262 triggering events*

	Political	Economic
Domestic	215	11
External	40	0

events are political, and though they may have some long-run relation to the economy, the connection is certainly not strong and direct.

This chapter has looked at 262 major political system changes in 170 countries between 1960 and 2015. The two sources – the Polity index and *The Economist* – agree on the timings of the changes. I then attempted to identify – within broad classes – the source of the triggering event in the 262 cases, using the relevant articles in *The Economist* in the identification. That, admittedly, is a narrow source, but it is available throughout the sample period (1960–2015) in a fairly consistent way, and the format of the magazine forces the journalists to concentrate on the important events.

The triggering events vary quite a lot, and they often enter into a complex process with other events. The sources are thin on some regime changes. In a few small countries, such as Burundi, military coups are (relatively) common, and they are barely mentioned. Other countries, such as Chile, have seen only one coup, which is covered by a handful of articles.

Still, one strong conclusion can be drawn: Seen from the perspective of development, triggering events are largely random. Previous work has demonstrated that once a triggering event occurs, the path of the democratic transition is an attractor for the resulting jump. That is why the transition curve is so apparent in the long-run data.

7

The Three Pillars Model for the Long Run

This chapter looks at the full Polity *P*-data set from 1800 to 2016, and presents The Three Pillars Model, explaining *why* the Democratic Transition comes about (s1). The long data series confirm equivalence (s2): The long data series tell the same transition story as the cross-country data in Chapter 4. The long run is illustrated by ten nutshell country stories (s3) and by some long-run descriptive graphs (s4). Finally, the long *P*-series are used to identify the spells of system constancy (s5), which allows a second look at regime consolidations (s6).

7.1 THE THREE PILLARS MODEL

The Democratic Transition has happened across the world, in countries with different cultures, religions, and history. Thus, there must be a basic theory that explains why development is very likely to cause a change to democracy.

Nearly all traditional political systems were some sort of kingdom that had been stable for a handful of centuries. It was based on *three pillars* that normally worked together: Pillar 1 was a hereditary *king* from a royal dynasty. Pillar 2 was the *feudal/military* class,[1] which provided the top of the military. Pillar 3 was the **Church**,[2] i.e., the organization of the national religion. Consequently, the ruling group was small. Sometimes power shifted between the pillars, and also dynasties were replaced, but the system was stable for at least a handful of centuries. Such systems are scored from −6 to −10 by the Polity index, and from 6 to 7 in the two Freedom House indices. In the old West, these systems existed in nearly all countries, and in South and East Asia systems were similar; see Figures 7.2c and 7.3a for Japan and Thailand.

Kings often managed to claim some "divinity" through their alliance with the Church, and the feudal lords had hereditary titles that made them "nobility" with special privileges, etc. As the top clergy also came from the nobility, they lived in similar splendor. This all helped to make the power structure in society deeply entrenched.

The new colonies of the Americas did not have the same old power structure, but big landowners soon developed and in the sub-tropical and tropical countries, landowners had slaves. In Latin America the Catholic Church was strong. The liberation of the colonies happened just before 1800 in the United States, and two decades later in Latin American countries during the Napoleonic Wars in Europe, when Spain was seriously weakened.

The Grand Transition undermined two of the three pillars in the traditional power structure. Pillar 2: The Agricultural Transition reduced agriculture from about 50% of GDP to less than 5%. As argued in the introduction, this is a long-run causal link from income. It greatly reduced the economic power of the feudal class, and the privileges of the nobility were abolished. Pillar 3: The Religious Transition reduced religiosity by a factor of 3. As will be discussed in Chapter 11, this is a long-run causal link from income. It reduced the power of the Church substantially.

Instead of agriculture, new sectors developed in trade and industry, mostly in the towns, which grew dramatically. New classes of capitalists and workers emerged, and with some lag, a big middle class developed. It became the main recipient of the vast increase in human capital. To the extent that the old feudal class managed to be captains of the new industrial and trading firms, they could hold on to power, but mostly they did not. The new classes wanted political representation, and as they were large and concentrated in the towns, they could exercise considerable

---

[1] The historical part of Binswanger et al. (1995) finds that most LICs had very durable feudal systems and so had the present HICs when they were LICs.

[2] Recall that for want of a better name "Church" is used for the organization of a religion, while "church" is a building.

TABLE 7.1. *The 23 countries covered in 1800/10 and their successor countries 2008/18*

	1800/10 mostly kingdoms			2008/18 mostly democracy		
No	Country	P	Political system	Country	P	Political system
1	Afghanistan	−6	Kingdom	Same	−1	Mixed
2	Austria	−10	Kingdom	Core of same	10	Democracy
3	Bavaria	−10	Kingdom	Germany	10	Democracy
4	China	−6	Kingdom	Same	−7	Communist
5	Denmark	−10	Kingdom	Same	10	Democracy
6	France	−8	Military/ Emperor	Same	9	Democracy
7	Iran	−10	Kingdom	Same	−7	Theocracy
8	Japan	−10	Kingdom	Same	10	Democracy
9	Korea	1	Kingdom	South Korea	8	Democracy
10	Morocco	−5	Kingdom	Same	−5	Kingdom
11	Nepal	−6	Kingdom	Same	6	Democracy
12	Oman	−6	Kingdom	Same	−8	Kingdom
13	Portugal	−10	Kingdom	Same	10	Democracy
14	Prussia	−10	Kingdom	Germany	10	Democracy
15	Russia	−10	Kingdom	Russia	4	More democratic
16	Saxony	−10	Kingdom	Germany	10	Democracy
17	Spain	−10	Kingdom	Same	10	Democracy
18	Sweden	−10	Kingdom	Same	10	Democracy
19	Thailand	−10	Kingdom	Same	2	More democratic
20	Turkey	−10	Kingdom	Core of same	4	More democratic
21	UK	−2	Kingdom mixed	Same	9	Democracy
22	USA	5	Democracy	Same	9	Democracy
23	Würtemberg	−7	Kingdom	Germany	10	Democracy
	Average	−7.4			5.3	

political pressures. Thus, it led to democracy, as illustrated by Table 7.1. The Three Pillars Model is certainly a strong model that explains why development causes democracy, but the mechanism is fuzzy. Traditional systems had many variants, and so did the reform process. Old groups often tried to hold on to power, and changes required triggering events. Such events are rather diverse, as shown in Chapter 6.

7.2 CONFIRMING EQUIVALENCE: THE TRANSITION CURVE IN THE LONG TIME SERIES

Figure 7.1 uses the data for the 25 countries (listed in the note to the table) where the (P, y)-data are available for more than 120 years. On average, the series have 172 observations.

As half the countries covered are Western and modernized early, the kernel-curve has a wide flat section at the top like the curve for West in Figure 4.8, but otherwise it looks very much like Figure 4.4a. This is not surprising given the findings mentioned earlier, and it confirms the equivalence hypothesis for the Democratic Transition.

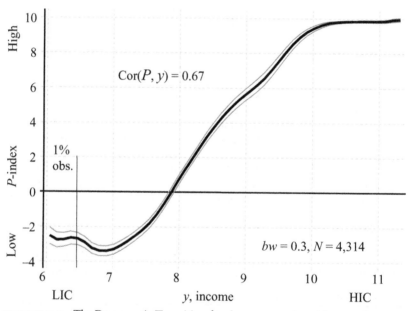

FIGURE 7.1. The Democratic Transition for the 25 countries with more than 120 observations

The 25 countries are Ecuador (120), Mexico (126), Bolivia (127), *Japan* (142), Argentina (145), Colombia (149), Uruguay (149), *Austria* (152), Peru (160), *Germany* (164), Belgium (165), Brazil (167), *Spain* (168), Greece (180), Norway (183), Venezuela (187), *Denmark* (192), *Portugal* (192), *France* (197), Netherlands (197), Chile (199), Italy (202), *UK* (217), *Sweden* (217), and *USA* (217). Parentheses hold the number of observations for each country. Germany and Italy are mergers of a handful of old countries in 1870 and 1860, respectively. The long series for the two countries are averages for the old countries. The eight countries in italics are also included in Tables 7.1 and 7.2.

7.3 THE TWO CENTURIES OF THE P-DATA: A SET OF NUTSHELL HISTORICAL CASES

The *P*-index covers 23 countries from 1800–10, where the average *P*-score was –7.4. Some of the countries have changed, but Table 7.1 compares the old countries to the same country or its successor. In 2008–18, they had an average *P*-score of 5.3. Table 7.2 compares the first spells in the data for countries that remained longer and shorter in the traditional steady state.

The graphs of Figures 7.2 and 7.3 show ten nutshell stories of the transition in countries where it is possible to create the long series by some interpolation of missing data, especially for income. The interpolated data appear as straight lines. This has caused some historical events to disappear, notably the Napoleonic wars that surely caused serious income losses in France and Spain. The same graphs have been created for Denmark, Italy, and Portugal – they look very much as the figures presented.

TABLE 7.2. *The first spell in countries that existed in 1800*

Late leavers of the traditional steady state				Early leavers of the traditional steady state			
Country	Data from	*P*-score	Spell	Country	Data from	*P*-score	Spell
Ethiopia	1855	4	75	Austria	1800	–10	47
Afghanistan	1800	–8	135	Denmark	1800	–10	34
Bhutan	1907	–10	98	France	1800	–8	14
China	1800	–6	109	Portugal	1800	–10	6
Japan	1800	–10	58	Spain	1800	–10	9
Korea	1800	1	111	Sweden	1800	–10	9
Nepal	1800	–6	48	UK	1800	–2	37
Thailand	1800	–10	132	USA	1800	4	9
Iran	1800	–10	106	Baden	1800	–7	22
Morocco	1800	–6	113	Bavaria	1800	–10	18
Oman	1800	–6	157	Prussia	1800	–10	33
Turkey	1800	–10	76	Saxony	1800	10	23
Russia	1800	–10	105	Würtemburg	1800	–7	19
Average		–6.7	102	Average		–6.2	22

Data for Ethiopia and Bhutan start in 1855 and 1907, respectively, but both countries are much older. The score of +4 for Ethiopia in 1855 seems high. It was the year Tewrodos II defeated Zemene Mesafint and became emperor.

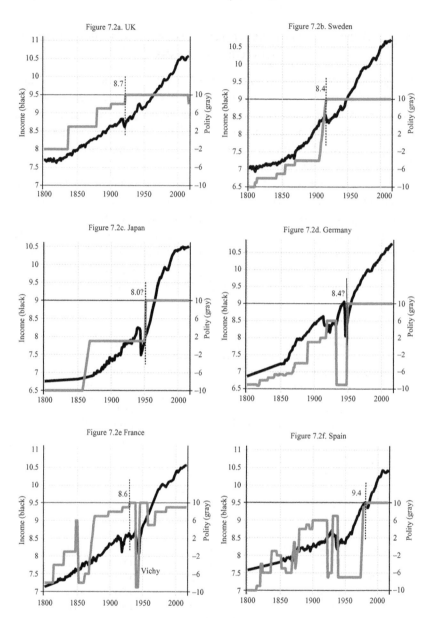

FIGURE 7.2. Some examples of the Democratic Transition, 1800–2016
The dashed vertical lines indicate where full democratization is reached. The number given is the income level where it happened. In most cases it shows about 100 years of democracy. The P-index for Germany before 1870 is an average for the five old German states. The ? indicates that the system change was influenced from abroad.

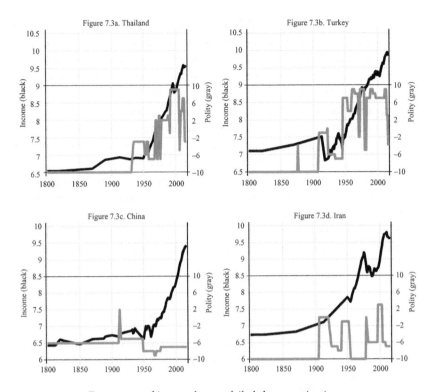

FIGURE 7.3. Four cases of incomplete or failed democratizations

Sweden, the United Kingdom, and Japan experienced one-way democratization, so that the G^P-ratio is 1 – there are no more movements in the P-index than necessary. The United Kingdom was the wealthiest country in the World in 1800, and also well ahead with the Democratic Transition. However, for the five other countries covered, the G^P-ratio is (much) larger than 1 – the P-index jumps up and down before it settles at the modern level (close to 10), and in some countries it has not settled yet.

Germany and Japan were democratized after some push from the occupation powers after the Second World War (hence the '?' on the graphs), but the income level grew rapidly at that time, and the democratization soon consolidated. All nine nutshell stories show that full democracy occurred at $y = 8.6 \pm 0.3$, which is an income level around $ 5,500, or for a family of four about $ 22,000 (in 2010 fixed prices). At this level of income, democracy consolidated in most countries.

Thailand (Figure 7.3a) and Turkey (Figure 7.3b) are countries in the process of democratization because of a late, but fast, modernization. They both look like a late and compressed version of France or Spain. My prognosis is that both countries will have consolidated democracies in 30 years, but both have passed the income of $y = 8.6$, where democratization took place in the old wealthy countries. Like most of the countries, they have gross movements in the P-index that are much larger than necessary for the transition, so that the G^P-ratio is (much) larger than 1. This is an important point in Chapter 13.

Finally, China (Figure 7.3c) and Iran (Figure 7.3d) are both very old countries with no traditions of democracy. However, both countries have made (unconvincing) attempts at some stage. My prediction is that they will try again, and eventually succeed. Both countries have reached an income level where most countries have democratized.

7.4 THE DATA FOR THE LONG RUN: SOME DESCRIPTIVE GRAPHS

As seen in Figure 7.4, the Polity-data only became widespread in 1960, and in the nineteenth century many of the (few) countries have no income data; see Figure 1.2.

As defined in Table 4.1, a *sequence* is a set of P-scores that change in the same direction in consecutive years; see also Chapter 5. The P-index reports reform processes that lead to a new system as a sequence of equidistant changes. Most P-scores that last one year only are part of a

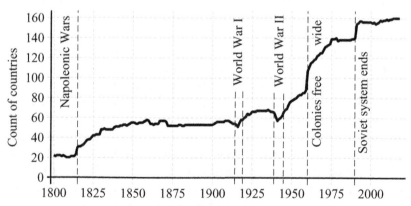

FIGURE 7.4. The number of countries included in the Polity index

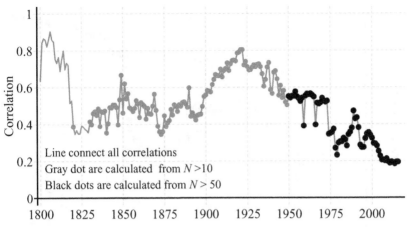

FIGURE 7.5. Cross-country correlations of P and y for each year from 1800 to 2016

The OPEC countries are deleted in the main calculation. If they are included, the curve shifts downward after 1950. When they are excluded, the correlation falls just before year 2000 as in Figure 4.9a.

sequence. I add all sequences that are followed by a constant P-score as part of the spell, also if one of the scores is zero. All spells found are reported in the net appendix, where sequences are highlighted in orange. The inclusion of the sequences increases the average spell by two years as most one-year spells disappear.

Table 1.3 reported that the correlation between the three political system indices and income is about 0.6. Figure 7.5 shows how the cross-country correlations vary over time. The average is close to 0.6. It is interesting that the correlation falls after 1990. The great wave of democracy makes the P-scores of countries more similar, even when income adjusts less quickly. It is noteworthy that the thin data before 1900 still have substantial correlations.

The averages of P and y across countries for year t are termed $\bar{P}$ and $\bar{y}$. Figure 7.6 shows the path over time of the $(\bar{P}, \bar{y})$-set. The country composition changes greatly, but the curve still has a clear upward drift. The period of the two world wars sees stagnation in the average income, and a rather chaotic period as regards political regimes. After the Second World War, the number of countries starts to rise and the average curve moves sideways. It is interesting to see that the big democratic wave in connection with the end of Soviet Socialism appears as an upward shift in the curve.

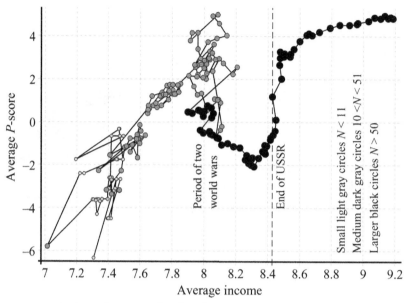

FIGURE 7.6. Annual averages for *P* and *y*

7.5 SPELLS OF CONSTANT REGIME, I.E., WITH A CONSTANT VALUE OF THE *P*-INDEX

A key fact of political regimes is that they often last a long time. To analyze how long needs long time series. Table 7.3 shows some statistics for the spells. While the rest of the book concentrates on the period 1960–2016, the full Polity dataset 1800–2018 is used to estimate the spells. Recall that sequences that lead to a new system are included in the spell.

The data file of Polity 2018 contains $N = 17,562$ observations, but some are blank. Consequently, only $N = 16,764$ observations are used. The last four columns are for spell interruptions: n is for new countries, t for truncated spells, s for countries that end, and $f = 100(n + t + s)/spells$ is the fraction (in %) of all spells that are interrupted.

The last four columns in the table are n for new countries, t for truncated spells, s for countries that end without a clear successor, and $f = 100(n + t + s)/spells$ is the fraction (in %) of all spells that are interrupted. China has data from 1800 to 2018, but China did not start in 1800 and did not stop in 2018, thus China has two t's. East Germany

TABLE 7.3. *Some counts and descriptive statistics of the Polity data set*

Country group (see net-appendix)	Countries	N	Spells	Avr	Std	n	t	s	f%
Africa, Sub Saharan	46	2,532	267	9.48	10.56	45	46	1	34.5
Asia and Oceania	28	2,461	179	13.75	22.78	20	35	1	31.3
Latin America include Caribbean	23	3,675	277	13.27	15.54	23	23	0	16.6
MENA, Middle East and North Africa	19	1,772	122	14.52	22.54	12	25	1	31.1
Post Socialist (see Table 3.1)	32	1,835	156	11.76	13.21	31	31	2	41.0
Western Europe and four overseas	24	3,882	158	24.57	29.47	12	35	1	30.4
Old German and Italian states before unification	11	607	31	19.58	15.87	7	4	11	71.0
Sums or averages for avr and std	183	16,764	1190	14.09	19.43	150	199	17	30.8

The data file of Polity 2018 contains $N = 17{,}562$ observations, but some are blank. Consequently, only $N = 16{,}764$ observations are used. The last four columns are for spell interruptions: n is for new countries, t for truncated spells, s for countries that end, and $f = 100(n + t + s)$/spells is the fraction of all spells that are interrupted.

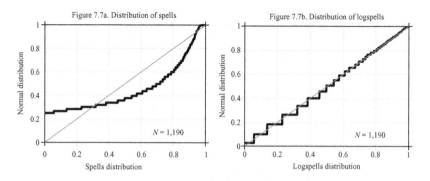

FIGURE 7.7. Probit diagrams analyzing the distribution of spells

started in 1949 and ended in 1989, thus East Germany has one n and one s. The sum $n + t + s = 386$ is twice the number of countries, as it should be.

No less than 31% of all spells are interrupted. The standard method to handle truncated spells is to multiply by two. When this is done for the 199 spells with a t, the average of **14.09** increases to **19.14**, but it does not seem reasonable for the 167 cases where the country is new (with n) or ends (with s) even when these cases do represent interrupted spells.

Figure 7.7 shows probit diagrams of the spells and the logarithmic spells. While the spells have a very skewed distribution, the log spell distribution is close to normal. However, formal tests reject normality, which is true also in the case of the logs. This is because of the integer representation of the P-score, which gives the step-curve shown. Consolidation takes time, and thus it gradually builds solid status quo equilibrium. Regime duration – i.e., spells – must be a function of the duration itself. This gives the spells the almost log-normal distribution shown in Figure 7.7b.

7.6 A SECOND LOOK AT REGIME CONSOLIDATION (CONTINUING SECTION 6.1)

The two basic steady states should show stability at the traditional steady state for low P-scores and at the modern steady state for high P-scores. This was shown by Tables 7.2 and 7.3, which looked at the traditional steady state as much as is recorded. It implies that the average spells are larger at the two ends, and less stable in between.

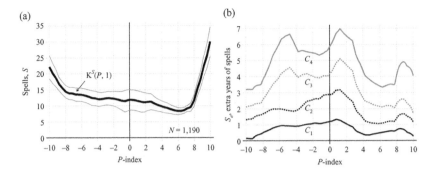

FIGURE 7.8. Explaining the spell S by P in two ways

Figure 7.8a reports the spells S as a function of P. Figure 7.8b analyzes how many extra years the spells gain after 1, 2, 3, and 4 years of consolidation. The extra spell for regimes that have survived one year is the consolidation curve C_1. It is found from the kernel K_1 for all spells lasting more than 1 year. The extra years are calculated as $C_1 = K_1 - K_0$. The consolidation C_1 is not much more than 1 extra year (on the S_e-axis). The second consolidation curve C_2 is calculated from the kernel K_2 of all spells lasting more than 2 years, and then the extra is $C_2 = K_2 - K_0$. Now there is a clear hump above $S_e = 2$. C_3 and C_4 are similarly calculated. The hump above 3 for C_3 is already larger, and the same is true for C_4. The hump over 4 is 2½ years extra for all Ps from −6 to +4. For $P = 4$, K_0 is 10 years. It rises from 10 to 16½ years, after 4 years of consolidation.

Figure 7.8a confirms that the spells are longer at the two ends of the distribution. Especially at the high-end, spells grow dramatically. Even during the transition, the average regime still lasts 10 years, or even 14 years, if the truncations are corrected for.

Figure 7.8b is an analysis of system consolidation. It shows how much longer the spell becomes if it survives 1 year, 2 years, 3 years, and 4 years. It does not matter much at the two ends, but it matters in the middle, where the average spell rises from about 10 years to 16½ years after 4 years of consolidation.

Table 7.1 showed that the standard deviation for the spells is larger than the average – no less than 19.4, but with 1190 spells, the standard error is still only 0.56, so the average is well established. The other chapters use the estimate that during the transition the average spell is roughly 15 years, when corrected for spell truncations. Both before and after the transition, system stability is measured in centuries.

PART IIB

THE TRANSITION OF THE ECONOMIC SYSTEM

The next two chapters deal with

Chapter 8 considers the *B*-index for *ownership preferences* from the World Values Survey, and Chapter 9 considers the *F*-index for *economic freedom* from Fraser Institute. The two indices are interpreted as measures for the preferences and the actual levels of capitalism vs feudalism/socialism. The indices are scaled to increase when capitalism rises, as it has done over the last 50 years.

TABLE IIB.1. *New terms and variables used in Chapters 8 and 9*

Variable	Definition and sources
New terms	
Welfare goods are goods with large positive externalities. The three big welfare goods are education, healthcare, and social protection. Infrastructure, law and order, and defense are others. goods.	
A *mixed system* has a large public part in the production of welfare goods, while private firms dominate operate in trade, agriculture, industry, etc.	

(*continued*)

TABLE IIB.I. (*continued*)

Variable	Definition and sources
Ownership preferences, B-index. Chapter 8	
Source	Item E036 from World Values Survey: www.worldvaluessurvey.org/wvs.jsp.
B_{it}	B-index. Excess preferences for private ownership to business. In percentage points.
$\pi^B(y_j)$	*Transition path*, estimated by $B = K(y, bw)$, with bandwidth bw, and slope $\lambda^B > 0$.
Fraser Index of Economic Freedom, F-index. Chapter 9	
Source	Fraser Institute: www.fraserinstitute.org/studies/economic-freedom.
F_{it}	F-index that measures the freedom to run a private business on a scale from 0 to 10.
$\pi^F(y_j)$	*Transition path*, estimated by $F = K(y, bw)$, with bandwidth bw, and slope $\lambda^F > 0$.

8

Ownership Preferences

The B-Index

The data available for analyzing the Transition in the Economic System are not made for the purpose. I use two indices: The present chapter considers the *B*-index of preferences for the economic system, and Chapter 9 considers the *F*-index measuring the actual system. The indices are weakly correlated, but they do tell the same story about the transition.

Both indices cover a short timespan only. Therefore, Chapter 8 starts with a brief survey of the history of economic systems in a longer perspective, suggesting that there is a transition (s1). Then the relevant theoretical literature is surveyed (s2). Next follows a description of the ownership item in the World Values Survey (WVS) explaining how the *B*-index is constructed (s3), and how to understand the index is discussed (s4). The transition curve is estimated for the 279 observations of the index (s5). Development over time in the index has some cyclicality due to big swings in ideology in the world (s6). The main direction of causality is from development to the *B*-index, but there is some simultaneity (s7). Finally, some multivariate results are reported (s8).

8.1 TRADITIONAL AND MODERN ECONOMIC SYSTEMS

Economic systems change during development, and in the end, all modern economic systems have converged to similar *mixed systems*, even when the way of reaching this system has differed considerably. This chapter and the next suggest that there is a general pattern.

The traditional economic system was feudal, with large landowners and tenant farmers. Income was low, and there was a large element of subsistence production. Thus, the fraction of produce sold in markets was limited, and hence towns were small.[1] Trade was taxed when goods left and entered towns. What are known today as industrial products were made in small quantities by skilled artisans who were members of guilds with monopoly power. Public sectors produced law and order, defense, and the conspicuous consumption required to glorify the royal house. Taxation was difficult to implement, and public sectors were small, 10–15% of GDP, except in times of war. The Church was the biggest supplier of the three important welfare goods – i.e., education, healthcare, and social protection – but it also had to pay for the Church itself. Church expenditures were financed by the tithe, voluntary donations, and income from land owned. This amounted to 8–12% of GDP, so expenditure on the three welfare goods was small, approximately 5% of GDP.

The modern economic system is a mixed system where trade and industry is private and a substantial public sector dominates the supply of welfare goods. The borderline between the public and private sectors is drawn a bit differently from one country to the next, but the convergence of the developed countries is also a convergence of economic institutions.

A great deal happened between the two steady state periods: The period between the Napoleonic Wars and the First World War is often termed the **Liberal Century** in the West, where industry developed and the feudal system vanished. In the rest of the world, this was the period of large-scale colonialism, when the West came to rule Africa and Asia, and Russia kept extending eastward until it reached Alaska. At the end of the century, the public sectors started to grow.

---

[1] Populations were small too. The whole of Western Europe had about 80 million inhabitants in year 1700, with France (21) and the area of present-day Germany (15) as the two largest populations. China and India had 140 and 165 million, respectively.

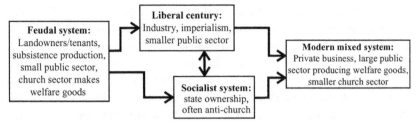

FIGURE 8.1. A nutshell history of the Transition of the Economic System
Chapter 11 discusses the decreasing role of the church sector.

In many countries, the transition included a detour via *Socialism*, i.e. public ownership of business, as sketched in Figure 8.1. This became a strong possibility after the establishment of the Soviet Union (discussed in Chapter 3) after the First World War.

The ex-colonies started their new life with economic systems formed by the colonial powers. The new countries wanted industrialization, and the infant industries idea argued that young industries needed protection to develop. The original argument was that protection should decrease once the firm was up and running.[2] However, protection generated *rents* with many beneficiaries, who quickly became addicted. Thus, many LDCs developed into rent-seeking societies, where the infant industries bloomed into bloated consumers of public funds, so that they became barriers to development.

The theory of Karl Marx stated that Socialism was the inevitable end result of the progression of economic systems caused by development; from the slave societies of antiquity to feudalism and on to capitalism, which inevitably leads to Socialism – a glorious goal that was only vaguely sketched. During the first half of the twentieth century, it appeared that the working class in advanced capitalist countries cared more about their increasing standard of living than about Socialism. This caused a big turn-around in the theory of Socialism; instead of being the goal of capitalism, Socialism became a proposal for a *short cut* to faster development that bypassed capitalism.

From the Socialist idea of the short cut to development, the infant industries became *SOEs*, State-Owned Enterprises. The goal of SOEs often developed into the creation of employment, which resulted in over-staffing, so firms came to need permanent protection. In the LDC-socialist model, the state leads development by taxing agriculture and

---

[2] The story of LDC Socialism is told in Paldam (1997). It includes rather sad descriptions of visits to ten SOEs in five countries. The World Bank (1995) is a large-scale study of the SOEs in the LDC-world. It documents that overstaffing of SOEs consumes substantial parts of public incomes that could be better used, e.g., for education, healthcare, and infrastructure.

foreign trade to acquire funds to build a modern industry of SOEs. Thus, there is no need for capitalism, which, as it was associated with the colonial empires, was viewed as a bad economic system. Therefore, large businesses were either nationalized or subjected to extensive regulation.

All LDCs have large informal sectors with a dense network of small firms (the bazar/market), which constitutes an important sector in the economy. The informal sector is difficult to regulate and tax. In the Soviet model of development, the informal sector was rigorously suppressed – even exterminated – especially in the countryside, although it was sometimes allowed in heavily controlled pockets of the economy. However, in other Socialist models it had/has a major role in the economy, providing dual development. The influential work of Hernando de Soto (2000) argues that the extensive regulation of private business, which also occurred in the informal sector, and the lack of secure ownership, including of land, caused many firms in the urban informal sector to be excluded from the banking system, which forced them to remain small and footloose.

Russia and China were poor countries, where, after bloody wars and revolutions, the communist parties won power and implemented Soviet Socialism (see Chapter 3). These two large countries claimed that they carried out successful and rapid modernization. Their extravagant claims were widely believed, especially in the LDC world.[3] During the 1960s, various versions of Socialism came to dominate in many countries in the form of African Socialism, Arab Socialism, Latin American structuralism, etc. Thus, there was a large-scale movement in poor countries from feudalism to some sort of Socialism. During the 1980s and 1990s, it became increasingly obvious that the Socialist road to development was a dead end.

A notable case is the story of African growth. The colonial powers left Africa with mixed market economies and moderate growth. From the early 1960s, most African countries started to implement African Socialism, as advocated by the OAU (Organization of African Unity). It took a decade to build, but once it was in full bloom, growth plummeted. The African growth tragedy lasted from 1970 to 1994, during which period income decreased in the average Sub-Saharan country. From approximately 1985, a whole wave of structural adjustments took place in order to move economic systems back toward the market. After a decade of reforms, growth resumed. Paldam (2017a) reviews the many explanations proposed for the tragedy. Most of these explanations are time-invariant, so they are inconsistent with the growth after 1994.

---

[3] It was also easy to convince many political leaders that they should control business.

The only consistent explanation I found is the large zigzag in the economic system. Thus, both when African countries adopted African Socialism and when they moved back toward the market, the policies were greatly influenced by growth expectations and growth experiences.

The reader may also consider the reforms in China in 1978 initiated by Deng Xiaoping. They were instituted in order to create development, and they were probably inspired by the great success of the Asian Tigers.[4] Once the reforms started to succeed, they were extended in all directions. And, after some time, they spread to Vietnam, India, and almost all East and South Asian countries.

8.2 THEORIES ABOUT THE LINK FROM ECONOMIC SYSTEMS/OWNERSHIP TO DEVELOPMENT[5]

In a democracy – even an imperfect one – people's preferences should cause the actual outcome. Hence, $B \Rightarrow F \Rightarrow y$. However, as argued in the previous section, it is likely that people's expectations/experiences shape their preferences, so that $y \Rightarrow B \Leftrightarrow F \Rightarrow y$, i.e., we are dealing with simultaneity.

People have a *natural tendency* to pursue *cost maximization* – especially when they are a cost themselves. If this tendency is allowed to develop, it destroys development, as the stories of many SOEs show. Thus, strong mechanisms are needed to prevent the natural tendency from letting the economy slide into inefficiency. In the Soviet model, a whole set of very labor-intensive central administrative controls were used for this purpose. In a market system, two decentralized mechanisms do the job: competition and property rights.

In the neoclassical theory of markets, competition punishes firms that give in to the natural tendency, so competition leads to competitive cost reductions. The property rights school has analyzed the importance of

---

[4] It is forgotten today that the four Asian Tigers, Hong Kong, Singapore, South Korea, and Taiwan, were ignored in the 1960s and 1970s, as they were barred from the organization of the (non-aligned/left leaning) Bandung Conference of less developed nations. Hong Kong and Singapore were British colonies that became trading nations, while South Korea and Taiwan were aligned with the United States, and hosted American military bases.

[5] The *general* sources used are Blaug (1997) on Marx and Marxism, and the readings in Pejovich (1997) on the property rights school. Interpretations of history in the light of property rights are found in North (2005) and Pipes (1999), which both contain good surveys of the literature. The cross-country pattern in property rights is discussed by de Soto (2000). Acemoglu et al. (2005) is a survey of the Primacy of Institutions view, by the main proponents. The Grand Transition view originated gradually from a set of essays republished in Kuznets (1965); see also Chenery and Syrquin (1975). Authors referred to in the general sources are listed with first names the first time they are mentioned.

ownership; see Pejovich (1997). The key idea is that when the owner is the decision-maker and the residual claimant, they can and will do much to turn the 'natural tendency' of cost maximization into cost minimization. It is debatable whether competition or private ownership is the strongest factor enforcing efficiency, but experience shows that it is difficult to make public firms compete. In practice, private ownership and competition go hand in hand, and deeply influence society. This suggests that the economic system – as measured by the B-index or the F-index – causes y: $B \& F \Rightarrow y$.

Several schools of thought broaden the property rights approach and argue that it determines the path of development. This was already a central part of Marx's theory, in which the economic 'basis' of ownership/ production shapes the 'superstructure' that includes politics and culture. The theory claimed that ownership systems contained dynamic processes, which generated irreversible stepwise system changes in the long run. The two final steps in Marx's long-run development model were (i) from feudalism to capitalism. As a result of the steady increase in the size of the working class during capitalism, it would (ii) turn into Socialism, which was seen as a highly desirable system. Thus, Marxism predicts that the correlation between the B-index and income is negative. In this chapter, it is found to be positive.

The research group behind the Fraser Index insists that countries (governments) choose policies, and argues that they should choose market-friendly policies with protection of property rights and free trade precisely to engender development. Here the choice of institutions is the exogenous element in development. However, success may be dynamic. The causality might be of the chicken–egg variety, where causation is circular. Once a government starts down a path, it will continue on this path if it is successful: $F \Rightarrow y$.

Theoreticians of history, such as Douglass North and Richard Pipes, have explored the broader macro-aspects to develop the links between political and economic institutions and economic development. Recently, the Primacy of Institutions (PoI) school of Daron Acemoglu and associates (ref) has considered how the property rights system (considered as the key institution for development) has developed. They use periods where fragmented political power existed to explain why fair enforcement of effective property rights arose. In contrast, societies where political power is concentrated in small elites fail to develop incentives to provide private property rights for the great mass of people. However, once development starts, it undermines the power structure; $F \Rightarrow y \Rightarrow F$, etc.

The argument so far has provided little clarity as regards causality. In the Three Pillars Model covered in Chapter 7, the key factor that changes political institutions is development itself, and it appears logical that these institutions also come to change economic institutions. The book argues that the underlying long-run causality is from development to institutions. However, the process of the Grand Transition is fraught with simultaneity and collinearity, as interacting transitions take place in many fields. Thus, it is a strong but fuzzy relation.

This gives rise to two predictions: Income is causal to the B-index, and this leads to the F-index.[6] Thus, the PoI and GT views lead to the same prediction with respect to the correlation between income and the F- and B-indices, but the correlation has reverse causalities. The causality tests find that the short-run results support the PoI school, while the long-run results support the GT view. The causality between institutions and development is complex.

Perhaps the discussion may be summed up as follows: If preferences were perfectly stable, and fell from the sky, the causal interpretation would be that B caused F, which caused development. The countries with the most capitalist preferences acquired more capitalism and hence became wealthier. This is the causal interpretation of the group behind the Fraser Index. Chapter 3 argued that the world has seen waves of opinion changes of a cyclical nature. If these changes are exogenous, the pure Fraser interpretation still holds.

However, if preferences change with income, the causal interpretation starts with income causing B, and then B causes F. We find that the long-run causality is from income to both F and B, and thus the pure Fraser interpretation becomes dubious.

An alternative explanation would be that development started in countries with a good location for trade. Trade is difficult to carry out as a public sector activity, and successful private trade created wealth that caused people to prefer liberal institutions, and then further success became dynamic. This interpretation is further discussed at the end of Chapter 9.

8.3 WVS OWNERSHIP PREFERENCE ITEM: DEFINING THE *B*-INDEX AND CALCULATING THE VALUES[7]

The WVS-questionnaire has received 513,529 respondents, of whom 420,083 have expressed an ownership preference; see Table 8.1.

---

[6] It has been discussed by many authors; see e.g. Knack and Keefer (1995), Acemoglu et al. (2005), de Haan (2007), Engerman and Sokoloff (2008), and Blume et al. (2009). On beliefs and values and development, see, e.g., Knack (2002), Uslaner (2002), and Bjørnskov (2010).

[7] The index is from Christoffersen and Paldam (2006). This part is based on Bjørnskov and Paldam (2012), who provide more details, especially on the relation between the index and other time series.

TABLE 8.1. *The waves of the World Values Survey*

Wave		Countries/polls	New countries	Respondents
W1	1981–84	24	24	32,964
W2	1990–94	43	20	62,771
W3	1995–98	69	26	118,943
W4	1999–2004	78	19	125,311
W5	2005–09	58	12	83,975
W6	2010–14	60	11	89,563
Sum		332 polls	112 countries	513,527

The ownership item is not covered by W1. It is polled 295 times in 110 countries of which 6 are *partial* states: Bosnia SrpSka, Cyprus N, Hong Kong, Northern Ireland, Kosovo, and Palestine. For three of these, income data have been interpolated. Bjørnskov and Paldam (2012) analyzed the representability of the sample. The 112 countries contain about 90% of the world's population, but they are about 30% wealthier than the average country. Also, the West and the post-socialist countries are overrepresented.

Economists like to think that important preferences are constant and cause the actual economic system, but it is hard to believe that preferences are unaffected by experience, and the index moves a great deal over time.

The item appears on a list about the preferences of the respondents for the way society should be organized. One of the items deals with the ownership of business – as it is part of a list, it does not read well:

Private vs state ownership of business and industry should be increased: Indicate preference on a scale from 1 to 10. 1 is strongest preferences for private and 10 is the strongest preference for public ownership.

The two sentences of the item are somewhat contradictory. The first sentence uses the word "increased," which points to a *change* of ownership. The second sentence asks people about their preferred *level* of ownership. The answers are interpreted in line with the second sentence. The next section demonstrates that this is in accordance with the answers of most respondents, but it adds a little uncertainty to the answers.

The answers are thus the preference for Socialism (low numbers) vs. capitalism (high numbers). This corresponds to the S- and the C-indices in Table 8.2. The C-index is used to give a measure that is positively correlated with the F-index discussed later. The answers are taken to measure mass *ideology* as an ownership preference.

The preference is measured in a period of considerable actual change. Table 8.2 shows the number of respondents giving each answer $n = 1, \ldots, 10$ and the frequencies in percent of the answers. The two

TABLE 8.2. *The ownership item: All 420,083 answers reported*

	Private									Public
n	1	2	3	4	5	6	7	8	9	10
Number	55,354	29,633	42,204	37,403	82,388	27,053	32,634	34,011	22,248	47,155
Percent	13.2	7.1	10.0	8.9	19.6	8.8	7.8	8.1	5.3	11.2
Data for	Cumulative preferences: $C = C(n)$ and $S = 100 - C(n - 1)$. Figure 8.2 shows the C-index as a curve									
C-index	13.2	20.2	30.3	39.2	68.8	67.6	75.4	83.5	88.8	100
S-index	100	86.8	79.8	69.7	60.8	41.2	32.4	24.6	16.5	11.2

The C and the S indices are the cumulative preferences for capitalism and Socialism, respectively. The item is V251 in Inglehart et al. (1998) and E036 in Inglehart et al. (2004). It is V117 in the root version of the WVS 2005–2006 questionnaire. Polls with 1–2000 respondents have measurement errors of 1–2 pp when the questions are clear and concrete. Items that are not salient to the respondent have larger measurement errors.

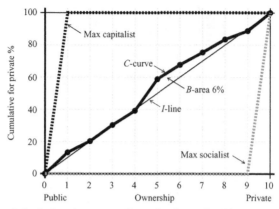

FIGURE 8.2. Calculating the *B*-area from the data of Table 8.2

indices give the *C-curve* and the *S-curve*, which are the cumulative frequencies for capitalism and Socialism, depicted in Figure 8.2. Per construction $C(n) + S(n+1) = 100$ for all n, so most of the discussion will use the C-curve only The C-curve is evaluated relative to the *I-line*, which represents indifference. The respondents are indifferent when they choose the ten possible answers $n = (1, \ldots, 10)$ with equal probability, so the expected frequency for each n is 10%. Hence, the cumulative frequency is the straight line from $(0,0)$ to $(10,100)$.

The C-curve is used for the B-index, which is the area between the C-curve and the I-line. With single-issue majority voting, the B-index reflects the ownership preference of the median voter. Under standard Downsian median-voting assumptions, all we need to see is if the C-curve is above or below the I-line at the intersection with the 50% line. However, logrolling is a fact of life, and decisions about property rights are typically made in the form of long-run political compromises involving other issues. Thus, the ideal B-index should also reflect the intensity of the preferences, which is measured as a distance relative to indifference, i.e., to the I-line. To measure the aggregate intensity, these intensities have to be added up. The sum is the area under the B-curve minus the area under the I-line. The first area is a set of trapezoids, which consist of rectangles with a triangle on top. The second area is a triangle, which is half the area of the whole graph. The steps between the n's are 1, and the curve starts in $C(0) = 0$ and ends in $C(10) = 100$, making the calculations rather simple:

$$B_1 = \int_0^{10} [C(n) - I(n)]\, dn = \sum_{n=1}^{10} \left[C(n-1) + \frac{1}{2}(C(n) - C(n-1)) \right] - \frac{1}{2} 10 \cdot 100$$

$$= \frac{1}{2} \sum_{n=1}^{10} [C(n-1) + C(n)] - 500 = \sum_{n=1}^{9} C(n) - 450 \qquad (8.1)$$

$$B = 100\, B_1/450 \qquad (8.2)$$

The index in Equation (8.1) is termed B_1. It has a linear relation to the average of the C-curve.[8] The final step is to calculate the index in percent. Figure 8.2 shows the two most extreme possibilities for the preferences: The *max capitalist* curve where all respondents answer "10" and the *max socialist* curve where they answer "1." The B_1 calculation for the max capitalist curve is 450, which is rescaled into the B-index by Equation (8.2), which is in percent. Equations (8.1) and (8.2) are used to calculate the 295 B-values listed on the data page. The C-curve on Figure 8.2 shows a small excess support for capitalism of 6%.

The B-index is anchored at zero for indifference between the answers, yet this is not the only way people can be neutral toward capitalism and Socialism. Neutrality means that the distribution of the answers is symmetric with respect to the mid-point, so that the two cumulative curves are exactly the same in reverse: $C(n) = S(11-n)$, for all $n = 1, \ldots, 10$. Thus, other neutral curves have symmetrical areas A over and B below the I-line, where $A = -B$. Hence, they deviate from the I-line by $A + B = 0$. This means that if the I-line is replaced with any neutral curve in the definition of the B-index, it will produce precisely the same index.[9]

Figure 8.3 shows the C-curves behind two of the most extreme B-values: The United States and China, which were the main powers with strong ideological stands, and thus the countries that most aggressively defended capitalism and Socialism.

In principle, the B-index ranges from −100 to +100. However, as each index is calculated from an average of all respondents to a poll, the law of averages tells us to expect the results to be non-extreme. The closeness of the cumulative curve to the neutrality line confirms this idea. The respondents in the full data set have a capitalist ideology, but only by 6%.

---

[8] The average C-curve is: $AvrC(n) = \left(\sum_{n=1}^{10} C(n) \right)/10$, so that $B_1 = \sum_{i=1}^{9} C(n) - 450 = 10(avrC(n) - 55)$.

[9] Imagine a neutrality curve that is zero until (answer category) 5 and then jumps to 100. Relative to the I-curve, the triangle with the corners (0,0), (5,50), and (5,0) is added, and the triangle with the corners (5,50), (5,100), and (10,100) is subtracted. As the two triangles are equivalent, the B-index does not change.

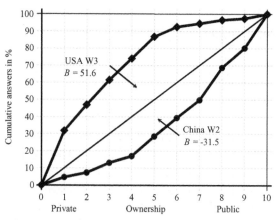

FIGURE 8.3. The C-curves for two extreme values of the *B*-index

8.4 THE LEVEL PROBLEM IN THE FORMULATION OF THE OWNERSHIP ITEM

The previous section mentioned that the WVS ownership item has a level problem due to the term *"increased"* in the first sentence of the wording of the item. This is contradicted in the second sentence, so two alternative hypotheses seem possible: (H1) People take the item as a question about the changes they want in the existing level of ownership. (H2) People consider the item as a question about their preferred level of ownership, as assumed until now.

Let us – for a moment – accept (H1). This leads to a prediction about the *B*-index in politically competitive democracies. Here the *B*-index must adjust to the will of people, so after some time the median voter will want no more changes. Thus, the *B*-index converges to zero.

This gives a prediction for three country groups: In the old West, *B* should have converged to zero. The *Convergers* are "new" Western countries that used to be middle-income countries (MICs) with little democracy. Thus, *B* might not have converged, and the same applies to the Asian Tigers, which are new democracies/developed countries (DCs) as well. The average *B*-index in these groups is 29.9, 11.6, and 13.0, respectively. This is the reverse of the prediction from the convergence-to-zero property. The consistently high positive indices in the oldest and most stable capitalist democracies are particularly revealing. These observations are inconsistent with (H1). Thus, most people must answer the question as a *level* item, as assumed.

8.5 THE TRANSITION IN THE B-INDEX

The distribution of the B-index values is displayed as a scatter over income in Figure 8.4a. It includes the six groups listed in the data page. Also, arrows point to the extreme countries from Figure 8.3. Figure 8.4a shows that the Bs have a range from –38 to +52, which is 90 pp (percentage points).

The transition-curve in Figure 8.4b, $\Pi^B(y)$, covers about one-fifth of this range and the correlation between income and the B-index is 0.32. The B-data scatter a lot around the curve, and the West stands out as the group of countries with the strongest support for capitalism. The $\Pi^B(y)$-curve is close to the linear estimates in the regression of Table 8.4, where the B-index increases by about 4–6 pp for each lp (logarithmic point). The full transition of 4.4 lp thus gives a B-change of about 18–25 pp. The positive slope on $\Pi^B(y)$ is contrary to Marxist theory, but it is in accordance with both PoI and transition theory. To distinguish between these theories, an analysis of long-run causality is needed, which will follow in Section 8.7.

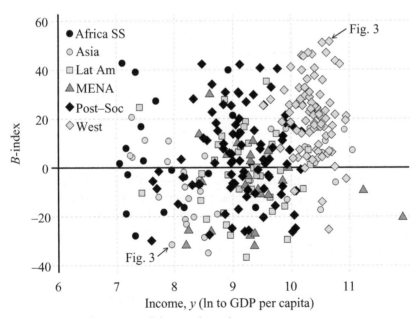

FIGURE 8.4a. The scatter of the B-index values

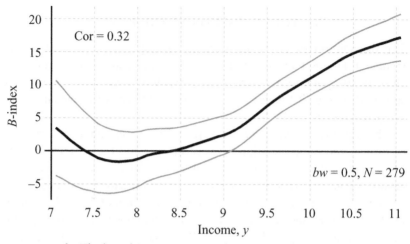

FIGURE 8.4b. The kernel $B = K(y, 0.5)$ in the Main sample

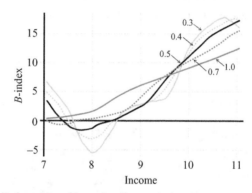

FIGURE 8.5a. Robustness of kernel to *bw*-variations

Figure 8.4b is estimated on $N = 279$ observations. This is too few to allow most of the robustness tests. However, Figure 8.5a shows that the form of the kernel is fairly robust to the bandwidth. Figure 8.5b is the beauty test. It is clear that the $B = K(y, 0.5)$ looks better than the reverse $y = K(B, 7)$-kernel, but the difference is not big.

8.6 THE PATH OF THE *B*-INDEX OVER TIME

The preference item started in 1990, which saw the triumph of capitalism: No less than 23 of the countries covered changed from Socialism to

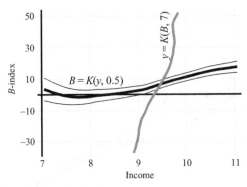

FIGURE 8.5b. Reverse kernels for beauty-test

capitalism, and many other countries privatized SOEs around that time, as discussed in Chapter 3.[10] The last two waves may be affected by the international bank/debt crises in 2007–12.

Figure 8.6 analyzes the path over time. The 92 countries are divided into three groups: *West, PCom,* and *All.* The figure reports two curves for each group: one for *all* observations and one adjusted for sample consistency, as explained in the note. The deviation between the two lines points to selection bias in the data, so it is reassuring that the deviations are small. Three observations follow from the figure,

(i) The *B*-index for all countries falls throughout the period, on average by almost 25 points. Even if 1990 was an unusual year, the shift toward Socialism is still substantial.

(ii) The *West* differs by being much more pro-capitalist than other country groups, just as in Figure 8.3. The fall is the same as for all countries, but it turns up at the end.

(iii) The post-socialist group was fairly pro-capitalist in W2 (1990–94), then the *B*-indices fell rapidly. The fall is probably caused by the high costs of the change of economic system. However, the *B*s turned up in W5 (2005–9), but in the last polls it has dropped one more time and it is now negative, i.e., pro-socialist. However, as seen in Figure 3.1, the economic development has been rather good since 2005, so it is surprising that the support for the system keeps falling.

[10] The privatization wave is analyzed in Parker and Saal (2003) and (for Western Europe) in Köthenburger et al. (2006); see also Megginson and Netter (2001).

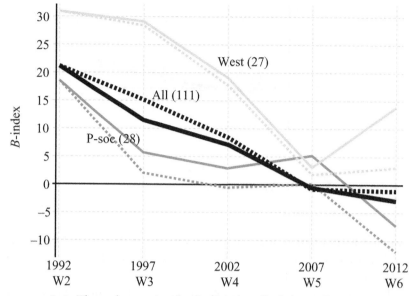

FIGURE 8.6. The path over time for the *B*-index, divided into three groups
Unbroken lines are all available observations. The broken lines are started from the average
in wave W2. The observation for wave W3 is reached by adding the average for all available
first differences W2/W3, etc.

8.7 THE DP-TEST FOR LONG-RUN CAUSALITY (FROM SECTION 2.8)

The DP-test shows that long-run causality is from income to the *B*-index, while the test the other way does not work (Table 8.3). However, there is a problem.

The TSIV-estimates in row (3) are larger than the OLS results in row (1). The average IV estimate is 9.5, and the OLS estimate is 6.5. Thus, the valid IV estimates are roughly 50% larger than the OLS estimates. The difference is significant in columns (3) and (4). As a minimum, this suggests that in addition to the long-run transition, other factors may operate in the short to medium run. The difference between causality in the medium run and very long run also applies to associations between income and other measures of institutions and basic political beliefs and values.

8.8 THE MULTIVARIATE ANALYSIS OF TABLE 8.4

A number of regressions have been run that try to explain the *B*-index. The explanatory variables are from three types of factors: (1) As usual,

TABLE 8.3. *The DP-test for long-run causality from income to the B-index*

Dependent variable: *B* Estimate No. of countries	Main model (1)	Robustness of model to instrument variation (2)	(3)	(4)	(5)
No. of countries	61	66	61	61	93
		OLS estimates			
(1) Income, *y*	6.19	7.30	6.19	6.19	6.69
t-ratio	(3.5)	(4.3)	(3.5)	(3.5)	(4.2)
(2) Centered R^2	0.16	0.22	0.16	0.16	0.16
		IV estimates: *y* is instrumented			
(3) Income, *y*	11.07	11.24	8.23	7.04	9.91
t-ratio	(3.4)	(4.0)	(2.8)	(2.6)	(3.7)
(4) Instruments	*biofpc, geofpc*	*bioavg, geoavg*	*animals, plants*	*axis, size, climate*	*coast, frost maleco*
(5) First stage partial R^2	0.34	0.41	0.37	0.42	0.36
(6) CD F-statistic	15.12	21.58	17.05	13.79	17.05
CD critical value	19.93	19.93	19.93	22.30	22.30
(7) Sargan test	0.67	0.54	4.71	3.72	2.17
p-value	0.41	0.46	0.03	0.16	0.34
		Hausman test for parameter consistency of OLS and IV estimates			
(8) C-statistic	3.90	3.65	0.77	0.17	2.39
p-value	0.05	0.06	0.38	0.68	0.12
		Check for reverse causality (none works and all are smaller)			
(9) CD F-statistic	6.84	8.68	6.09	3.11	5.22

The observations are averages of waves 2–6 of the World Values Survey. All specifications include a constant term (not reported).

development is operationalized as *income, y*. (2) Fixed effects for the main country groups defined as listed in the Countries file on the data page. (3) Fixed effects for the waves of the WVS.

Table 8.4 is a set of regressions using the three sets of variables available for all 295 polls. The table shows that income and the waves of the WVS have little collinearity, while income and the country groups have strong collinearity. One of the groups, the *West*, can be replaced by income. The coefficient on West is thus fully explained by the relative income.

TABLE 8.4. *The B-index explained by income, culture, and WVS-waves*

Included	Income	Waves		Country groups		Waves and groups	
	(1a)	(2a)	(2b)	(3a)	(3b)	(4a)	(4b)
Income	6.12 (5.5)	6.33 (6.2)	6.21 (6.1)	1.88 (1.3)	2.04 (11.5)	3.78 (2.8)	3.79 (2.8)
Africa				−9.67 (−0.8)	−10.81 (−2.7)	12.76 (2.8)	13.63 (3.3)
Asia				−18.47 (−1.4)	−19.90 (−6.4)	0.18 (0.1)	
La Am				−18.42 (−1.4)	−19.86 (−6.5)		
MENA				−24.67 (−1.8)	−26.12 (−7.2)	−4.03 (−1.0)	
Post-soc				−12.52 (−1.0)	−13.95 (5.8)	4.11 (1.4)	4.94 (2.2)
West				1.65 (0.1)		14.72 (4.3)	14.53 (5.4)
W2		−39.35 (−3.9)	22.52 (7.6)			−23.36 (−1.8)	−24.16 (−1.9)
W3		−47.59 (−4.9)	14.25 (5.5)			−29.94 (−2.4)	−30.63 (−2.5)
W4		−52.23 (−5.4)	9.63 (3.9)			−34.29 (−2.7)	−35.38 (−2.8)

W5		−59.69 (−6.1)				−42.02 (−3.3)	−42.75 (−3.4)
W6		−63.83 (−6.4)				−42.37 (−3.2)	−43.65 (−3.3)
Constant	−51.10 (−4.8)		−60.68 (−6.2)				
N	295	295	295	295	295	295	295
Adj R²	0.09	0.34[dl]	0.26	0.32	0.32	0.41	0.41

The fixed effects for country groups and for waves sum to 1, so when either is in the table, the constant is excluded. The gray areas show excluded variables. Regressions (2a), (3a), and (4a) are the starting ones. They are modified in (2b) and (2c) by being tested down to significant coefficients only, and in (2c) and (3c) there is a tested down version, which starts with all country groups except the least significant.

The effect of income falls from 6 to 4 when relations (1a) and (4) are compared, and the coefficients on the country club dummies change even more when (3b) and (4b) are compared. This means that the group-coefficients also reflect the average income differences between the groups.

The fact that the high B-indices of the West seem to result from the high income of the West is interesting for three reasons. (1) It confirms that the B-index is a preference for a level of property rights. (2) It contrasts to the West-is-different story presented by de Soto (2000). (3) The West is the best example of a *convergence club* of countries that have achieved much the same standard of living, and globalization has historically been particularly strong within the Western group. This has caused the B-index to cluster as well – as appears in Figure 8.3.

9

Economic Freedom

The F-Index

The Fraser Index measures the freedom to run a private business.[1] It has the following five components: government size, legal quality, stable money, free trade, and regulations. It started in 1970 with data for 54 countries, since then it has increased to 162, as seen in Figure 9.1. From 1970 to 2000, it was reported with 5-year intervals, since then it has been annual. The Fraser Index is carefully made in a transparent way, but it is built in the spirit of libertarianism, and the group behind the index is keen to state that it shows that more freedom causes higher income.

    The eight sections of Chapter 9 start with some descriptive statistics for the *F*-index (s1). Then the transition curve is estimated, and it is demonstrated that it is rather robust (s2). The causality tests show that while the causality in the short run is from *F* to development, the long-run causality is from development to *F* (s3). Finally, the *B*-index (from Chapter 8) is compared with the *F*-index (s4). While the two indices have a weak correlation, they do tell the same story about the transition.

---

[1] The Fraser Index was defined in Gwartney et al. (1996). See also the annual volumes, the latest of which is Gwartney et al. (2018). It is used as a measure of the economic system of countries. As I look at the Socialism/capitalism dimension, it may be acceptable.

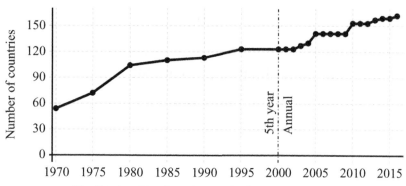

FIGURE 9.1. The *F*-index: Number of countries from 1970 to 2016

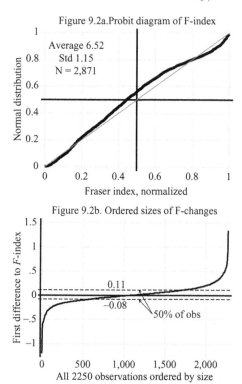

FIGURE 9.2. Some descriptive statistics for the *F*-index

9.1 SOME STATISTICS AND THE DEVELOPMENT OVER TIME OF THE *F*-INDEX

Figure 9.2a shows a few descriptive statistics for the *F*-index. In principle, *F* goes from 0 to 10, but half of the scale contains 95% of the observations. The 2,871 observations for the index have an almost normal distribution with an average of 6.5 and a standard deviation of 1.2. Figure 9.2b reports first differences of the index. It is rarely constant, but 50% of the changes are in between –0.08 and 0.11. Economic systems are always changing, but most changes are small. Only 0.13% of the changes are larger than ±1 F-point, and 2.78% exceed ±0.5 F-points.

The two graphs of Figure 9.3 report the development of the Fraser Index over time. Figure 9.3a shows that there were small movements in the first 20 years of the index, but for the next 10 years, 1990–2000, there was a big rise in connection with the end of Soviet Socialism.

Since 2000, the data are annual, and once again there are small movements only. The figure shows an average rise of about 1.6 Fraser points. From 1970 to 2016, income has grown about 1 log point. Thus, a crude estimate is that the change caused/inspired by the end of the Soviet system was almost 1 Fraser point in the group of Others, while the underlying change caused by the rise in income was about 0.6 ± 0.2 Fraser points per income point.

Figure 9.3b shows the change out of the Soviet model from 1990 and the increase in economic freedom in the rest of the world for comparison. The data from 1970 to 1990 contain few countries from the Soviet bloc. Hungary starts in 1980, while Bulgaria, Poland, and Romania start in 1985. These countries give two strange points on the graph. I think it is unlikely that Romania in 1985 (F 5.58) had more economic freedom than South Korea (F 5.49) and Costa Rica (F 5.33). The index for China (F 3.64) in 1980 seems much more reasonable.

Paldam (2002b) tries to assess how the F-index for the Soviet bloc countries would have looked by using a comparison with the transition index from the EBRD. The assessment is that the countries of

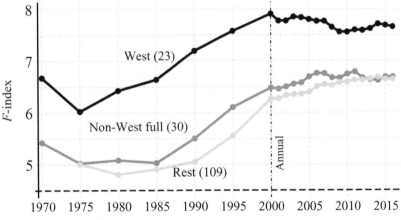

FIGURE 9.3a. The Fraser Index for three country groups

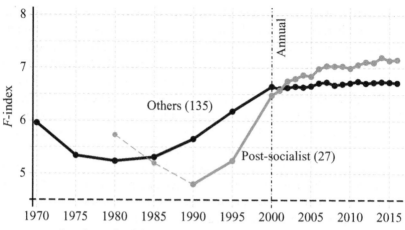

FIGURE 9.3b. The path of the post-socialist countries compared to the rest

the Soviet bloc would have been at $F = 3.5$ (+0.5) in 1970–80 if data had existed.[2] Today they are at 7.1, so a large system change amounts to 3.5 Fraser points. Even in the countries that made the greatest efforts to change, such as Estonia, it took 7 years.

To sort out the time-series movements in the data, an annual cross-country regression explaining F by y is run. Figure 9.4 reports the coefficient, b, on income – it is positive every year. Its average size is 0.60 with a standard error of 0.03, so the relation is robust, even though it changes a bit over time. Thus, as predicted by the equivalence hypothesis, the results tally rather well. A rise of y by 1 point gives an F-change of 0.6 points either way it is measured.

9.2 THE TRANSITION CURVE $\Pi^F(y)$ AND ITS ROBUSTNESS

Figure 9.5 is the kernel estimate of the transition curve $F = \Pi^F(y)$. The curve is almost linear – like the kernel of the B-index – with only weak signs of convergence at the two ends, where data are fairly adequate.

---

[2] The European Bank of Reconstruction and Development helps finance the change of economic system in the post-socialist countries in Europe. The components of the transition index differ from these of the Fraser Index, so the assessment of what the size of the change would have been in the Fraser Index is quite uncertain.

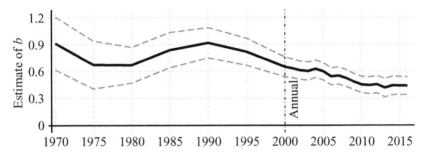

FIGURE 9.4. The coefficient, *b*, on income in annual cross-country regression explaining *F*

A few countries have *F*-index observations, but no income, so the number of countries is 3–5 lower than on Figure 9.7. The figure reports the cross-country coefficient on income from regression (1): $F_{it} = a_t + b_t y_{it} + \varepsilon_{it}$, estimated for each *t* from 1970 to 2016. The dashed curves are the 95% confidence interval.

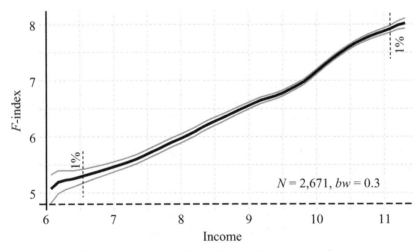

FIGURE 9.5. The transition curve for *F*, Fraser, the Main sample

The curve shows that *F* rises three points. This is, once again, a rise of 0.6 Fraser points per income point. Thus, the results from the various methods tally rather well. The near-linearity of $\pi^F(y)$ causes collinearity when both income and the *F*-index are used as explanatory variables in Chapter 10. The robustness tests are reported in Figure 9.6.

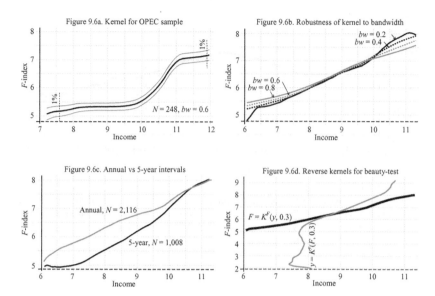

FIGURE 9.6. The robustness of the transition curve for *F*
The 5-year data are from 1970, 1975, to 2015. The annual data are from 2000 to 2016.

Figure 9.6a reports the curve for the OPEC sample. It is estimated on $N = 248$ observations, so it has wider confidence intervals. It has a strange bend, and the transition comes later and is slower. Figure 9.6b shows that the curve for the Main sample is robust to the bandwidth; while Figure 9.6c shows that the time interval between the data matters a little, though the form of the curve is the same.

9.3 THE THREE CAUSALITY TESTS (FROM SECTIONS 2.7 AND 2.8)

Figure 9.6d shows the beauty test, where the reverse curve and the transition curve are shown together. The $K^F(y, 0.3)$ is the clearest, but the $K^y(F, 0.3)$ curve may also make some sense. Thus, there may be causality both ways.

Figure 9.7 reports the average correlogram for the 118 countries where the data are complete for the period. The correlations are in the range from 0.05 to 0.25. The form of the curve supports the view that causality is from Fraser to income, but this is a short-run result, and the transition theory deals with the long run.

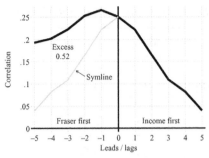

FIGURE 9.7. Correlogram of Income and the Fraser index with 11 leads/lags
The curves are the average correlogram for 118 countries where the data from 2000 to 2016 are complete. The 118 correlations for each lead/lag have a standard error between 0.052 and 0.056 for the 11 leads/lags, so the correlations above 0.11 are statistically significant. It is all correlations from −5 to 3, but the form of the bend is not well determined.

The result of Figure 9.7 indicates that liberalizations have positive effects on income within just a few years. This contradicts the analysis in Chapter 3 that dealt with the very big liberalization in the post-socialist countries, where the short-run effects were very negative, giving substantial reform costs before the positive effects came to dominate. Most of the big change in the post-socialist countries is not covered by the data used for Figure 9.7.

The DP-test reported in Table 9.1 finds that in the long run causality is strongest from income to the Fraser Index. The reverse test for causality from the *F*-index to income sometimes has strong instruments too, so there is simultaneity. However, the instruments are always strongest from income to the *F*-index. Also, the average size of the OLS estimates of the coefficient on income is 0.53, while it is 0.55 for the TSIV estimates, so they are very close.

9.4 COMPARING THE *B* AND *F* INDICES

The two chapters on the Transition in the Economic System yielded the same qualitative conclusion: Both the *B*-index and the *F*-index showed that the main causal flow in the long run is from *y* to *B* and *F*, though there is some causality the other way in the shorter run.

The two transition curves $B = \Pi^B(y)$ in Figure 8.4b and $F = \Pi^F(y)$ in Figure 9.5 look similar: They are approximately linear and have a positive slope. One hundred observations for each of the two transition curves have a correlation of $\mathrm{cor}(K^B(y), K^F(y)) = 0.95$, so the transition path is

TABLE 9.1. *The DP-test for long-run causality from income to the F-index*

Dependent variable: F	Main model	Robustness of model to instrument variation			
Estimate	(1)	(2)	(3)	(4)	(5)
No. of countries	96	101	96	96	131
	OLS estimates				
(1) Income, y	0.53	0.55	0.53	0.53	0.49
t-ratio	(11.7)	(12.8)	(11.7)	(11.7)	(10.6)
(2) Centered R^2	0.59	0.62	0.59	0.59	0.46
	IV estimates: y is instrumented				
(3) Income, y	0.50	0.55	0.50	0.57	0.61
t-ratio	(7.5)	(9.5)	(7.5)	(9.2)	(9.2)
(4) Instruments	biofpc,	bioavg,	animals,	axis,	coast,
				size,	frost
	geofpc	geoavg	plants	climate	maleco
(5) First stage partial R^2	0.47	0.55	0.47	0.54	0.51
(6) CD F-statistic	40.65	59.22	41.57	35.63	43.22
CD critical value	19.93	19.93	19.93	22.30	22.30
(7) Sargan test	0.12	*3.41*	*0.01*	2.21	3.72
(p-value	0.73	0.06	0.93	0.33	0.16
	Hausman test for parameter consistency of OLS and IV estimates				
(8) C-statistic	0.39	0.00	0.47	*1.00*	7.70
p-value	0.53	0.99	0.49	0.32	0.01
	Check for reverse causality (2 work but all are smaller)				
(9) CD F-statistic	15.07	26.50	15.05	*18.64*	*26.56*

The observations are averages of 2005–2010. All specifications include a constant term (not reported).

the same, but this does not mean that the observations for the two indices are the same. The *B*-index can be combined with the corresponding values of the *F*-index and income for 254 of the 295 observations. Table 9.2 shows the correlations. They are all significantly larger than zero, but the correlation of the two system-indices is only 0.20.

Figure 9.8 shows how the scatter of the two indices looks. If we interpret the Fraser Index, as the original research team thought, as the freedom to run a private business, the aggregate index should surely be correlated to preferences for capitalism. The weak connection between

TABLE 9.2. *Correlations of the corresponding 254 observations for all three series*

	Income	B-index	F-index
Income	1		
B-index	0.29	1	
F-index	0.59	0.20	1

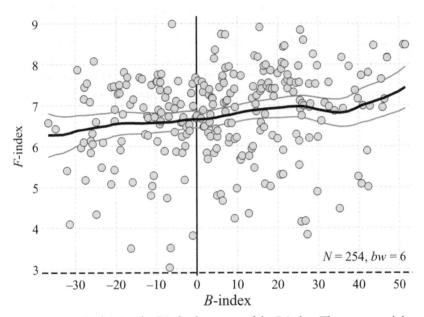

FIGURE 9.8. Explaining the F-index by means of the B-index: The scatter and the kernel

The coefficient, b, on B in the regression. $F = a + bB$ is nicely significant, but in $F = a + bB + cy$ the coefficient b becomes insignificant. The two system variables are only related because of the common transition.

the two indices is thus a bit of a puzzle. It can be explained in two ways: (i) The indices do measure something different: In particular, it is possible that preferences (B) and realities (F) differ. (ii) They have large uncorrelated measurement errors.

(i) It is possible that components of the F-index are better correlated than the aggregate index. As shown in Bjørnskov and Paldam (2012), the B-index is better correlated to the legal quality component of the index than to the other component.

(ii) The B-index is based on 295 polls of about 1,600 respondents each. The question posed was not very clear, and it is possible that many respondents had given little thought to the economic system they preferred. The reader may wonder how well an African farmer would be able to answer the said question. The dimension of saliency is important for the B-index.

However, for all of that, it is still satisfactory that the long-run transition curves in the two indices are so similar. It would be neat if it could be demonstrated that the preferences led to the system and that this caused the development, but from the above it is clear that the data are too weak for the purpose. In the long run, development causes system changes, and successful systems lead to preferences for the system. However, we also find simultaneity even in the long run. In the short run, the causality is rather from the economic system to income.

PART IIC

THE TRANSITIONS IN TRADITIONS AND BELIEFS

The next two chapters deal with

The variables in the two chapters are so different that they will be listed in the chapters.

The Transition of Corruption

The corruption index, T, has a scale, where T rises when corruption falls. It aggregates polled measures of perceptions of corruption/honesty. Section 2.2 found that the T-index, income (y), the Polity index (P), and the Fraser index (F) have one strong positive common factor. Thus, the four variables are confluent, and it is difficult to untangle the effect of each variable. As both P and F have a transition, it is no surprise that T has one as well. Corruption is an *embedded tradition* that is difficult to change, the T-transition happens relatively late, and it is influenced by the prior transitions in P and F. We are dealing with a strong, but fuzzy relation with substantial lags. The T-index is negatively correlated to the first differences to income (g), Polity (dP), and Fraser (dF). This is a strong J-curve effect, which lasts no less than a dozen years.

TABLE 10.1. *Variables used in Chapter 10*

Variable	Definition and source
Transparency's Corruption perception T-index.	
Source	Transparency International: www.transparency.org/.
T	The T-index [0, 10] for corruption to honesty. It rises when corruption falls.
Θ^T	The deviation of the T-index from the transition path: $\Theta^T = T - \Pi^T.(a)$
$\Pi^T(y)$	*Transition of Corruption.* Estimated by the kernel $K^T(y, bw)$ that has a positive slope.
Variables from other chapters	
P, dP	Polity index and its first difference from Chapter 4. (b)
F, dF	Fraser index and its first difference from Chapter 9. (b)

Notes: (a) Θ^T is a tension variable as defined in Section 2.6. (b) The two first difference variables, dP and dF, are defined as the average numerical change.

The ten sections of Chapter 10 proceed as follows: First, the index is discussed (s1), and the robust transition curve is estimated (s2). A short literature survey follows (s3), and a correlation analysis (s4). The causality tests show that the main direction of causality is from income to corruption (s5). It is demonstrated that institutions have an independent role in explaining corruption (s6–7). Finally, four examples show that economic and institutional uncertainty and crisis generate excess corruption.

10.1 THE CORRUPTION PERCEPTION INDEX FROM TRANSPARENCY INTERNATIONAL

The corruption index uses a scale that rises with honesty, so that it becomes a goal for countries to increase the index. As shown by Figure 10.1, it started in 1995 with 41 countries – since 2007 it has been around 175, and there are data for 188 countries, but most have gaps in the series. Table 10.2 provides some descriptive data.

The transparency index aggregates data from many primary data by a double process explained in Lambsdorff (2007). First, the primary data are calibrated to the same scale, and then an average is calculated. Thus, it is difficult to interpret the first difference in the series, and also the method has changed, notably in 2012; see Gründler and Potrafke (2019).

Figure 10.2 shows the path of the two relevant correlations. (i) The top line for cor(T, y) is stable at a level just above 0.7. (ii) The lower line for cor (T, g) is quite variable. It is positive before 2001, where the range of the data was small, but even after 2003 the results are not fully stable.

TABLE 10.2. *Descriptive data for the Transparency corruption index, T*

	Main	OPEC	All	Average	Std	Min	Max
All 1995–2016	2,730	247	2,977	4.4	2.2	10.0	0.4
Country averages	173	15	188	4.1	2.0	9.4	1.0

The data are for countries and years having an income observation in the Maddison project database

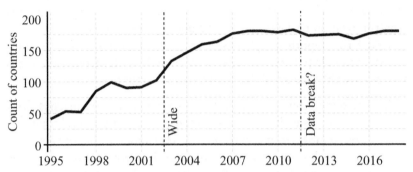

FIGURE 10.1. The number of countries included in the *T*-index per year 1995–2018

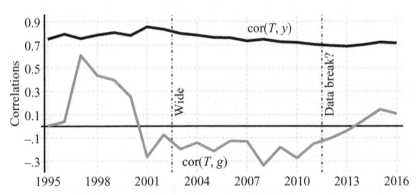

FIGURE 10.2. Looking for data-breaks in two annual cross-country correlations *Wide* indicates that the data cover countries at all income levels. The wide data cover only 13 years of observations. The two graphs on Figure 10.2 are the annual correlations of the corruption index to income and growth.

(iii) There is no break in 2011/12, so for the present study the data revision does not matter. The cor(T, g)-line suggests that the corruption data have measurement problems, but Sections 10.2–10.7 are based on cross-country averages over $N > 100$, so the error should be divided by $\sqrt{N} > 10$.

10.2 THE TRANSITION CURVE AND ITS ROBUSTNESS

It has long been known that *development* is the strongest explanation of the cross-country levels of perceived corruption/honesty – high income and modern institutions go together with honesty.[1] The available historical narrative provides the same story. A couple of centuries ago, when the present developed countries were poor, they were as corrupt as countries at the same level of income today.[2] Thus, both the cross-country and the long-run relation of development and honesty are positive.

Figure 10.3 reports the (T, y)-scatter and the kernel $T = K^T(y, 0.3)$ for the Main sample (where T is the corruption index, y is income, and 0.3 is the bandwidth). The graph highlights two observations:

(i)   The kernel estimate $K^T(y, 0.3)$ shows a transition curve that has all six properties listed in Table 2.2, so it qualifies as a beautiful transition curve. It moves from a corruption level at about 2½ in poor countries to a level close to 9 in wealthy countries. It diverges from the low level at an income of about $y \approx 8$, but the rise is slow before $y \approx 9.5$.[3]

(ii) The black circles are for the oldest developed countries. They have a corruption level close to 9. These countries have adjusted to wealth. This suggests that when countries join the group of HICs, they will gradually move to the same level.

Figure 10.4 reports 15 additional kernel curves showing the robustness of the basic path. Figure 10.4a shows the robustness of the kernel curve to the bandwidth, *bw*. As usual, the kernel is a bit wobbly for small bandwidths and becomes more and more linear (and flat) for large bandwidths, but the basic form is robust. Figure 10.4b reports that the curve is stable over time – though it does move marginally to the right. Figure 10.4c shows that the transition curve has the same form in the Main sample and the OPEC countries. As the OPEC countries are relatively wealthy at each level of development, the K-curve shifts to the right for these countries.

---

[1] The income effect on the cross-country pattern of corruption has been known since Treisman (2000) and Paldam (2002a), who also found a weakly negative effect of growth. These results are confirmed by the meta-study by Ugur (2014).

[2] The 20 authors of Kroeze et al. (2018) cover the historical evidence in the literature that is listed over 42 pages.

[3] The value for income 8 equals $ 3,000 like Kenya, and 9½ equals $ 13,500 like Brazil in 2016.

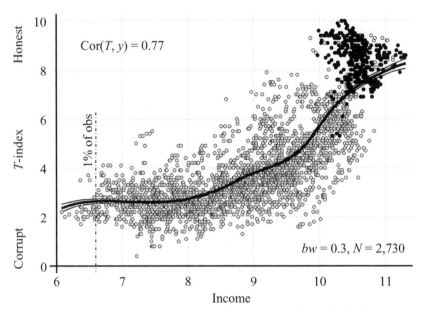

FIGURE 10.3. Corruption–income scatter for Main sample, with the kernel $K^T(y, 0.3)$

$K^T(y, 0.3)$ is the kernel with $bw = 0.3$, and 95% confidence intervals, $N = 2,730$. The vertical dotted line shows that the leftmost 10% of the curve is supported by 1% of the observations only. The kernel rises from 2.5 to 8.5, when income increases from 6.5 to 11, thus the slope is $6/4.5 = 1.33$. The kernel is used to calculate $\Theta^T = T - \Pi$. The black circles are from the Old West: Australia, Austria, Belgium, Canada, Denmark, Finland, France, Germany, Iceland, Ireland, Luxembourg, Netherlands, New Zealand, Norway, Sweden, Switzerland, United Kingdom, and United States.

Figure 10.4d is more complex, as it reports the informal beauty test for causality discussed in Section 2.7. It compares the transition curve, $T = \Pi^T(y) \approx K^T(y, 0.3)$, which assumes causality from y to T with the reverse $y = \Lambda^y(T) \approx K^y(T, 0.3)$, which assumes causality from T to y. While $K^T(y, 0.3)$ looks as predicted by the transition theory, $K^y(T, 0.3)$ is difficult to explain, and it has bends that are not expected from the sand theory (discussed in Section 10.3).

10.3 THE LITERATURE ON CORRUPTION AND DEVELOPMENT (CONTINUED IN SECTION 10.6)

Scattered corruption data started to be collected in the 1980s, and the T-index was started in 1995. The old literature before that was theory

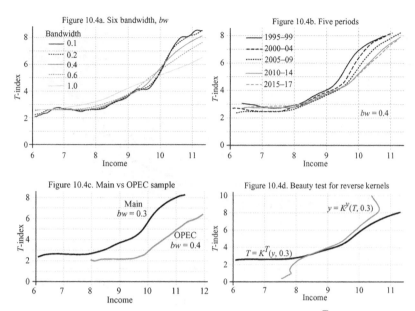

FIGURE 10.4 Analyzing the robustness of the kernel-curve, $K^T(y, bw)$, from Figure 10.1

Figures 10.2a, 10.2b, and 10.2d are based on data from the Main sample.

based on anecdotal evidence.[4] After data became available, a new literature emerged. Two large books survey these literatures and republish the main papers: Heidenheimer et al. (1989) for the old literature, and Dutta and Aidt (2016) for the new.

The first question in the old literature is how to delimit corruption from other types of fraud and rent-seeking. A number of definitions have been proposed. The paper uses Transparency's definition: *Corruption is the abuse of entrusted power for private gain*. This definition implies a principal agent framework, with an agent who deals with a third party. Corruption occurs when the agent colludes with the third party to

---

[4] The old literature suffered from politeness. Though it was widely known, it was considered impolite to mention that the level of corruption is higher in poor countries. Consequently, most papers in Heidenheimer dealt with the United States, and the 1,776 pages of volume 1 of the *Handbook of Development* (Chenery and Srinivasan 1988–89) did not mention corruption. This changed after data appeared, as seen already from the title of Dutta and Aidt (2016).

defraud the principal. The longest chains of agents and sub-agents exist in the public sector. Hence, it is particularly prone to corruption.

The first question in the new literature is the quality of the measurement: Aidt (2003) provides a survey of the early measurement discussion; see also Gutmann and Paldam (2021) for a comparison of four corruption indices. While they differ as to the order of many country pairs, they all show a similar transition pattern.

The transition pattern can be explained from both the demand and the supply side: *The demand theory* sees honesty as an intangible good with positive income elasticity. It speaks for this theory that it can be extended to a whole family of intangibles, such as democracy, generalized trust, and various cultural goods. They are "nice" to have, but not really necessary, so the demand for these goods increases when income rises. Most poor countries are weak on honesty and democracy, and have few art museums. The consumption of other intangibles, such as religion, decreases when income rises. Thus, intangibles may have both positive and negative income elasticities. Such goods are poorly measured, not sold on the market, and their prices are difficult to impute. Thus, the parallel to goods is a bit of a construct – it is, at best, a rather fuzzy relation. In this theory the causality is: $y \Rightarrow T$.

The supply theory sees corruption as *inefficiency* in all transactions. It has to be hidden from the principal, and this takes time and effort. In poor countries, many deals involve a lengthy process of haggling, where some part may be a secret part of the deal. In modern mass production, such inefficiency is squeezed out. Corruption may change to be a fixed commission or a tip that appears on invoices. Hence, it ceases to be corruption. This is, once again a rather fuzzy relation, which might be interpreted as a causal relation: $y \Rightarrow T$. However, the transaction theory may also be interpreted as saying that corruption is an extra cost that delays development. Thus, a reduction in corruption may increase development.

The demand and transaction theories see corruption as a social ill that vanishes over time as countries develop, but the transition theory may also provide a double argument to fight corruption. It is not only a social ill in itself, but also *sand* in the machine of development. Many authors, notably Lambsdorff (2007), stress this theory and provide some evidence. The key argument is that corruption is an extra cost of transactions and thus production. This should give a positive correlation of T and growth, contrary to the evidence that $\text{cor}(T, g) < 0$.

Given the evidence, it is possible that corruption works as *grease* in the machine, increasing efficiency. Thus, from a growth perspective corruption is either sand or grease in the machine.[5] In other words, a briber may see the bribe as a cost or as a cost-saving device. Especially as regards public regulations, it is easy to come up with examples supporting either view. The examples hinge on externalities:

Many regulations improve welfare, so corruption reduces the improvement. Examples are compulsory inoculation programs to eradicate epidemic diseases,[6] or regulations reducing air pollution, etc. Even if corruption allows both individuals in the transaction a short-run welfare improvement by circumventing the regulation, this has (large) negative externalities disregarded by the individual.

Other regulations harm welfare, so corruption limits the harm: It is easy to mention regulations that mainly serve to produce rents to politically influential groups. This, e.g., applies to most tariffs. Also, in many less-developed countries it is a problem that the time and effort needed to obtain legal property rights to a business are far too large; see de Soto (2000).

Grease-cases certainly exist, but they often have dynamic side effects that may change the conclusion: Perhaps the risk of corruption has made it necessary to have several layers of expensive controls that slow down the administration, so it is corruption that turns corruption into grease! A further aspect of the story is that the regulators may slow down administrative processes precisely to extract bribes. To understand such cases needs a complex model, where the solution is fragile depending on the case-dependent details of the model.[7]

Several researchers have tried to estimate reduced form models, with both grease terms and sand terms. Normally they both become significant, but they are hard to sort out; see Méon and Sekkat (2005) and Méon and Weil (2010) for somewhat different results.

Many papers, starting perhaps with Andvig and Moene (1990), argue that corruption is dynamic: Corrupt countries tend to become more so, and honest countries become more so as well. Thus, corruption has a high and a low equilibrium. Paldam (2002a) gives an overview of some mechanisms that have this "seesaw" dynamics:

---

[5] The sand theory is, as mentioned, much more popular. The grease theory goes back to Leff (1964).

[6] The author once visited a vaccination clinic in the "African bush" that gave a choice of either a vaccination and the WHO-stamp in your vaccination booklet, or just the stamp. The latter was cheaper and less painful.

[7] As the negative effect of growth on corruption is small, it is possible that it can be turned to become positive by effective policies to combat corruption, as discussed in many papers. In October 2020, Google Scholar showed 120,000 hits to "anti-corruption policies."

(i) It is impossible to punish everybody if they are all corrupt, but if few are corrupt, they can be punished. (ii) The corrupt needs to announce his business and this is typically done by conspicuous consumption – driving a Mercedes Benz is the classical method in poor countries. With low corruption, such advertisement announces a criminal. (iii) Jobs have different potential for corruption, and the jobs with the highest potential see wages competed down, so that the honest seek other jobs. Thus, the corrupt and the honest sort themselves out in jobs by high and low potential for corruption – this increases corruption.

This suggests that corruption is stuck at rather low T-values in most countries, as seen later, but once it starts to fall, the rise in T-values is quite large. This helps explain why the transition of corruption happens late in the process of development; see Section 10.6.

10.4 CORRELATIONS AND THE θ^T-INDEX FOR CORRUPTION NET OF THE TRANSITION[8]

Table 10.3 shows the correlations between the levels of the four variables: the corruption index T, income y, and the two system variables P (Polity) and F (Fraser). The left-hand panel is for the Main sample, and the right-hand panel is for the OPEC sample. The first three variables (T, y, and F) have similar correlations in the Main and the OPEC sample, while the correlations to the P-index have opposite signs and similar numerical sizes in the samples. As expected from the factor analysis in Table 2.2, a strongly confluent pattern appears. The correlations of corruption and the three other level variables (y, F, and P) add up to two, so crudely stated the three "explanations" of the T-index explain the same thing twice.

The column of correlations of the four level variables and growth gives results that are more modest. The only significant result is that cor(T, g) is negative.[9] The correlation between growth and income is insignificant and positive, as in the literature on absolute convergence.

The first row in Table 10.4 shows that the correlations to the T-index are almost the same if calculated for the country averages for all

---

[8] The θ^T-*index* is a tension variable, like the θ^P-*index*.

[9] The same contradiction appears when the L2FE estimation model (with a lagged endogenous variable and two fixed effects) discussed in Section 2.3 is estimated for $T = T(y)$. The short-run results are too small to be consistent with the long-run results from a pure cross-country estimate; see Paldam (2021a).

TABLE 10.3. *Correlation for all observations between level variables*

	Main sample, avr. N = 2,830				OPEC sample, avr. N = 254			
	Income	F-index	P-index	Growth	Income	F-index	P-index	Growth
(1) T, Corruption	0.774	0.726	0.450	−0.092	0.790	0.740	−0.488	−0.046
(2) y, income	–	0.738	0.441	0.022	–	0.629	−0.542	0.026
(3) F, Fraser		–	0.461	0.024		–	−0.289	−0.016
(4) P, Polity			–	−0.031			–	−0.016

Each correlation is for all overlapping observations available between 1995 and 2016. This makes N vary by 15%. A consistent sample is about 30% smaller, and gives much the same results. Estimates are bolded if they are significantly different from zero at the 5% level. The gray columns show the correlations between the four level variables and the first difference variable growth.

166

TABLE 10.4. *Correlations for country averages between level variables and first differences*

Correlations	Level variables			First difference variables		
$N = 144$	y, income	F, Fraser	P, Polity	g, growth	dF, dif F	dP, dif P
T, corruption	0.75	0.74	0.41	−0.10	−0.48	−0.48
Θ^T, net of transition	−0.05	0.39	0.40	−0.03	−0.25	−0.17

See Table 10.3. Data are Main sample for 2000–16. The two dif-variables are the average numerical change.

observations. The right-hand panel shows the correlation between the corruption index and the first difference variables. They are all negative and two of them are even significant.

The analysis until now has shown a lot of confluence. To reduce the confluence, the Θ^T-index of relative corruption is defined as the T-index net of the transition, i.e., the Θ^T-index is:

$$\Theta^T{}_{it} = T_{it} - K^T(y_{it}, 0.3) \quad \text{where } K^T(y_{it}, 0.3) \text{ is the estimate of}$$
$$\Pi^T(y) \text{ from Figure 3} \tag{10.1}$$

Θ^T is negative if the country has "too much" corruption ("too little" honesty), and it is positive if the country has "too little" corruption ("too much" honesty) at its level of development.

Table 10.4 shows what happens when the T-index is replaced by the Θ^T-index: The income effect disappears, as it should; the correlation to the Polity index remains almost the same; but the correlation to the Fraser index falls to half. The fall is due to reduction in confluence. The problematic correlation to growth also falls to become insignificant, but it is still negative, so the contradiction becomes weaker, but it remains. The right-hand panel of the table deals with the relation between corruption and the first difference in the three variables. The correlations to the Θ^T-index are always smaller, but the correlations to dF and dP remain significant.

The average number of observations for T and Θ^T per country is 18.1. Thus, a t-ratio can be calculated for each country to test if the Θ^T s are above or below the transition curve.

Figure 10.5a shows the frequency distribution of the 166 t-ratios. The white bars for t's in the interval [−2, 2] are the countries that do not deviate significantly from the transition path. The dark gray bars are significant – they are 64% of the countries. Thus, most countries deviate systematically over several decades from the long-run path. They are either too corrupt or too honest. Section 10.7 provides some examples of such countries, and shows that they are explained by economic and political instability.

Figure 10.6b looks at the slopes in the T-index for the countries. Few of these slopes are significant, which tallies well with the high t-ratios of the Θ^Ts. Thus, both parts of Figure 10.5 show that corruption is a variable with a lot of inertia, and so has institutions as discussed.

Another possibility for explaining the inertia of corruption is culture, which is a soft concept where measurement is difficult, and a great deal is discussed by way of examples. A typical example is the difference in corruption between North Western Europe with Anglo-Germanic culture and Southern Europe with Latin-Mediterranean culture. The present analysis suggests that the difference is caused by the fact that Northern Europe became wealthy first, but culture may play a role too. It has also been

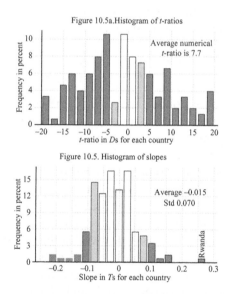

Figure 10.5a.Histogram of t-ratios

Average numerical t-ratio is 7.7

t-ratio in Ds for each country

Figure 10.5. Histogram of slopes

Average –0.015
Std 0.070

Slope in Ts for each country

FIGURE 10.5 Frequency distribution for the t-ratios and slopes for Θ^Ts of 166 countries

Empty bars are for insignificant observations, and light gray are for mixed significant and insignificant.. For the slopes the significance does not only depend on the size but also on the variation. The t-ratios are truncated at ± 20. At the negative end, the extreme countries are Taiwan, North Korea, and Paraguay. At the positive end it is New Zealand, Cape Verde, Sweden, and Denmark.

suggested that culture can be proxied by religion, as analyzed by Paldam (2001), who found that countries with Protestant Christianity stick out as relatively honest, but the Protestant countries seem to be the only ones that differ. Neither Catholics nor Muslims differ when income is controlled for.

10.5 TWO MORE CAUSALITY TESTS (SEE SECTIONS 2.7–2.8)

Chapter 2 presented three causality tests. The first was the informal beauty test that was applied in Figure 10.5d. The two remaining tests are the correlogram test and the TSIV-test using the DP-instruments. They are run in the present section.

Figure 10.6 reports the correlogram tests. The correlograms are calculated independently for each country with enough data. The figure shows the averages. The intersections with the vertical axis for no leads or lags for the T-index are the correlations from Table 10.3. The left-hand side of the graphs shows the effect of corruption on growth, while the right-hand side of the graphs shows the effect of growth on corruption.

Figure 10.6a contains a strong trend resulting from almost linear transition – it is difficult to interpret. The trend disappears in Figure 10.6b, which uses the Θ^T-data. Thus, the trend of Figure 10.6a is a result of the transition. Figure 10.6b is much easier to interpret. At the left-hand side, there is no significance, but the right-hand side looks precisely as it should when it shows causality. It lasts about 12 years before it disappears. Thus, the contradiction between the short- and the long-run is temporary.

The formal DP causality test for the long run is reported in Table 10.5. Here the results are clear. The causality from y to T is highly significant, and the tests are all as wanted (except the last Sargan test). However, the TSIV estimates of the income effect are larger than the OLS estimates – sometimes even significantly so. In addition, the CD-tests show that the instruments work in reverse as well. They are not as strong as in the main direction, but still acceptable.

Thus, the three causality tests show that the main direction of causality is from income to corruption both in the short and the long run, but there is some simultaneity in the relation.

10.6 INSTITUTIONAL EXPLANATIONS: THEORY AND EMPIRICS

Both political and economic institutions should impact on corruption. Already in Section 2.2 it was demonstrated that the T, P, and F indices

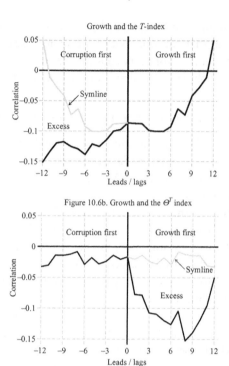

FIGURE 10.6 Correlogram between growth, g, and corruption, T and Θ^T
The unlagged correlation is made on $N = 2,783$ observations, and for each lag to either side about 160 observations are lost. The two curves are for all countries, with more than six observations. I assess that the 5% level of significance is about ± 0.09; see Section 2.4.

are confluent, but there are likely to be more than the common transition. The Θ^T-index is corruption net of the transition – it should eliminate confluence.

Corruption and political institutions: It is likely that democracy and honesty reinforce each other. When civil servants are honest, people are more likely to trust elections, and hence the elected politicians. Thus, the correlation of the T-series and the P and Θ^T-indices is likely to be more than spurious.

Corruption and economic institutions: The Fraser index was announced as a measure of the freedom to run a private business. Thus, F is linked to corruption in another way: Corruption is often used to evade public regulations, and high values of the Fraser index indicate that few such restrictions exist.

TABLE 10.5. *The DP-test for long-run causality from income to the T-index*

Dependent variable: T Estimate No. of countries	Main model (1)	Robustness of model to instrument variation			
		(2)	(3)	(4)	(5)
	101	106	101	101	142
		OLS estimates			
(1) Income, y	1.31	1.41	1.31	1.31	1.26
t-ratio	(13.3)	(14.3)	(13.3)	(13.3)	(13.2)
(2) Centered R^2	0.64	0.66	0.64	0.64	0.55
		IV estimates: y is instrumented			
(3) Income, y	1.51	1.60	1.48	1.37	1.25
t-ratio	(10.0)	(11.5)	(9.8)	(9.8)	(9.2)
(4) Instruments	biofpc, geofpc	bioavg, geoavg	animals, plants	axis, size, climate	coast, frost maleco
(5) First stage partial R^2	0.44	0.52	0.44	0.50	0.50
(6) CD F-statistic	39.03	55.05	39.05	32.06	45.32
CD critical value	19.93	19.93	19.93	22.30	22.30
(7) Sargan test	0.23	2.49	1.09	3.09	13.06
p-value	0.63	0.11	0.30	0.21	0.00
		Hausman test for parameter consistency of OLS and IV estimates			
(8) C-statistic	3.34	4.03	2.18	0.34	0.03
p-value	0.07	0.04	0.14	0.56	0.86
		Check for reverse causality (3 works but all are smaller)			
(9) CD F-statistic	29.58	41.62	27.64	17.89	20.40

The observations are averages of 2005–2010. All estimates include a constant (not reported).

The first difference variables dP and dF are measures of institutional instability/uncertainty as demonstrated in Chapter 13. There is a parallel to the effect of poverty. Uncertainty is another hardship that is likely to increase corruption. Unfortunately, instability also has the problem of confluence. As already shown in Table 10.4, the level variables have a strong positive correlation to corruption, while the first difference variables have a negative (but smaller) correlation to corruption.

The F index started as an annual index in 2000. Therefore, this section works with *the overlapping sample* (with $N = 1,965$) that covers the 17 years from 2000 to 2016 and 131 non-OPEC countries.

Table 10.6 is not meant as an estimate of a model, but as an attempt to sort out the confluence. It reports 14 regressions. The seven (T)-regressions explain the corruption index by means of the variables in the left-most column; for example, regression (T4) is $T_i = a + bP_i + cF_i + u_i$, where a, b, and c are the estimated coefficients reported. The seven (Θ^T)-regressions are the same, except that T is replaced by Θ^T, the corruption net of the transition.

Two of the variables give fairly stable estimates, though they are not always significant. The first is P, the Polity index, which gives a small positive effect on corruption by both T and Θ^T. Democracy does increase honesty, but not much. The second is growth, which is always negative. The betas for both variables are about 0.15. The coefficients on the remaining five variables change substantially. The purpose of the table is to study the pattern in the changes.

Income and the Fraser-index have high collinearity to income when explaining T. The betas sum to 0.83 in equation (T2), while beta for T alone is 0.80 in (T1). Thus, the two variables explain almost the same, but income is better alone in (T1) than Fraser alone in (T3). From the corresponding Θ^T-estimates, it is clear that the confluence is generated by the transition, as expected from Section 2.3. The two first difference variables dP and dF are always negative when significant, and mostly also when insignificant. Thus, institutional instability increases corruption in the short run, as does growth. However, the dP and notably the dF variable also have a great deal of collinearity with the level variables. In the last section of the table with both the levels and the dif-variables, only one coefficient to dP is significant – this happens when income y is omitted.

I interpret the positive effect on corruption of the two institutional variables and the negative effect of the instability of the same two institutional variables as follows: A transition is a process of system change. The changes are mainly for the better, so in the longer run corruption decreases. However, the changes also cause instability, so in the short run they increase corruption. This is a story of short-run costs versus long-run gains, i.e. a J-curve effect. It points back to the positive effect of income and the negative effect of growth from Section 10.3. If part of the transition is caused by the transitions in the institutional variables, it reinforces the idea that the main direction of causality is from development to corruption, not the other way around.

This corroborates the finding from Figure 10.3 that the old wealthy countries of the North West stood out as unusually honest. This is an

TABLE 10.6. *Seven OLS regressions explaining T and* Θ^T

Explaining T-index, corruption

	(T1) Coef.	t-ratio	Beta	(T2) Coef.	t-ratio	Beta	(T3) Coef.	t-ratio	Beta
y, income	1.33	(14.9)	0.80	0.88	(7.0)	0.53			
P, Polity				0.03	(1.5)	0.09			
F, Fraser				0.72	(3.9)	0.30			
y, income							0.06	(2.5)	0.17
F, Fraser							1.57	(9.7)	0.65
Constant	-7.55	(-9.4)		-8.61	(-9.2)		-6.63	(-6.4)	
R²	0.63			0.69			0.57		

	(T4) Coef.	t-ratio	Beta	(T5) Coef.	t-ratio	Beta
y, income	1.21	(10.6)	0.72			
g, growth	-0.11	(-2.1)	-0.12	-0.17	(-2.4)	-0.18
dP, dif P	-0.46	(-1.4)	-0.09	-2.13	(-5.3)	-0.40
dF, dif F	-1.90	(-1.1)	-0.07	-9.57	(-4.5)	-0.34
Constant	-5.72	(-4.7)		6.80	(15.7)	
R²	0.65			0.34		

Explaining Θ^T-index, net corruption

	(Θ^T1) Coef.	t-ratio	beta	(Θ^T2) Coef.	t-ratio	Beta	(Θ^T3) Coef.	t-ratio	Beta
y, income	0.11	(1.5)	0.13	-0.29	(-2.8)	-0.34			
P, Polity				0.03	(1.7)	0.16			
F, Fraser				0.64	(4.4)	0.54			
y, income							0.02	(1.1)	0.10
F, Fraser							0.37	(3.3)	0.31
Constant	-0.99	(-1.5)		-1.95	(-2.6)		-2.59	(-3.6)	
R²	0.02			0.19			0.14		

	(Θ^T4) Coef.	t-ratio	Beta	(Θ^T5) Coef.	t-ratio	Beta
y, income	-0.04	(-0.5)	-0.05			
g, growth	-0.06	(-1.5)	-0.13	-0.06	(-1.5)	-0.13
dP, dif P	-0.49	(-1.8)	-0.19	-0.43	(-1.8)	-0.16
dF, dif F	-2.73	(-2.0)	-0.19	-2.46	(-2.0)	-0.18
Constant	1.11	(1.1)		0.67	(2.6)	
R²	0.08			0.08		

(continued)

TABLE 10.6. (continued)

	Explaining T-index, corruption						Explaining Θ^T-index, net corruption					
	($T1$) Coef. t-ratio Beta						(Θ^T1) Coef. t-ratio beta					
	($T6$)			($T7$)			(Θ^T6)			(Θ^T7)		
	Coef.	t-ratio	Beta	Coef.	t-ratio	Beta	Coef.	t-ratio	Beta	Coef.	t-ratio	Beta
y, income	0.84	(6.4)	0.50	0.05	(1.9)	0.13	−0.34	(−3.2)	−0.41	0.01	(0.8)	0.07
P, Polity	0.02	(1.0)	0.06				0.02	(1.4)	0.13			
F, Fraser	0.86	(4.2)	0.36	1.49	(7.4)	0.62	0.65	(4.0)	0.55	0.40	(2.7)	0.33
g, growth	−0.13	(−2.7)	−0.14	−0.17	(−3.1)	−0.18	−0.08	(−2.0)	−0.16	−0.06	(−1.5)	−0.13
dP, dif P	−0.20	(−0.7)	−0.04	−0.76	(−2.2)	−0.14	−0.29	(−1.2)	−0.11	−0.07	(−0.3)	−0.02
dF, dif F	0.78	(0.5)	0.3	−0.65	(−0.3)	0.02	−0.66	(−0.5)	0.05	−0.07	(−0.1)	−0.01
Constant	−8.72	(−6.1)		5.2	(−3.4)		−1.09	(−0.9)		−2.53	(−2.3)	
R^2	0.70			0.61			0.22			0.15		

All regressions are calculated for a consistent sample of 131 non-OPEC countries. The explanatory variables have different scales. To make the effects comparable, the standard estimates are supplemented with beta coefficients, for normalized series. The first difference variables are dif P and dif F.

effect of time on the internal dynamics of corruption. Once countries become honest, they gradually become more honest over time.

10.7 FIGURE 10.7 COMPARING THREE TRANSITIONS: π^T, π^P, AND π^F

Section 10.4 analyzed the Democratic Transition, $\Pi^P \approx K^P(y, 0.3)$, and Chapter 9 analyzed the Transition in the Economic System, $\Pi^F \approx KF(y, 0.3)$. Figure 10.7 compares these transitions with the Transition of Corruption, $\Pi^T \approx K^T(y, 0.3)$. The figure is estimated based on the overlapping data for 2000–16. Even when the data is shorter, the three curves are virtually unchanged.

The K^T-curve and the K^P-curve have similar paths, but the K^T-curve is one full log-point of income later than the K^P-curve. This is a difference in GDP per capita of 2.7 times, which is 20–50 years' worth of growth. Thus, first the political system becomes more democratic, and after several decades corruption falls. The K^F-curve is less clear. It has a positive slope throughout, and the confidence intervals (not shown) are narrow, so it does represent a systematic change.

The K^F-curve looks like a typical (log-linear) income curve. This explains the high collinearity of F and y. However, given that the F-curve is interpreted as a transition curve, it is clear that it starts to rise well before the K^T-curve. Thus, it can explain the K^T-curve, and support the conclusion that the Transition of Corruption is late and due to transitions in other variables, notably institutions.

10.8 SIX EXAMPLES ILLUSTRATING THE EFFECT OF INSTABILITY ON CORRUPTION

Instead of long series, six examples are provided. The first three are for country pairs on three continents, where each pair has many similarities and a clear difference in the levels of stability and corruption. Table 10.7 provides data for the country pairs shown in Figures 10.7–10.10, while Figure 10.10 looks at three countries with spectacular crises. The four figures are drawn for the Θ^T-data, so the transition curve is horizontal at $\Theta^T = 0$ per definition.

Argentina and Chile. The two neighboring countries in the Southern Cone are both Spanish ex-colonies, with much the same immigration history, language, religion, etc. They are also at the same income level, although Chile has grown much faster.

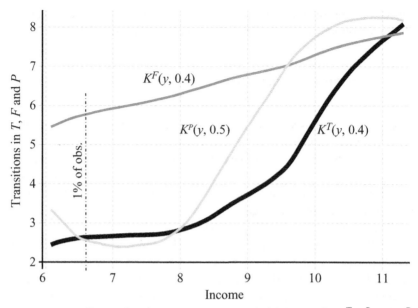

FIGURE 10.7. Comparing three transition curves in Main sample: K^T, K^P, and K^F Estimated for $N = 1,965$ for the years 2000–16. F is the Fraser index (Figure 9.5), P is the Polity index (Figure 4.4), and T is the corruption index (Figure 10.3). The confidence intervals for K^P and K^T overlap below 8.2.

Still, the level of corruption differs by 4.2 points. The two institutional indices show that Argentina has had less democracy and economic freedom. Argentina has also had much more volatility both in the political and economic system – and the differences started long before the indices. Thus, it fits our story perfectly well. It is difficult to explain why the two countries had such a different history, but once things started going awry in Argentina, there was an amazing lack of brakes.

Estonia and Latvia. The two Baltic countries Estonia and Latvia have had much the same history – at least since 1795 when they both were integrated into Russia as provinces. They were independent from 1918 to 1940, when Russian rule returned. After the brief German occupation, they returned to Russian rule until liberation in 1990/91.

In spite of this common history, and a similar income level and population size, the two countries have a difference of 1.6 points in the level of corruption. The level of the institutional variables are higher in Estonia, while there is no difference in the instability variables, but perhaps it is not so much the actual instability that counts as the potential one: Latvia is a

TABLE 10.7. *The institutional variables for three country pairs*

	Argentina	Chile	Latvia	Estonia	Côte d'Ivoire	Ghana
P	8.12	9.65	8.00	9.00	1.88	7.29
Z^P	0	0	0	0	0.16	0.02
V^P	1.00	0.52	0.43	0.46	0.27	1.12
F	5.78	7.75	7.55	7.80	5.73	6.53
V^F	0.26	0.07	0.13	0.08	0.11	0.15
Start	1995	1995	1998	1998	1998	1998

The period ends in 2017. The values are averages for the periods. The most corrupt of the pair is first and shaded.

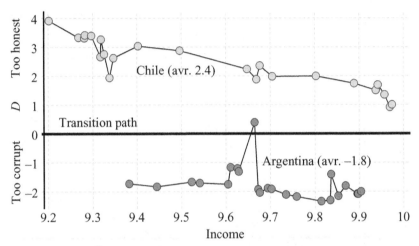

FIGURE 10.8. Θ^T-levels over income in Argentina and Chile, 1995–2017

much more divided country, both as regards ethnicity and religion. This causes some uncertainty.

Côte d'Ivoire and Ghana are (also) neighbors, at roughly the same size and income level, but they differ as to colonial history, languages, and ethnicity. The T-index differs by 1.3 points. As regards the institutional variables, there has been a dramatic shift: In the 1970s Ghana was a much more unstable country, but now it is the other way round. The level of the institutional indices is (much) higher in Ghana, while the volatility variables provide a less clear picture. The Z^P-variable is 0.26 in Côte d'Ivoire. This reflects that the country has had about 5 years of civil war in the period. That the difference in the level of corruption is not larger is probably because of the previous period, where Ghana fared badly. Note also that the two low-

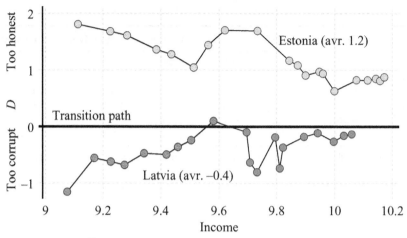

FIGURE 10.9. Θ^T-levels over income in Estonia and Latvia, 1998–2017

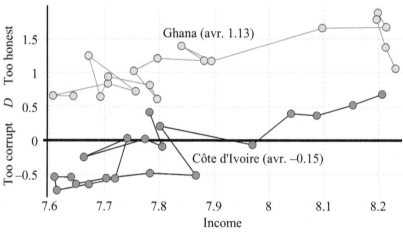

FIGURE 10.10. Θ^T-levels over income in Côte d'Ivoire and Ghana, 1998–2017

income African countries have had more volatile economic development than the middle-income countries of the previous pairs.

Three crises: Greece, Venezuela, and Zimbabwe. Figure 10.11 shows the development in the Θ^T-index in three countries (on different continents) that have experienced very big economic crises: Greece, Venezuela, and Zimbabwe. Their Θ^T-indices are depicted with time on the horizontal axis. Note that as the Θ^T-index is used, the curves do not reflect differences in

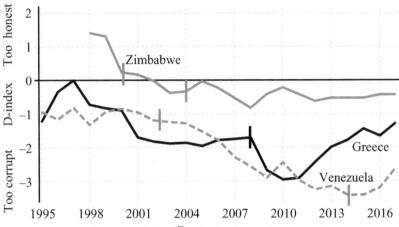

FIGURE 10.11. The story of the Θ^T-index in three crisis-countries

corruption, but in corruption relative to other countries at the same income level.

The crises in the three countries were preceded by at least a decade of inconsistent economic policies that sober observers soon found irresponsible. At some stage, the policies caused galloping debt, balance-of-payment deficits, and increasing inflation, and finally a large fall in *gdp*. This sequence led to a fall in the Θ^T-index in all three cases where the index turned negative. The small vertical lines indicate main events.

Greece became relatively corrupt around 2000, maybe because Greeks became cynical as regards the policies pursued. Corruption further increased, but temporarily only, during the full scale crisis of 2008–13. However, Greece remains a relatively corrupt country.

Venezuela has fared rather poorly for a long time in spite (or because) of its oil wealth. This led to the political victory of the populist Hugo Chavez, who was president from 1999 to 2013. Maybe 2002 was the turning year when his policies became unsustainable. The economic balance in Venezuela gradually worsened, and corruption that was already too high increased by a further two points. After the death of Chavez, power went to his vice-president Nicolás Maduro, who continued his policies with catastrophic results. The upturn in the last two years of the Θ^T-index is due to the large fall in the income level. The *T*-index remains constant at 1.7–1.8, making Venezuela the most corrupt country in Latin America.

Zimbabwe was known as a relatively honest country until the rapid socialization program was started in 2000, but then corruption increased by about 2 points. During the dramatic debacle of the economy, corruption remained rather trendless.

When this evidence is summarized, it is clear that an economic crisis increases corruption, but the timing is not so clear. It probably depends on the extent to which people understand what is going on.

10.9 CONCLUSIONS

This chapter has shown a strong transition in the level of corruption as measured by Transparency International's T-index. Poor countries are rather corrupt, but they become honest as they grow wealthy. The change is a complex process that interacts with institutions. They also have transitions, so the relations examined contain a great deal of collinearity. When the transition path is deducted from the T-index – to give the Θ^T-index – it greatly reduces the collinearity, and allows identification of the substantial genuine effect of institutions.

The Transition of Corruption happens relatively late in the development process. The lateness argues that the transition, and hence T, is caused by development and not the other way around. This is also confirmed by the three causality tests reported in Sections 10.2 and 10.5.

A main reason for the late transition is that development creates many changes that inevitably result in uncertainty, which causes setbacks in the corruption index. Such setbacks are temporary, and when institutions stabilize and countries become stable, wealthy, liberal democracies, honesty comes to dominate. Thanks to the short-run reverses and the internal dynamics of corruption, the process takes time.

I I

The Religious Transition

The chapters until now have looked at transitions of institutions that are clearly related to the economy. I now turn to religion, which, on the face of it, is a long way from the economy, but even then, religiosity has a highly significant transition. The chapter distinguishes between the qualitative variable religion and the quantitative variable religiosity,

Religion is a "package good." It is a binary choice whether people buy into the package. Most people know and readily say what their religion is. It has a large element of tradition – it is typically the same within a family for many generations. The package is complex, and it changes a little over time. Religions are produced in two ways: by Churches and within families. It is used as a factor of production and for consumption.

Religiosity is the *amount* of the good used/consumed, reflecting inten-sity. It is the weight of (any) religion in all aspects of life. The stock of religious beliefs may be constant, but the relevance of these beliefs for decision-making changes depending on the level of development, which is also the level of education and knowledge.

Religiosity has been discussed from many perspectives. In this book, the perspective is growth and development economics. First, religiosity is attached to this frame of reference (s1), and the relevant literature is discussed (s2). The *R*-variable for religiosity follows from the definition of religiosity that is reached from a factor analysis of 14 items in the World Values Survey (s3). The 332 observations for the *R*-variable allow an estimate of the transition curve $R = \Pi^R(y)$(s4). The DP-test shows that

TABLE 11.1. *New variables and terms used in Chapter 11*

Variable	Definition and source
Main concepts	
Church	Organization of a religion. Term used for want of a better one. Covers all religions.
church	Building used for religious services. May be a mosque, temple, synagogue, wat, etc.
Religion	Binary variable of belonging. People know which religion they belong to, if any.
Religiosity	Quantitative variable of intensity. The importance of religion in all aspects of life.
Religiosity variable R, Sections 3–8.	
Source	World Values Survey: www.worldvaluessurvey.org/wvs.jsp.
R	*Religiosity index* in percent, factor one in factor analysis of 14 religiosity items.
$\Pi^R(y)$	*Transition path.* The transition is 50 pp (percentage points), slope $\lambda^R = \partial \Pi^R / \partial y \approx -9.5$
$K^R(y, bw)$	*Kernel regression* with bandwidth *bw*. Estimate of transition curve, $K^R(y, bw) \approx \Pi^R(y)$.
Church s-proxy for religiosity. Historical data, Sections 9–10 (a)	
Source	Own compilation from several sources; see Paldam and Paldam (2018).
S, s	*Supply* of churches. The stock of churches, which per capita is termed *church density*
D, d	*Demand* for churches Aggregate and per capita; d_t is unobserved
κ	*Capacity* utilization, relative to stock: $S_t = D_t(1 + \kappa)$, in equilibrium $S_t^* = D_t$
$d \approx aR$	Relation between the two measures of religiosity, where *a* is approximately constant.

Note (a). The church data are for every 5th year 1300 to 2016. For Denmark only.

the main direction of causality is from income to R (s5). The changes in R over time show some cyclicality, especially in the post-socialist countries (s6). The slope of the transition-curve proves to be quite robust (s7), even when China and the United States are conspicuous outliers (s8). The per capita density of churches is a historical religiosity proxy. It is available for Denmark only, but for seven centuries. From casual observation, I think that it may generalize to other countries. It confirms equivalence (s10).

11.1 RELIGIOSITY IN THE THEORY OF GROWTH AND DEVELOPMENT

Religion is used as a ***consumption good*** when people pray/meditate (often in churches, i.e., places of worship) to achieve (existential) peace of mind. Section 10.3 discussed the theory of demand for intangible goods. When religion is seen as one such good, we need (at least) an income elasticity to understand how religiosity reacts to development. One explanation of the Religious Transition may be that the elasticity is negative. This tallies with the idea that religion is a necessity that becomes less important when the choice space widens as a result of rising income. This theory seems likely, but it is difficult to substantiate.

Religion is used as a ***factor of production*** when people pray for good health or a good harvest,[1] and when political leaders are blessed by religious ceremonies. The theory of growth and development sees the economy as Equation (11.1) a macro production function, F, which produces GDP, Y, by means of factors of production: labor, L, human capital, H, physical capital, K, and knowledge, A, which enters production through K and H. Religion/religiosity has an important, but rarely discussed, role in the theory. In the traditional steady state, A_t was stationary and dominated by traditions that were greatly influenced by religion. This is written as Equation (11.2), where A_t is the sum of Ω the religious part and Z_t the secular one.

$$Y_t = A_t F(L_t, H_t, K_t), \quad t \text{ is time.} \tag{11.1}$$

$$A_t = \Omega + Z_t, \quad \text{religious knowledge } \Omega \text{ has no time index.} \tag{11.2}$$

The importance of religion in knowledge is thus

$$R^A = \Omega/A_t = \Omega/(\Omega + Z_t) \tag{11.3}$$

---

[1] The author has experienced a whole town in the Sahel zone (in Africa) united in a communal prayer for rain, when the rainy season was delayed. In the Developed World, farmers drill boreholes and irrigate.

Z_t grows rapidly in modern society, while Ω is roughly constant. Modern growth, therefore, is a process in which the importance of religion in production falls relative to Z_t, the stock of secular knowledge, notably within science and technology. Equations (11.1) to (11.3) are developed into a full growth model in Gundlach and Paldam (2012). Technical progress is driven by knowledge that follows Equation (11.3). The model uses CES technology to catch the substitution process. Thanks to the productivity of scientific knowledge, it generates a transition path with an endogenous growth component that provides a link between the elasticity of substitution $\sigma_{\Omega Z}$ and the transition. If $\sigma_{\Omega Z}$ is sufficiently high, all growth becomes endogenous.

When causality is analyzed, the endogenous component means that causality becomes simultaneous. Development causes a falling share of Ω in knowledge as per Equation (11.3), but the substitution causes extra growth so that income rises. In the long run, it must be y that causes R, but within a medium time horizon causality between y and R becomes simultaneous.

Figure 11.1 is a preview of our findings about the Religious Transition. Though it is relatively noisy, it looks the same as any other transition. The decline of religiosity is similar to the decline of corruption in the process of development discussed in Chapter 10. To get some intuition as to the modern level, R^M, which may keep falling or converge to a steady level, we have to look at demand and supply at the micro level.

Religion is **demanded** for two main reasons that serve to give (practical) peace of mind,

(i) To give divine protection against risks to life and property. The Grand Transition has doubled the expected life span from about

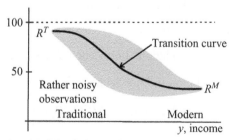

FIGURE 11.1. A sketch of the Religious Transition

As before, the horizontal axis is income, i.e., the logarithm to GDP per capita. R is the measure of religiosity discussed in the text. The superscripts T and M designate the traditional and modern level

40 to 80 years. It also allows people to save for pensions and insurance, public transfers appear, etc. All this reduces the risk and its effects. Thus, the need for divine protection falls, and so does the demand for religion.[2]

(ii) To provide explanations of the unknown. Here science has become an alternative, as mentioned. Science has made substantial progress in reducing the unknown, thereby reducing the realm of religion. In the post-transition world, people have largely ceased to associate diseases with evil spirits and magic spells. Thus, there may also be a time index on Ω in Equation (11.2), so that Ω does not only fall relatively when Z increases, but falls absolutely. It is no wonder that many churches have fought to uphold religious explanations against the onslaught of scientific explanations. It is likely that these components will level off, so that there may be convergence, but it is difficult to predict a steady state level.

The *supply* of religion takes place through several *channels*. Churches supply religious goods *directly* by means of religious services, and in the form of high-quality ceremonies for the rites of passage in the important stages in life: birth, maturity, marriage, and death. Religious goods have also been supplied *indirectly* as a joint product with the three big welfare goods: education, healthcare, and social protection, which consequently are three *extra channels*.

In poor societies, the tax base is small, and most tax revenue is used to finance the power structure holding the state together against internal and external enemies. Churches often owned a great deal of land and had a religious claim to taxes (tithes), but they typically managed to collect only parts of what they claimed. When income from church land and bequests were added, the Church probably did succeed in collecting something like 12% of GDP in taxes.[3] It financed the Church itself and the (small) production of the three welfare goods.

The Grand Transition changed the production of the three welfare goods. Their share of GDP increased about five times from around 3–5% to approximately 20–25%. This exceeded the financial capacity of Churches, and the state had to take over, and hence control over

---

[2] The demand for divine protection against an event e is proportional to $\rho \cdot W$, where $\rho(e)$ is the risk that the event occurs, and $W(e)$ is the welfare cost of the event if it occurs. If $W(e)$ is constant, the conclusion is as stated in the text, but if $W(e) = f(1 - e)$, i.e., welfare is a function of non-occurrence, the conclusion no longer holds.

[3] See the detailed assessments/estimates in Paldam (2017a).

production moved from the Church to the state. When the state took over, it used the provision of welfare goods to supply its own secular ideology. Thus, Churches lost the three extra channels.[4]

11.2 CONTROVERSIES ON SECULARIZATION AND REVERSE CAUSALITY (FROM R TO y)

Religion is an emotional subject for many people, and Churches are (still) large organizations, so the Religious Transition is surrounded by controversies.[5]

A major controversy deals with the unclear concept of secularization.[6] It originated as a component of the theory of *modernization* that goes back to Marx, Freud, Weber, Durkheim, and others. They predicted that economic development would cause religions to vanish. Consequently, religiosity would vanish too. Religion has remained rather stable, and perhaps this is why Stark and Iannaccone (1994) claim that "secularization is a myth."

By contrast, McCleary and Barro (2006) apply a quantitative approach and find that various indicators of religiosity fall with rising income. In this chapter, their results are generalized to much more data, and a rationalization is provided.

As religiosity falls with development, Churches have a (second) interest in resisting development. This leads to the second macro controversy: The family of theories that deals with the causal role of various religions for development, i.e., with reverse causality.

Most reverse theories argue that a certain religion is socially conservative and hence delays development. For a long time, East Asian countries had no development, and in the interwar period, theories appeared about the anti-developmental nature of the belief systems in East Asia,[7] but then things changed. A more recent literature sees Islam as a rigid religion,

---

[4] In most countries, these sectors also have private firms, but they will be disregarded. The take-over by the state varies greatly by country. See also Section 7.1 on the Three Pillars Model and Section 8.1 on the Transition of the Economic System. The channel argument is inspired by Puchades-Navarro and Montoro (2009).

[5] The literature is enormous and written by authors from many trades; see Iannaccone (1998) and Ekelund et al. (2006) for surveys of the much more limited economics literature.

[6] Wikipedia lists about ten definitions of secularization, some of which are quite different. Secularization is a fact if the reader agrees that my analysis is an operational version of the secularization hypothesis.

[7] The theory was developed by J. H. Boeke, 1884–1956. The main argument was about backward-bending labor supply curves. His books are only partly translated (from Dutch), but a summary is available in Higgins (1959).

preserving belief-based traditions from the seventh century, such as the traditional gender roles that keep women out of the labor market; see Paldam (2009). A different reverse theory was proposed by Weber (1904/5), who argued that certain religious minorities, precisely because they are in opposition to mainstream conservative religion, have had a causal role in economic development, notably in the rise of capitalism.

At present, this is not our subject, but it is touched on indirectly as follows: The estimate of the transition slope, λ, is controlled for reverse causality and for the main religious affiliations. The results suggest that belief-based traditions do not have strong anti- or pro-developmental effects in the long run.

The micro theory of the economics of religiosity does not explicitly address the religious transition, although links may be developed on the demand side: Azzi and Ehrenberg (1975) consider the time allocation to religious and non-religious activities at the household level in response to changes in the budget constraint. Durkin and Greely (1991) study the relationship between the demand for religion and the prevalence of risk in modern society. Lipford et al. (1993) investigate the link connecting religiosity to social behavior.

The supply side is dominated by the *competition theory*; see Finke and Iannaccone (1993) and Stark and Iannaccone (1994).[8] Here, religiosity is a function of the degree of competition in the market for religion, with competition increasing the efficient supply of religious goods, which generates its own demand. The theory explains why religiosity differs across countries at the same income level, but it does not address the religious transition.

11.3 THE RELIGIOSITY VARIABLE, R: THE FACTOR ANALYSIS

The Religious Transition is the relation $R = \Pi^R(y)$, as in the previous chapters. Thus, one point of change in y is a change of *gdp* of e ≈ 2.7 times. The explained variable is religiosity, R. If K variables were used to measure the importance of religion in all aspects of life, R would be the largest common factor in all these variables. The actual R-variable is estimated by means of a factor analysis of $K = 14$ items from the *World*

---

[8] The theory was used to provide an explanation of the remarkably high religiosity of the United States, but Opfinger (2011) reports that the theory fails in a cross-country perspective, using our R-variable.

Values Survey (WVS); see Inglehart et al. (1998, 2004). The items are chosen to span as much of the aspect space as possible.

The WVS questionnaire was developed as an English master version, which defines the terminology used. Experts in each country have translated the master into their languages and cultural environments. Key concepts, such as *God* and *church*, are easy to translate for monotheistic religions, but seem less relevant in other belief systems. However, the countries of South and East Asia fit well into the general pattern. All items disregard the respondent's religious affiliation, if any, but ask about religion's importance in various spheres of life. The number used from each poll is the fraction (as a percentage) of the respondents giving the high importance answer. The aggregate R-score is in percentages as well. Changes in R are thus in percentage points.

A complete panel for 111 countries and 6 waves would contain 666 polls, but our sample contains only 332 polls.[9] Thus, the gaps in the panel are substantial, which limits the gain from using the panel structure. The regression analysis uses either the cross-country sample of 111 country averages, R, or the full sample of 332 Rs with controls for waves and selected groups of countries and religions.

Table 11.2 shows that the missing observations are not random.[10] The 1982 wave covered countries, mainly in the West, which were three times as rich as the average country in the world. The next waves came to contain many post-socialist countries to catch the effects of the collapse of Communism. As time passed, the sample changed to include more Muslim countries. Consequently, each wave of the WVS has a skewed country sample of countries, and the skewness changes over time. The cross-wave stability of the R-factor is therefore quite remarkable. Representativity is better once all waves are taken together. The last column of the table reveals that the 111 countries included in at least one poll hold 86% of world population and are only 57% richer than the average of all countries.

The time span is only 30 years, so the analysis hinges crucially on the *equivalence hypothesis* that the *within* (time-series) slope is the same as the *between* (cross-country) slope. Thus, I assume that countries had a

---

[9] In addition to countries that are dropped in the polls, some items are dropped. For 666 polls, complete coverage would demand 9,324 polled items, but we only have 3,260, so 65% of the cells in the (111, 14, 6)-panel are empty.

[10] The changing composition of the country sample probably reflects public concerns at the time of the wave. It is difficult to fund such a large project as the WVS, and funding depends on the public interest.

TABLE 11.2. *The representativity of the sample of R-data*

	W1	W2	W3	W4	W5	W6	Polls	Countries
			Countries included: All and grouped in two ways					
All	24	43	68	78	58	60	332	111
West	18	20	23	24	16	8	109	27
Post-socialist	1	12	24	24	10	13	84	28
Others	5	11	21	31	32	39	139	56
Christian	22	37.5	57	55.5	39.5	32.5	244	72.5
Muslim		1.5	6	15.5	10	18.5	51.5	28
Others	2	4	5	7	8.5	9	35.5	10.5
	The share (in %) of the sample						Average	All
World Countries	13.6	22.1	34.9	40.0	29.4	30.5	28.4	57.0
World Population	20.1	58.6	71.5	74.8	72.3	69.0	61.1	86.2
	Excess income (in %) in countries of sample						Average	All
GDP per capita	219	161	96	74	64	54	111	57

In four countries, about half the population is Muslim: Ethiopia, Lebanon, Malaysia, and Nigeria.

rather similar level of development about 300 years ago, so the cross-country differences in present income levels reflect the long-run path of development since then; see Section 11.9.

Table 11.3 provides a short version of the question asked in the 14 items and the number of times it has been asked in each of the five waves. The 3,260 polled items in the sample have three dimensions: $j = 1, \ldots 14$ are the items, $i = 1, \ldots, 111$ are the countries, and $t = 1, \ldots, 6$ are the waves. The aggregate answer for item j in country i and wave t is A_{jit}. When aggregated across countries it is A_{jt}, and when further aggregated across waves it becomes A_j. Column (8) shows the A_js, representing the average share of "high importance" attributed to each item by the respondents. The grand average of all A_js is 53.0%, which is thus the fraction of the respondents in all polls that declare themselves (rather) religious. Column (9) shows the coefficient of correlation of the A_{it}'s and income y_{it} for each j. All correlations – except the one to item 14 – are statistically significant, negative, and substantial in size.

Table 11.4 reports a factor analysis of the religiosity items. The factor analysis is based on the pairwise correlations within each wave, so it uses as many observations as possible. I have also run the analysis on balanced samples. It is debatable which estimate is the best. However, the results are virtually the same. Also, an aggregate factor analysis has been made by joining the individual waves together in one matrix. It also gives much the same results. The factor analysis is done independently for each wave. Our criteria for accepting one factor as the religiosity variable are, as follows: Its loadings to all items are *positive*, *large*, and *stable*. The stability is given by the cross-wave t-ratios in the right-hand column.

Factor 1 fulfils these criteria: It is the dominating factor with an average eigenvalue of 8.2 and a cross-wave t-statistic of 10.8. All items have positive and mostly large loadings to factor 1. The cross-wave t-ratios are in the range from 6.9 to 118.8. Factor 1 taps into a latent variable that is very salient for the respondents. Thus, factor 1 is our R-variable.

Factor 2 has an average eigenvalue of 1.74. However, all but one factor loadings are unstable across samples. This factor mainly loads to items that reflect the relations of the respondents to the organization of the Church, and will not be discussed further. The third and higher factors are of no consequence.

Row 15 in Table 11.4 shows that factor 1 always loads negatively to income. Even if it rises a little as the sample comes to cover more of the income range, the cross-wave stability is still −13.7. Thus, the correlation of income and the dominant first factor is robust and negative.

TABLE 11.3. *The 14 religiosity items: Short definitions and some counts*

Content of item	(1)	(2)	(3)	(4)	(5)	(6)	(7)	(8) Avr.	(9) Cor
	Included in N polls						All	A_j	(A_{it}, y_{it})
Wave	W1	W2	W3	W4	W5	W6			
Period for polls in wave	81/84	90/94	95/98	99/04	05/09	10/14		%	(a)
1 God very important in life	23	39	67	76	58	58	321	57.5	−0.51
2 Family should teach children the faith	23	43	69	77	58	60	330	34.0	−0.41
3 Religion important in life	–	43	69	77	57	60	306	40.3	−0.45
4 Believes in God	23	37	66	73	–	54	253	83.3	−0.39
5 Has moments of prayer and meditation	16	37	33	65	50	–	201	67.9	−0.37
6 Non-believers are unfit for political office	–	–	33	72	49	–	154	33.0	−0.67
7 Churches answer family life problems	16	33	33	74	51	–	207	49.8	−0.51
8 Churches answer social problems	–	35	33	74	51	–	193	40.2	−0.49
9 Better if people are strongly religious	–	–	33	33	49	–	115	38.2	−0.62
10 Churches answer moral problems	8	35	33	74	51	–	201	55.0	−0.57
11 Churches answer spiritual needs	16	35	33	74	51	–	209	76.5	−0.52
12 Attends religious service regularly	24	40	67	76	57	57	321	40.2	−0.44
13 Is a religious person	23	42	66	74	58	59	322	68.5	−0.43
14 Belongs to religious denomination	16	40	33	45	–	–	134	76.5	0.01
Sum or averages	188	459	668	964	640	348	3,267	53.0	−0.45
Number of countries in wave	24	43	69	78	58	60	332(b)	111(c)	
Missing observations, in % of total possible	44.0	23.8	30.8	11.7	21.7	58.6	29.7		

The order of the 14 items is per the factor loading in Table 11.4. The variable is the answer that says that the respondent is (very) religious. The polls of each wave are paired with the average income for the period.

Notes: (a) correlation of all poll averages and income for each item. Thus in row (1) $N = 321$. (b) Number of polls. (c) Number of countries (or similar) included in at least one wave.

191

TABLE 11.4. *A factor analysis of the 14 items*

Content of item	Results for individual wave						Across waves	
Wave	W1	W2	W3	W4	W5	W6	Avg.	t-ratio
Eigenvalue for factor 1	7.16	7.80	9.27	10.58	9.33	4.86	8.17	10.8
Eigenvalue for factor 2	1.67	2.53	2.63	2.49	0.86	0.49	1.78	5.1
Eigenvalue for factor 3	1.35	0.50	0.73	0.93	0.50	0.35	0.72	5.3
	Factor 1 loading						Avg.	t-ratio
(1) God very important in life	0.95	0.95	0.96	0.97	0.90	0.91	0.94	88.7
(2) Family should teach children faith	0.94	0.91	0.89	0.93	0.92	0.88	0.91	118.8
(3) Religion important in life		0.93	0.87	0.82	0.94	0.92	0.89	45.9
(4) Believes in god	0.96	0.84	0.85	0.96		0.82	0.88	32.2
(5) Has moments of prayer and meditation	0.93	0.88	0.80	0.94	0.83		0.88	35.3
(6) Non-believers are unfit for political office			0.80	0.96	0.87		0.88	23.1
(7) Churches answer family life problems	0.86	0.75	0.84	0.90	0.90		0.85	33.6
(8) Churches answer social problems		0.74	0.84	0.87	0.83		0.85	22.9
(9) Better if people are strongly religious			0.79	0.80	0.93		0.82	35.3
(10) Churches answer moral problems	0.85	0.62	0.77	0.98	0.85		0.81	15.5
(11) Churches answer spiritual needs	0.88	0.65	0.77	0.87	0.73		0.78	20.5
(12) Attends religious service regularly	0.90	0.81	0.72	0.43	0.80	0.78	0.73	12.3
(13) Is a religious person	0.39	0.79	0.72	0.66	0.80	0.87	0.70	11.0
(14) Belongs to religious denomination	0.31	0.60	0.61	0.76			0.57	6.9
(15) Income (ln to GDP per capita)	-0.55	-0.42	-0.40	-0.56	-0.66	-0.62	-0.53	-13.7

The t-ratio in the right-hand column measures the cross-wave stability of the factor loadings. When the cross-wave stability of the loadings to factor 2 and 3 is analyzed in the same way, only a couple of cross-wave estimates have t-ratios above 2, and hence they are bolded. A joint factor analysis of all 332 polls gives much the same results as the average column, though with slightly higher values throughout.

192

The calculations in row (15) of Table 11.4 and in column (9) in Table 11.3 are performed quite differently. It is reassuring that the results are similar. This already suggests a strong religious transition – however, it is still a measure of correlation only.

The standard method of weighting a set of correlated items is to use principal components. Parallel to Table 11.4, a table of principal components has been calculated. They are very similar, so I have just calculated the average of the percentage scores. The 68 factor loadings in Table 11.4 have an average of 0.82 with a standard error of 0.05, so the aggregate is rather robust to the weights used. Finally, it should be noted that the average wave contains 11.7 items, so by using the averages of the items, uncorrelated measurement errors are reduced by a division with $\sqrt{11.7} \approx 3.4$.

11.4 THE TRANSITION CURVE π^R

Figure 11.2 shows the (R, y)-scatter of the data points. The graph includes a kernel curve $R = k(y, 0.4)$ that is an estimate of the transition curve π^R. It has a highly significant negative slope, and some convergence at both ends, but it is estimated on $N = 332$ only. Figure 11.3 shows the (satisfactory) robustness of the kernel curve to the bandwidth.

The few low-income countries in the sample have Rs of about 80 percentage points, and the measure of R can hardly be higher than 90%, so the traditional level $R^T \approx 80\%$ is well determined.

The decline in the curve and hence the adjustment path is obvious, but the modern equilibrium level R^M is not yet clear. It is surely below 40%, but stability has not yet been reached. Perhaps the decline has slowed down, so it will probably cease, but it is difficult to predict whether it will stabilize at 30% or fall below that.

The data points are considerably scattered around the average curve, so the Religious Transition explains only some of the observed variation. China and the United States are depicted as large diamonds. Section 11.8 points to these countries as the most extreme ones. They are outliers reflecting inertia in religiosity. A more detailed study of the cross-wave observations for each country shows that they are often quite similar relative to the general trend, indicating path dependency.

11.5 THE DP-TEST FOR LONG-RUN CAUSALITY
(SEE SECTION 2.8)

In the part of Europe where the author lives, the dominating religion has changed twice in the recorded history of the last dozen centuries. Religion

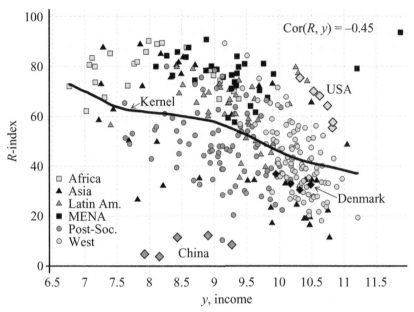

FIGURE 11.2. The transition path: $R = \Pi^R(y) \approx K(y, 0.4)$, $N = 332$ polls
The large diamonds are the five obs. for China and the six obs. for the United States; the small diamonds are the four obs. for Denmark referred to in Section 11.9. The correlation of R and income within the groups are Africa –0.23 (22), Asia –0.44 (45), Latin America –0.21 (42), MENA –0.01 (30), post-socialist –0.40 (84), and West –0.45 (109), where the parentheses hold the number of observations.

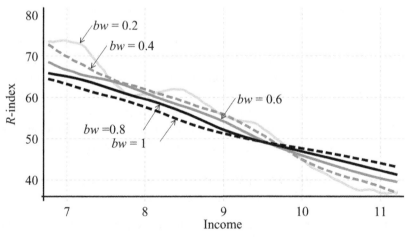

FIGURE 11.3. Robustness of kernel from Figure 11.2 to the bandwidth

has been similarly stable in most other parts of the world. This suggests that religiosity may also change slowly. Thus, the Grand Transition framework deals with the long-run relation $R = \Pi^R(y)$, where it has to be shown that y is causal to R. To this end, the long-run DP-causality test from Chapter 2 is used. The long-run results may hide more complex short-run interactions.

The limited sample is probably the main reason why the coefficient on y is about 30% larger in Table 11.5 than in the other tables; i.e., it is -12 in Table 11.5 vs. -9.5 in the other tables. When the sample increases to $N = 94$ in column (5), the coefficient on y falls to the usual size.

TABLE 11.5. *The DP-test for long-run causality from income to the* R-*index*

	Dependent variable: *R* Estimate No. of countries	Main model (1)	Robustness of model to instrument variation			
			(2)	(3)	(4)	(5)
		62	67	62	62	94
	OLS estimates					
(1)	Income, *y*	−12.13	−12.04	−12.13	−12.13	−8.75
	t-ratio	(−7.0)	(−7.3)	(−7.0)	(−7.0)	(−5.1)
(2)	Centered R^2	0.44	0.44	0.44	0.44	0.22
	IV estimates: *y* is instrumented					
(3)	Income, *y*	−14.94	−17.33	−15.07	−14.30	−16.20
	t-ratio	(−5.0)	(−6.4)	(−5.3)	(−5.4)	(−5.2)
(4)	Instruments	*biofpc, geofpc*	*bioavg, geoavg*	*animals, plants*	*axis, size, climate*	*coast, frost maleco*
(5)	First stage partial R^2	0.36	0.43	0.39	0.44	0.37
(6)	CD F-statistic	*16.49*	*23.73*	*18.74*	*15.15*	*17.32*
	CD critical value	19.93	19.93	19.93	22.30	22.30
(7)	Sargan test	5.57	1.51	2.60	0.66	7.32
	p-value	0.02	0.22	0.11	0.72	0.03
	Hausman test for parameter consistency of OLS and IV estimates					
(8)	C-statistic	1.46	7.67	1.82	1.22	11.05
	p-value	0.23	0.01	0.18	0.27	0.00
	Check for reverse causality (all are smaller but one works)					
(9)	CD F-statistic	12.15	21.89	11.95	7.33	*16.03*

The observations are averages of waves 2–6 of the World Values Survey, thus $N = 62$ to 94. All specifications include a constant term (not reported).

The Sargan test reveals that the instruments are valid and correctly excluded from the estimation equation in three out of five cases. The Cragg-Donald (CD) test statistics are above or at the critical value – the instruments are thus reasonably strong. Hence, the IV-results are statistically valid and identify the *causal* effect of income on religiosity.

All five IV-estimates of the slope are highly significant and rather similar: $\lambda_{IV} \approx$ –15. As before, the favorite combination of instruments is in column (1). It uses the principal components of the geographical variables and the biological variables as the two DP-variables, but statistically the test results are better in column (2).

It looks as if $\lambda_{OLS} < \lambda_{IV}$. This is formally tested by the Hausman C-test, which rejects the difference in three cases and accepts it in two. The conclusion is that the simultaneity bias in the OLS-estimate of λ is of dubious significance. Finally, section (9) of Table 11.5 tests for reverse causality. The CD-test statistics are smaller than for the main causal direction in all cases and larger than the critical value in one case only. This confirms that our instruments show that the main direction of causality is from income to religiosity, but there appears to be some simultaneity, as expected from the theoretical discussion.

11.6 AN ANALYSIS OF THE 201 CHANGES R FROM ONE WAVE TO THE NEXT

The analysis of the trends over time is based on first differences across waves. With a growth of 2.4% per year, the growth from wave to wave is 13%. The R-changes are $\Delta R_{iw} = R_{iw} - R_{iw-1}$, where i is country and w is the wave. The measure demands that an observation is available for both R_{iw-1} and R_{iw}. This provides 201 changes. They have an average value of –1.3, which is the change of the R-variable from one wave to the next. This is difficult to observe. For the West, the average fall is three times larger. The post-socialist countries are particularly interesting, as the Communist regimes until Wave 2 were anti-religious and (often) suppressed religion. The first two waves after the end of Communism consequently showed a return to "normality." However, the last two changes are much like other countries. Another interesting group is the Muslim group. It is often alleged that religiosity has increased in the Muslim world in the last quarter century, but this is not confirmed.

The average changes in the religiosity items for the *West* are significantly negative, and the decline is –3.7 percentage points, on average, per wave (i.e., over five years). The decline is somewhat erratic, but perhaps it slows, suggesting that the transition may converge to a stable level. For *Others* the fall is smaller and (even) more erratic.

11.7 A REGRESSION ANALYSIS OF THE STABILITY OF THE TRANSITION SLOPE λ TO COUNTRY GROUPS

The first part of the robustness analysis is reported in Table 11.7, which provides estimates of the slope λ after including binary dummies for the main country groups and religions. Row (1) is the *base model* for the full sample of 332 polls. It gives an estimate of $\lambda \approx -9.6(9.2)$. Row (13) shows the average of the 11 regressions (2)–(12) and two *t*-ratios: the average of the 11 *t*-ratios and the cross-regression *t*-ratios. For λ it is -9.3 (8.9), with a cross-regression *t*-ratio of 30. Thus, the transition slope of **-9.5** is very robust, and 13% of -9.5 is -1.24, as in Table 11.6.

Rows (2) to (7) report results for six regressions of religiosity on a constant and *one* of the country (group) dummies. Column (A1) controls the estimate for income, but column (B1) is without this control. All of the country group dummies are significant in columns (A1) and (B1), except

TABLE 11.6. *Changes in religiosity items across waves, 1982–2005*

	Difference	W1–W2	W2–W3	W3–W4	W4–W5	W5–W6	All
		Part A: Aggregate results					
All countries	Average	-2.53	-2.73	1.39	-7.10	3.16	-1.29
	N	23	42	59	40	37	201
		Part B: Divided into country-groups					
West	Average	-5.15	-6.07	-0.04	-8.06	2.76	-3.67
	N	17	19	21	13	8	78
Post-socialist	Average	22	1.29	5.38	-7.06	1.65	1.88
	N	1	12	22	10	7	52
Others	Average	1.19	-1.36	-2.22	-6.38	3.69	-0.88
	N	5	11	16	17	23	72
		Part C: A Muslim exception					
Muslim incl. 50%[(a)]	Average		6.84	-5.40	-5.00	4.62	-1.15
	N		2	6	8	7	23

Averages in bold are significant at the 5% level. Averages in bold and italics are significant at the 10% level. The table uses all available observations on item changes. The first observation in the post-socialist row refers to a date before the fall of Communism. The Muslim group is quite thin, so I have included the four countries where about half the population is Muslim: Ethiopia, Lebanon, Malaysia, and Nigeria.

TABLE 11.7. *The effect on R of income and country groups, (2 × 11) + 1 regressions*

N = 332	(A) Regressions with income included				(B) Regressions without income		
	(A1)	(A2)	(A3)	(A4)	(B1)	(B3)	(B4)
	Country group	Income	Constant	R^2	Country group	Constant	R^2
(1) Income	–				–	None	
(2) Africa	**4.52 (3.4)**	**−7.95 (−7.0)**	**126.95 (11)**	0.231	**27.15 (6.6)**	**50.75 (47)**	0.117
(3) Asia	**−13.06 (−4.7)**	**−10.27 (−10.0)**	**151.61 (15)**	0.254	**−9.33 (−3.0)**	**53.83 (46)**	0.026
(4) Lat Am	**10.10 (3.5)**	**−9.37 (−9.1)**	**140.12 (14)**	0.232	**11.89 (3.7)**	**51.08 (44)**	0.039
(5) MENA	**24.67 (7.9)**	**−9.13 (−9.5)**	**136.86 (14)**	0.331	**26.54 (7.6)**	**50.15 (47)**	0.149
(6) Post-soc	**−11.57 (−5.3)**	**−10.79 (−10.4)**	**157.69 (15)**	0.265	**−6.63 (−2.7)**	**54.24 (43)**	0.021
(7) West	−1.85 (−0.7)	**−9.05 (−6.8)**	**138.87 (11)**	0.205	**−12.73 (−5.8)**	**56.75 (44)**	0.092
The Muslim exception – compare with estimate for Mena group							
(8) Muslim	**18.28 (6.8)**	**−7.42 (−7.2)**	**119.97 (12)**	0.301	**24.37 (8.8)**	**48.77 (45)**	0.192
(9) Arab	**26.24 (7.4)**	**−9.12 (−9.3)**	**137.10 (14)**	0.317	**28.56 (7.2)**	**50.57 (48)**	0.135
Other exceptions							
(10) China	**−55.10 (−7.4)**	**−10.53 (−10.7)**	**153.13 (16)**	0.317	**−45.06 (−5.3)**	**53.24 (50)**	0.077
(11) USA	**24.92 (3.4)**	**−10.23 (−9.8)**	**149.05 (15)**	0.231	12.7 (1.6)	**52.33 (47)**	0.007
(12) Nordic	**−11.78 (−3.1)**	**−8.74 (−8.1)**	**136.20 (13)**	0.226	**−20.12 (−5.0)**	**54.02 (49)**	0.070
Cross-estimate stability							
(13) Average	**2.31 (3.4)**	**−9.33 (8.9)**			**3.40 (5.2)**		
(14) t-ratio	(0.3)	(−30)			(0.5)		

The parentheses contain *t*-ratios. The bottom row provides the cross-regression *t*-ratio. Coefficient estimates with *t*-ratios above 2 are bolded. In Column (13) the average *t*-ratios are calculated for the numerical values. Note that while most group dummies get significant *t*-ratios, they are different, while both *t*-ratios for income are highly significant.

West in column (A1). This means that all of the low religiosity in the West can be explained by the high income. The reverse story applies to the United States. Here the coefficient to the country dummy is insignificant without income control, but it is significant when income is controlled for. Thus, the United States is a very religious country at its income level.

While row (13) shows that income has a very stable coefficient, this does not apply to the country group dummies; although most of the estimates are significant, they are, as they should be, different both in columns (A1) and (B1).

11.8 THE ROBUSTNESS OF THE TRANSITION SLOPE λ TO OBSERVATIONS FROM INDIVIDUAL COUNTRIES

Table 11.8 contains the multivariate regressions where (1) and (2) correspond to (A1), and (3) and (4) correspond to (B1). The results are much as expected, and it is nice to see that regression (2) has an R^2 score of 0.57.

The 12 estimates of the transition slope, λ, in Table 11.7 have an average of about −9.5 and a std. of 8.6, and the results in Table 11.8 are very similar. Given that the causality issue is settled, it is possible to use all data for a more detailed and precise analysis. To confirm the robustness, I analyze how the estimate of λ reacts to the deletion of individual countries and in particular to suspicious countries. The 332 polls have one to six polls for each of the 111 countries. The base model (1) becomes

$$R_j = \alpha + \lambda y_j + D_i + \mu, \quad \text{for } j = 1, \ldots, 111 \text{ and } \mu \text{ are the residuals.}$$

$$D_i \text{ is a dummy} \quad \text{for the observations for country } i. \quad (11.3)$$

The base regression with all 332 observations has no D-variable. It provides the estimate λ_{all}. It is possible that the size of the estimated λ hinges on the inclusion of one or a few outliers. Therefore, 111 estimates, $\lambda_1, \ldots, \lambda_{111}$, are generated, where λ_i is estimated on the sample after excluding the observations for country i, by means of the dummy D_i. These estimates differ from λ_{all} by the effect $\eta_i = \lambda_i - \lambda_{all}$. Figure 11.4 shows the distribution of the 111 estimates of the country effect η_i. Except for a few outliers – notably China and the United States – the distribution of the ηs is nicely normal with a rather small standard deviation. Only 7 of the 111 countries exceed $-0.3 < \eta < 0.3$. This means that if there is some measurement error in the data for one country, this normally influences the estimate of λ by less than 3%. The estimated ηs are approximately

TABLE 11.8. *The effect on R of income and country groups - four multiple regressions*

	Income	Asia	MENA	Post-soc	West	China	USA	Nordic	Constant	R^2
(1) Coef.	-8.59	-21.01	12.29	-18.13	-11.86				144.16	0.453
t-ratio	(-7.7)	(-7.2)	(3.7)	(-7.3)	(-4.2)				(14.3)	
(2) Coef.	-9.63	-15.40	12.74	-17.84	-9.39	-47.62	23.55	-10.34	153.37	0.574
t-ratio	(-9.6)	(-5.8)	(4.3)	(-8.1)	(-3.6)	(-7.6)	(4.2)	(-3.4)	(17.0)	
(3) Coef.		-32.71	-14.23	-29.59	-33.18				77.20	0.378
t-ratio		(-10.2)	(-4.3)	(-10.7)	(-12.5)				(35.4)	
(4) Coef.		-28.17	-14.23	-29.59	-31.71	-40.85	19.56	-11.60	77.20	0.77
t-ratio		(-9.3)	(-4.7)	(-11.6)	(-12.3)	(-6.0)	(3.2)	(-3.4)	(38.5)	

See Table 11.7. Both the African and Latin American country groups become insignificant in the multiple regressions.

200

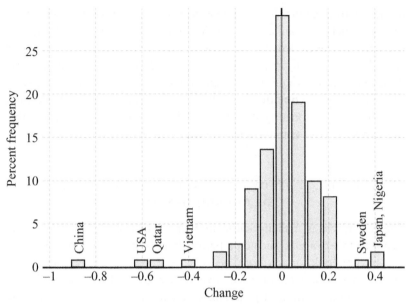

FIGURE 11.4. The distribution of the country-effect η_i on λ of the deletion of one country

additive, so that the effect of deleting two countries is the sum of the effect of the deletion of each.

The effect of deleting a country altogether places an upper bound on the effect of a possible measurement error in the polls for the country. The true effect of a measurement error affecting the data of the country is likely to be (much) smaller.

The two largest outliers have ηs of about −0.9 (China) and −0.6 (United States). As seen in Figure 11.2, China is (still) a relatively poor country with low religiosity, and the United States is a rich country with high religiosity, so their effects on the estimate of λ are much the same. If the two outliers are both deleted, the estimated transition becomes −1.4 points faster, so that λ changes from −9.5 to almost −11.[11]

Religiosity polls for some countries are *suspicious*. This applies to polls made under authoritarian antireligious regimes, such as China and Vietnam, but note that the poll from Hong Kong is not much different

---

[11] The effect of excluding the one observation from Qatar is almost as large as excluding the six observations for the United States, so Qatar is really extreme.

to the one from China. In the same way, polls from authoritarian religious regimes, such as Iran and Saudi Arabia, may be suspect. If the two countries are excluded, the effect is to change the estimated transition slope by +0.4. If all 17 polls from the nine Middle Eastern and North African countries are deleted, the effect is +0.68, which is much the same as the effect of deleting the five polls from the United States. While some polls may have reporting skewness, I believe to have demonstrated that this can have only a minor effect on the main pattern found.

11.9 A PILOT STUDY OF LONG TIME SERIES: THE PROXY OF CHURCH DENSITY

The R-variable is a theory-close measure. However, it only covers 30 years, and there are no such data before that. To find long time series, it is necessary to look for a proxy. The variable found is the per capita density of churches. The data compiled covers my country, Denmark, only, but over 700 years. I think it generalizes to other countries, but it needs to be confirmed.

A large project "Danmarks Kirker" (ref) at the Danish National Museum has until now covered two-thirds of all churches, including closed churches, in great detail. As the project uses a published sampling plan, and as the present churches are registered on a carefully updated home page run by the Church, it was possible to project the present *church stock* for the geographical area of present-day Denmark for every fifth year from 1300 to 2016. The data include the opening and closing of churches, their sizes, and all changes to the buildings.[12]

Figure 11.5 shows the church stock both in plain numbers and size-weighted. The two curves are virtually parallel, and show a pattern of no trend from 1300 to 1850, where the population and income were rather stable. The reformation changed the religion from Catholicism to Lutheranism, which is less church intensive. This resulted in a drop in density of 9%. From 1750 and until today, the church stock has increased by 26%. However, the population has increased six-fold since

---

[12] Paldam and Paldam (2018) gives references to the sources used, which are mainly in Danish. The project would have been impossibly large without the 50 years of work by a dozen researchers in the "Danske Kirker" project. It seems that the project is unique. Thus, it is lucky that the project was possible for Denmark. Part of the luck is that old Danish Churches are sturdy stone buildings and that few wars have been fought on Danish territory.

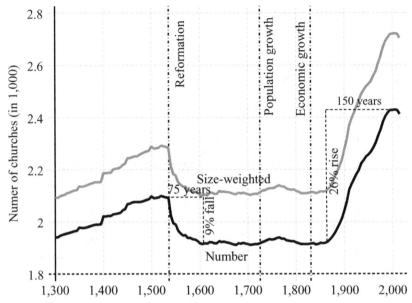

FIGURE 11.5. The church stock, *S*, in Denmark, 1300 to 2015

1750.[13] Thus, there has been a fall in per capita *church density* during the Grand Transition. The fall is almost five-fold.

Figure 11.6 shows the church density and income from 1750 to 2016. The two series have a correlation of −0.95, so we are dealing with a strong relation. Before 1950, more than 98% of the population were members of the national Church (Folkekirken), and this number is still 75%. As the average size of the churches has grown only marginally, there has been no increase in the efficiency of church use. However, there has been a large fall in the attendance rate at services. For all we know, the church capacity was fully used in 1750, while this is not the case in 2015, where only about 1.5% of church members go to church on an average Sunday.[14] Thus, the fall may be even larger than the five times shown. It should be

---

[13] It is a bit unclear when the Grand Transition started in Denmark, as data for the period 1750–1820 are weak.

[14] The rough numbers are: In 1750, the stock was 1,970 churches with app. 300,000 seats. The population was 850,000 and all were Lutheran. All seats would be full if 60% of the adult population went to the Sunday service. Today, the number of churches is 2,390 with about 400,000 seats. The population is 5,700,000, of which 75% are Lutheran. About 1.5% or 65,000 go to church on an average Sunday. Thus, they occupy 16% of the available seats.

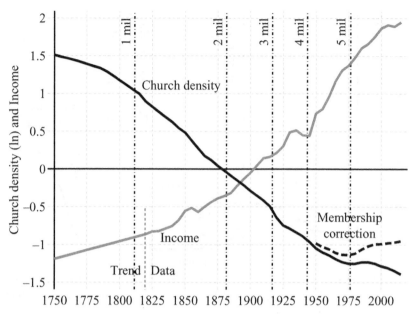

FIGURE 11.6. The church density, *s*, and income, *y*, 1750 to 2015

The church density is also in logs. Income data before 1820 are a trend only. The vertical lines show when the population reaches 1 million, 2 million, ..., 5 million. The population will reach 6 million in 2030

intuitively clear that church density is a fine proxy for religiosity in the longer run, but it is worth formalizing the connection. First, two claims are stated,

Claim (C1): The church stock is demand driven. The church stock is the capital used in the production of religion. The theory of production claims that with a given technology, the capital stock equals demand in equilibrium. The capital stock adjustment model (i.e., the accelerator model) shows how supply adjusts to demand. Thus, (C1) makes sense in the longer run.

Claim (C2): A religion-package is consumed in fixed relations. Section 11.3 showed large factor loadings on the national *averages* for the items. The item "attends religious service regularly" has an average factor loading of 0.73. This means that even though church attendance may not be a good measure at the individual level, it appears to be a good measure at the aggregate level. It follows that the demand for churches $d_t = a R_t$, where a is a "technical" coefficient. Thus, (C2) makes sense at the aggregate level.

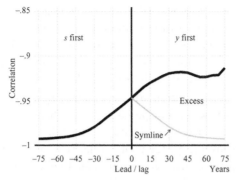

FIGURE 11.7. The correlogram analysis of the (s, y)-data used for Figure 11.6
The format of the figure is discussed in Section 2.5. Note that the observations are
5 years apart, so the 31 leads/lags analyzed cover 150 years, as indicated on the
horizontal axis.

The two level variables are the church stock S_t, and the population
Pop_t. The demand for services $d_t = d(R_t) \approx a R_t$. Thus, the macro
demand for churches is $D_t = a R_t Pop_t$, which equals the desired church
density $s_t^* = a R_t$. However, the actual church density is the supply of
churches $s_t = S^S_t / Pop_t$. Thus, in the short run, demand comes to equal
supply $S_t = D_t(1 + \kappa)$, via κ, which is the capacity utilization for churches.
If the supply is too small, κ represents the amount of queuing for seats at
the services. If the supply is too large (as it is today), κ represents the
fraction of vacant seats at the weekly service.

The capital stock adjustment model describes the adjustment process
of supply to demand. In the short run, the church stock is fixed, for
physical and institutional reasons. With under-capacity, $\kappa > 0$, more
churches are built; with over-capacity, churches are closed. It easily takes
20 years from under-capacity being observed to a new church being
opened. It takes even more years of obvious over-capacity before a church
can be closed.[15] The convergence to the long-run equilibrium causes the
long-run stock to be demand driven. The demand is a function of income
and religion.

The Danish data provide the correlogram test for causality. This nicely
confirms the DP-test in Table 11.5. There is no doubt that income, y, leads
church density, s.

While the cross-country analysis based on Figure 11.2 showed a transition where religiosity falls about three-fold, the time-series analysis

---

[15] The Danish national Church is reluctant to record church attendance.

based on Figure 11.6 suggested a transition where religiosity falls by a factor of about five. Part of the difference may be that the fall has been large in Denmark. Figure 11.2 shows that Denmark is below the average transition line. In addition, the s-proxy considers the national Church only, while R catches all religiosity, including non-official "outside" beliefs that exist in addition to the official ones. The evidence about "outside" beliefs is weak, but perhaps it has fallen less strongly. Outside beliefs are a mixed bag. They include other religions than Lutheranism and beliefs that are independent of formal religion. While folk superstitions fall during the transition, it is possible that spirituality increases.

A simple fact from the study of Danish churches is that 51% of the churches were already built in 1300. My subjective impression from many journeys in Europe is that a similar number would be reached in most countries. In some countries (such as Sweden), most churches are built of wood, so they have to be replaced from time to time. In other countries (such as Germany), many churches have been destroyed by war, but most have been rebuilt. It would surely be nice to have the data for a few more countries, but until then, the default is that the Danish story generalizes.

11.10 CONCLUSION: EQUIVALENCE CONFIRMED

As far as the historical data show, equivalence is confirmed. This can be interpreted by the substitution process discussed in Section 11.2, and the growth model in Gundlach and Paldam (2012). Maybe the increase in scientific and technological ideas driving out traditional (religious) beliefs is a driver of development.

Figure 11.8 is an illustration of the story told in this chapter. The two columns are drawn for R, which covers everything religion may be used for. By the percentage scale of R, the two columns are equally high. The R-index measure covers all religion, while the church-density proxy only covers official church use. The large change in the figure is the increased trust in science and technology. In the past, and in most poor countries today, traditional beliefs based on religion explain things people don't understand, whereas people in wealthy countries today use modern science, which they know is developed by humans.

The religious transition is the decline of religiosity caused by development. Most of the analyses use a new composite index of religiosity R, but supporting evidence from studies using long time-series is also reported.

The transition causes R to fall from about 80% to about 35%. The transition is still not complete in the developed countries, although it has

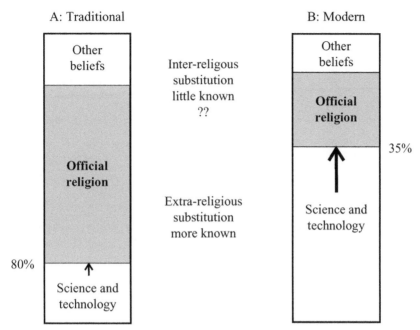

FIGURE 11.8. A stylized picture of the transition, as measured by the *R*-variable Drawn to visualize how a reduction in the *R*-variable from 80% to 35% looks.

slowed down. It will probably continue to reach 30% or go even lower. The estimated slope of the transition, $\lambda \approx -9.5$, proved robust. The full transition normally takes one to two centuries, so the change per year is only 0.2–0.5 percentage points, which gives 1–2 percentage points over the five years between WVS-waves. Hence, the religious transition is easy to overlook in the perspective of five to ten years, especially as religiosity data vary considerably across countries.

To establish the micro foundations of macro regularity is notoriously difficult. When income rises, the demand for religion as a factor of production may converge to zero in the limit, while the demand for religion as a consumption good may converge to a level well above zero. The loss of control by religious institutions over the provision of collective goods also appears to be a powerful mechanism in the religious transition.

I conclude that the religious transition is a substantial phenomenon that has general explanations, even if many details of these explanations differ across countries and between religions. As argued in Chapter 7, the Religious Transition is a key part of the Three Pillars Model, which explains why traditional political systems turn into democracies.

PART III

THE GRAND TRANSITION

12

The Hump-Shaped Transition Path
for the Growth Rate

Part II of this book has shown that a handful of socioeconomic variables have underlying transition paths. Many other socioeconomic variables have such paths. This chapter demonstrates that the aggregate GDP data has a transition too. Development is a process that diverges from the traditional steady state and converges to the modern one. Thus, the growth rate moves from zero to approximately two. If countries catch up, there must be, at least, one peak in between. This is indeed the case, and hence countries do catch up.

The eight sections of Chapter 12 start by presenting the data (s1). Then the hump-shape is estimated (s2), and its robustness is demonstrated (s3). Next, the theoretical consequences are discussed – the key point is that the form found rejects the standard one-sector model (s4), but it is easy to explain by means of the good old two-sector model with a traditional sector that is gradually replaced by a modern sector (s5–6).[1] Finally, the hump-shape is replicated with nonlinear panel regressions; the form is significant, but the explanatory power of the shape is small (s7).

12.1 DATA AND FOUR SAMPLES: ALL, BASIC, MAIN, AND OPEC

This chapter uses GDP-data only. As before, the real per capita GDP is the *gdp*. It is the *cgdppc* data from the Maddison Project. The *gdp* is used to calculate the growth rate, $g = \Delta gdp/gdp_{-1}$, and income, $y = \ln gdp$. These data are used to estimate the relation between the annual growth rate of a country, g_{it}, and the income level, $y_{it(-)}$, at the beginning of period t. The countries included account for more than 95% of world population. As no other series is used in the chapter, the wide sample goes back to 1950, when roughly 60 countries, notably in Africa, were still colonies. Thus, the time dimension is 1950–2016.

The sample of *All* data is reduced to the *Basic* sample by a deletion of outliers, defined as all observations in the first and in the 99th percentiles of the growth rates and the income levels; see Figure 12.1. This procedure discards observations of growth rates above 26% and below –21% and *gdp* levels below $610 and above $57,250, where *income* is 6.4 and 11, respectively. As before, the Basic sample is divided into the *Main* and the *OPEC* samples. Table 12.1 gives some descriptive statistics for these samples.

Extreme negative growth rates often reflect (civil) wars, the breakdown of the Soviet Union, or large negative changes in oil prices. Extreme positive growth rates are due to the exploitation of newly discovered natural resources and mean reversion after large negative shocks. A *gdp* level of $610 is compatible with the lowest *gdp* levels that are recorded in the Maddison Project Database for pre-industrial times: The first percentile of *gdp* is at $650 (where $y = 6.5$) for all countries and all years before 1750. Hence, still lower income levels are extreme by historical comparison. Income levels beyond the 99th percentile are also extreme. Extreme high-income observations are dominated by OPEC countries with a small population.

---

[1] In Chapter 10 T was used for the corruption index (from Transparency International), but in the present chapter T is used for the traditional sector.

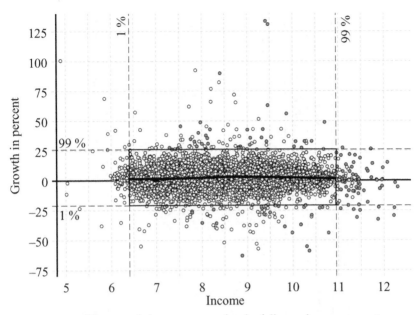

FIGURE 12.1. The growth-income scatter for the full sample, 1950–2016
The inner square is the Basic sample used for the estimated kernel of Figure 12.2. See Table 12.1. The gray observations are from the OPEC countries excluded from the Main sample

12.2 ESTIMATING THE HUMP, THE BEST ESTIMATE OF THE TRANSITION CURVE, $g = \Pi^g(y_{(-)})$

Figure 12.1 shows a scatter plot of the correlation between the growth rate and the income level. Each dot represents one of the 10,329 country-year observations for pairs of g and initial $y_{(-)}$ for 1950–2016. The dashed vertical and horizontal lines identify observations above and below the first and the 99th percentiles of the growth rate and the income level. Gray dots represent observations for OPEC countries, which account for a large fraction of the outliers. The inner rectangle gives the observations for the Basic sample, where outliers have been deleted.

The wild scatter of the data points and the packed rectangle mean that any presumed growth path can only explain a small fraction of the variation at best. The thick black line through the middle of the inner scatter is the **best** kernel regression estimate of the transition-path, Π^g, for the sample without outliers (Basic). With a range of the vertical axis

TABLE 12.1. *Descriptive statistics for alternative samples, 1950–2016*

Sample name	ALL (10,329)			Basic (9,931)			Main (9,137)		
Deleted	None			Extreme (398)			OPEC (794)		
	gdp_{it-1}	y_{it-1}	g_{it} %	gdp_{it-1}	y_{it-1}	g_{it} %	gdp_{it-1}	y_{it-1}	g_{it} %
Mean	9,401	9.15	2.5	8,666	9.07	2.5	8,563	9.06	2.5
Standard dev.	13,292	9.49	8.2	9,971	9.21	6.4	9,935	9.20	5.8
Maximum	220,71	12.30	133.6	56,319	10.94	26.0	56,319	10.94	26.0
Minimum	134	4.90	-62.9	609	6.41	-21.0	609	6.41	-21.0
1st percentile	608	6.41	-21.0	701	6.55	-14.8	695	6.54	-14.5
50th percentile	4,592	8.43	2.5	4,580	8.43	2.5	4,381	8.39	2.5
99th percentile	57,244	10.96	26.0	44,308	10.70	19.6	44,281	10.70	18.9
Years	66			66			66		
Max N (countries)	169			168			153		
Min N per year	139			130			119		

The real GDP per capita in 2011 US$ is termed *gdp*. It is the *cgdppc* series from the Maddison Project (2018). *Income*, *y*, is the logarithm to *gdp*. *Growth*, *g*, is for *gdp* in year *t* compared to year *t-1*. Extreme observations are below the first percentiles and above the 99th.

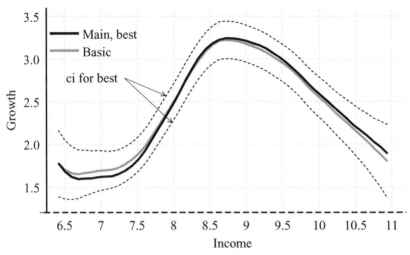

FIGURE 12.2. The enlarged growth-income path for the Basic and Main samples. The black curve is taken as the best estimate of the transition curve $g = \Pi^g(y_{(-)})$ Both curves are estimated for the bandwidth chosen by Stata, which is 0.32 and 0.31 for the two samples. It gives virtually the same curves to use $bw = 0.3$ in both cases. The 95% confidence intervals are drawn for the Main sample. The curves are within the confidence intervals of each other. As usual, the 95% confidence intervals (ci) are rather narrow thanks to the large number of observations. All curves within the confidence intervals are hump-shaped, but the peak is only determined within the interval from $y = 8.2$ to 9.7, and for $g = 3$ to 3.4.

(annual growth rate) from +125% to –75%, the reported kernel line looks flat.

Figure 12.2 gives an enlarged picture of the same growth-income path, where the scatter points are suppressed. Zooming in reveals a hump-shaped growth curve. It picks up at an income level of about 7.3, peaks with a growth rate above 3% at an income level of about 8.7, and thereafter falls toward a potential steady state growth rate slightly below 2%. Growth at the low end is 1.5% and thus well above the historical growth rates before modern growth started. This means that the transition has started even in the poorest countries, as argued in Section 1.8. However, the path at the low end (from 6.3 to 7.3) is flat. There seems to be no low-level equilibrium trap. It is not easy to start growing, but Malthus' mechanism is not evident; see also Figure 1.1b at the start of the book.

The graph also shows that it does not matter for the estimated growth path whether OPEC members remain in the sample or not as long as extreme observations are deleted. There is an almost perfect overlap between the paths estimated on the Basic sample (black line) and the Main sample (gray line). The estimated rule-of-thumb bandwidths are both close to 0.3 (used from now), and the confidence intervals are so similar that only one is shown. The best estimate of the transition curve $\Pi^g(y_{(-)})$ is based on the slightly less noisy Main sample (no outliers, no OPEC countries). The reported confidence interval is sufficiently narrow to rule out any line where the slope has the same sign over the full income range. Thus, the workhorse model does not work for the full range. Hence, the main empirical result is that the growth-income path is hump-shaped, with a sign change in the middle.

This means that from an income level of 7.5, low-income countries do catch up with high-income countries. However, the growth of the average less developed country peaks at 3.25%, which gives a catch up rate of only 1.5%, so the time necessary to close a gap of say 25 times is a little more than 200 years.

12.3 ROBUSTNESS OF THE BEST Π^G-CURVE FROM FIGURE 12.2

As in the previous chapters, a set of experiments are made to show that the transition curve is robust. Figure 12.2 uses the annual data – most growth studies use a longer time unit, such as 5- or 10-year averages. Figure 12.3a shows that it matters little for the form of the curve. The peak is a little lower for a longer time unit, and as N falls, the confidence interval widens.

Figure 12.3b demonstrates how alternative bandwidths affect the estimated kernel line. The kernel line becomes quite wobbly for a low bandwidth of 0.1 and approaches a straight line for a high bandwidth of 0.9. In between, the hump-shaped transition path remains. The kernel line for $bw = 0.1$ *to* 0.5 is almost completely within the confidence interval for the reference kernel.

Figures 12.3c and 12.d report experiments showing what happens when time periods or country groups are excluded. In Figure 12.3c, the peak is a little higher when the years since 1991 are excluded. In Figure 12.3d, the largest effect of exclusion happens when Africa (Sub Saharan) is excluded. This makes the sample quite thin at the low end, and the form changes somewhat. However, it is still hump-shaped.

Most chapters have found that the OPEC countries have a different transition. Thus, Figure 12.3e compares the reference curve in the Main sample with the curve for the OPEC-countries of $N = 794$ observations,

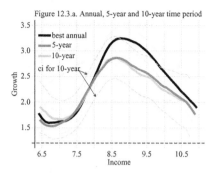

Figure 12.3.a. Annual, 5-year and 10-year time period

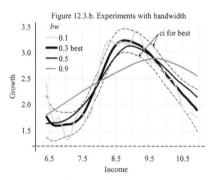

Figure 12.3.b. Experiments with bandwidth

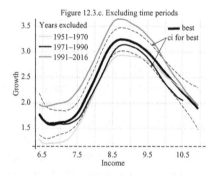

Figure 12.3.c. Excluding time periods

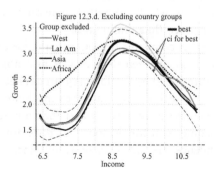

Figure 12.3.d. Excluding country groups

FIGURE 12.3. Robustness of the best Π^g-*curve* from Figure 12.2, shown as the bolded black curve

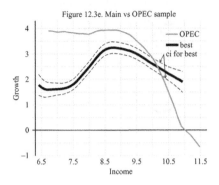

Figure 12.3e. Main vs OPEC sample

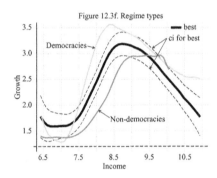

Figure 12.3f. Regime types

FIGURE I2.3. (*cont.*)

which excludes extreme growth rates and income levels higher than 11. A few OPEC members (especially Qatar) have even had income levels beyond 11.5 for some years. With income above 11.5, the confidence interval of the estimated OPEC kernel line explodes, so the income range has been limited at the high end. Apart from the much wider confidence interval (not shown), the estimated OPEC kernel line differs from the main empirical result. Instead of a hump, the OPEC growth-income path tends to fall throughout, which is a pattern consistent with a return to the steady state after a shock (like finding oil).

Finally, Figure 12.3f compares transition paths for alternative political regimes. To distinguish between democracies and non-democracies, the dichotomous measure coded by Cheibub (1996) has been used. The transition graphs for the two regime types have the same hump-shape. The graph suggests that democracies grow a little faster than non-democracies.

The growth-income path for democracies does not differ much from the reference confidence interval. Since most high-income countries (apart from some OPEC members) are democracies, the confidence interval of the kernel line for non-democracies becomes rather wide beyond income levels of about 9, and extremely wide after income levels of about 10 (widening confidence interval not shown). So the reported kernel line for non-democracies is based on a sample that excludes two relatively rich non-OPEC oil countries (Bahrain and Oman) and Singapore, which is the only non-oil high-income country that is not a democracy.

12.4 SOME CONSEQUENCES OF THE HUMP-SHAPED GROWTH DIAGRAM

All transition curves in the book have a large variation around the central kernel curve. This is also the case for the scatter on Figure 12.1, which has Figure 12.2 as the underlying transition path. However, the data sample is large, and the transition path is well determined. The fact that the central curve looks like the one in Figure 12.2 has a number of consequences that are far from trivial.[2]

One consequence deals with the concept of β-convergence in the literature on growth empirics. It starts from a simple log-linear estimation equation:

$$g_{it} = \alpha + \beta y_{it} + u_{it}, \qquad \text{the absolute convergence equation, where } g$$
$$\text{is growth and } y \text{ is income } (\ln gdp), \text{ while } u$$
$$\text{is the residual term} \qquad (12.1)$$

When Equation (12.1) is estimated on a wide cross-country sample, the sign on β tells us whether the countries converge or diverge. The sign is minus for convergence, and plus for divergence. Equation (12.1) is known as the *workhorse* model, which can be derived from a one-sector Solow model. The model has the modern steady state as the only equilibrium. The further below the steady state equilibrium countries are, the faster should growth be. Growth is even a hyperbolic function of the deviation from the steady state. Poor countries are far below the said steady state, and thus they should grow particularly fast. Thus, the theory predicts that the sign is negative on β. However, the standard result from estimates of Equation (12.1) is that β is positive, but insignificant. Thus, countries have

---

[2] The presentation in Section 12.4 follows standard growth theory as, e.g., covered in Jones and Vollrath (2013). Barro and Sala-i-Martin (1995, 2004) have a much more detailed discussion of convergence, but nothing about divergence.

a vague divergence. This also follows from the fact that the income differences between countries have been growing.

If the growth diagram looks like Figure 12.2, the estimate of Equation (12.1) will give an insignificantly positive slope, precisely as found. If the sample is thin for high-end countries, the slope may be positive, and if it is thin for low-end countries, the slope may be negative, precisely as happens in Figures 11.3a and b in the previous chapter. This sign pattern also occurs in studies of convergence/divergence for the provinces/states within rich and poor countries. They converge in rich countries such as the United States, and diverge in poor countries such as India and China.

This argues that the underlying model does not apply. Solow (1965, 1970) stressed that his model was created to explain why developed countries grow along log-linear growth paths, and return to their path even after large shocks such as wars, earthquakes, or economic crises. The model is not relevant to countries in the middle of the transition, which are far from a steady state. The well-known growth paths of China and India, shown in Figure 12.4, illustrate this. The two countries are trying to catch up. After some rather unsuccessful experiments, they both found a (similar) path that seems to work. It is not a steady state path, so growth cannot be understood as cycles around a steady state path. In addition, both countries are undergoing massive structural change.

As Equation (12.1) did not show convergence, it was amended to Equation (12.2), which contains the []-set of variables that is chosen to control for country heterogeneity. Alternatively, the constant, α, can be broken into fixed effects for countries.

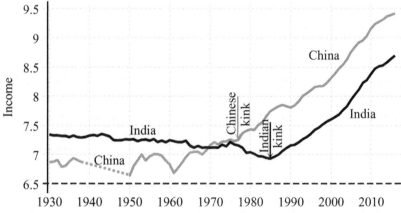

FIGURE 12.4. The growth paths of China and India over the last 86 years

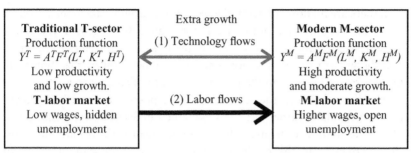

FIGURE 12.5. The basic two-sector (dual) model, with dual labor markets
Recall from Chapter 11 that Y is GDP, A is knowledge, L is labor, K is real, and H is human capital. The number of equations grows rapidly once we leave the one-sector approach, e.g., by adding the relations to the rest of the world, capital flows, or policies that are (much) easier to implement in the M-sector. The original Solow model disregarded H, and made L and A exogenous, so all that was necessary was the production function and an accumulation function for K, for everything to be solvable. With two sectors, this doubles and doubles once again when flows between the sectors are added. In addition, the two-sector model with flows makes it difficult to set wages equal to marginal productivities in the two sectors

$$g_{it} = \alpha_{it} + \beta y_{it} + [\gamma_1 z_{1it} + \ldots + \gamma_n z_{nit}] + \varepsilon_{it},$$
the conditional convergence equation   (12.2)

With the right control-set or fixed effects for countries, β does become significantly negative. This suggests that if countries were alike, they would converge, which seems to be a tautology. However, since they are not, they do not converge. This opens up a long story, which will not be told at present. It concentrates on the nonlinear form of the transition curve.

12.5 TWO-SECTOR MODELS GENERATE HUMP-SHAPED DEVELOPMENT PATHS[3]

Several chapters in this book have claimed that two-sector models where a traditional T-sector and a modern M-sector coexist give a picture with a growth peak in the middle. Figure 12.5 is a sketch of the basic model.

---

[3] The two-sector (or dual) model of development goes back to Lewis (1954) and Ranis and Fei (1961). For a lucid survey of the origin and later development of the model, see Gollin (2014).

If there are no flows between the sectors, the growth rate in the economy is just the weighted sum of the two growth rates. As the growth rate in the modern sector is the same as the one of the fully modernized rich countries, and the growth of the traditional sector is (much) lower, this "internal" growth rate is lower than the growth rate of the rich countries.

The flows between the sectors open the possibility for extra growth that is potentially rather large. As explained in Section 1.7, a transfer of 1% of the labor force from hidden unemployment in the traditional sector to employment in the modern sector generates a growth premium of 5–8%, if the productivity gap is 5–8 times. Thus, the growth rate increases from below 2% to about 8%. Normally, the sectoral transfer is smaller, and many problems may occur; see Chapter 13.

It is also a political temptation to use the potential growth to generate rents to distribute to clients building support for the regime. With enough rent-seeking, the growth premium vanishes; see Krueger (1974, 1990). The main theoretical property of the two-sector model is that it has no steady state as long as both sectors exist. It starts from the traditional steady state before the modern sector appears,[4] and it ends in the modern steady state when the traditional sector is fully absorbed. In order to exist as disequilibrium, it needs some brake that limits the flows between the sectors.

(1) The technology flows go both ways. With large differences between the prices of labor and capital in the LDCs and DCs, the optimal choice of techniques in the M-sector differs in the two types of countries, so bits and pieces of traditional techniques will be used in the modern sector, and some modern techniques will seep into the traditional sector.

(2) The resource flows, of which labor is the main one, go from the traditional to the modern sector. Obviously, the possible wage gain from this sectoral migration is a driver of labor flow. However, it is offset by the welfare losses from moving from hidden unemployment in the traditional sector to open unemployment in the modern sector, as modeled by Harris-Todaro (1970), which provides temporary equilibrium solutions for the flows.

The traditional sector has low wages, and even when wages in the modern sector are higher, they are (much) lower than in the high-income countries abroad. Thus, the modern sector has a competitive advantage

---

[4] An important point to note is that the M-sector produces using international techniques imported from abroad.

on the world market. If it can sell its product, it will be rather profitable and can expand rapidly, absorbing resource flows from the traditional sector – notably labor. This might still be the case even when labor has less human capital and the goods produced are slightly behind in style and technological refinement.

A much-analyzed complication occurs when some of the firms in the M-sector are branches of (large) foreign firms from the DCs. Such companies are under political pressures to pay similar wages in the LDC branch as those that they pay at home. In addition, they often create product chains in which the most labor-intensive part of production is located in the low-wage LDCs. In other versions of the model, the T-sector is the export sector, while the M-sector consumes the import.[5] Thus, the two-sector model has been developed in many directions, and maybe there are more than two sectors.

At present, I want to argue that the whole family of such models normally produces a hump-shaped transition path. Initially, when the modern sector is small, it cannot absorb more than a tiny flow. In addition, it takes time to develop the market for modern goods and the necessary human capital for mass production. In the end, when the traditional sector is small, it cannot generate much of an outflow. In addition, once resources are squeezed out from the traditional sector, it is likely that it will modernize rapidly, so that the sectoral gap vanishes.

Thus, it appears very likely that the greatest potential for rapid modernization and high growth occurs somewhere in the middle, where both sectors have a substantial size. It is often assumed that the traditional sector is agriculture, so the slope of the curve for the Agricultural Transition, as estimated by the kernel in Figure 1.1a, illustrates the size of the flow. The slope is low at the start of the transition, high at mid-income (between $y = 7.5$ to 8.5), and as income increases, it falls.

12.6 A NEW TWO-SECTOR MODEL THAT DOES PRODUCE A HUMP-SHAPED DEVELOPMENT PATH

Two-sector models became increasingly complex during the 1980s, and then they disappeared from the literature during the 1990s, when interests

---

[5] One version of the distinction is to speak about the *informal* and the *formal* sectors, where firms in the informal sector have no legal title to their business. This makes it difficult to use property as collateral for loans from the banking system. Consequently, this acts as a barrier to business growth.

changed to endogenous technical progress, processes of substitution between capital, labor, and resources, etc. In order to handle these issues, the complexities of two-sector models were unnecessary. Thus, the literature turned back to the workhorse one-sector Solow model. In the process, many authors seem to forget that the Solow model was not designed to explain development.

The two-sector model made a brief reappearance with Lucas (2009). The Lucas two-sector model contains a number of innovations relative to old two-sector models. It is designed so that it is easy to collapse the model to the one-sector workhorse model. The model has "city" and "farm" as the two sectors, which both produce a single output good that adds up to GDP. Cities are the centers of intellectual exchange. The contribution of the city sector to GDP depends on the level of human capital multiplied by its employment share; it is assumed to generate a positive *agglomeration externality* as a result of the exchange of productive ideas in cities.

In addition, the city sector produces a *productivity externality* that spills over to the farm sector. This makes farm output and its employment share functions of the level of human capital in cities. Assuming mobility of labor across sectors, the model predicts a declining share of farm employment with rising levels of human capital.

Growth enters the two-sector model in the form of catching up with a frontier economy, which is assumed to grow at a constant rate. As in the workhorse model, the income distance to the frontier has a positive effect on the growth rate of the follower economy, but this effect is assumed to be conditioned by an *openness externality*, such that more open follower economies should grow faster than more closed follower economies, all else being constant. The model is sufficiently parsimonious regarding parameters to allow a complete set of simulations that can be reported within a paper; see Gundlach and Paldam (2020). The simulations demonstrate that *all* non-collapsed versions of the model have a hump-shaped growth path.

12.7 NONLINEAR PANEL REGRESSIONS WITH FIXED EFFECTS

The kernel regression that generated the main empirical result from the previous section omitted many potentially important variables and the panel structure of the data. To address both concerns, the hump-shaped growth path is approximated with panel regressions that include country- and time-fixed effects together with a quadratic income term to allow for nonlinear effects. In addition, the marginal income effects are checked to

TABLE 12.2. *Nonlinear panel regressions*

	Dependent variable: annual growth rate in %			
	(1)	(2)	(3)	(4)
Income	6.63	8.90	7.55	9.59
	(0.9)	(1.3)	(1.9)	(1.9)
Income squared	−0.37	−0.51	−0.47	−0.65
	(0.1)	(0.1)	(0.1)	(0.1)
Observations	9,137	9,137	9,137	9,137
Countries	153	153	153	153
R-squared (adjusted/overall)	0.01	0.07	0.00	0.02
Country-fixed effects	no	No	yes	Yes
Time-fixed effects	no	Yes	no	Yes
Marginal income effects at:				
$y = 7.3$ ($1,500)	1.25	1.46	0.63	0.15
	(0.1)	(0.2)	(0.4)	(0.4)
$y = 8.3$ ($4,000)	0.53	0.46	−0.30	−1.12
	(0.1)	(0.1)	(0.2)	(0.2)
$y = 9.2$ ($10,000)	−0.15	−0.47	−1.17	−2.30
	(0.1)	(0.1)	(0.2)	(0.3)
$y = 10.1$ ($25,000)	−0.82	−1.40	−2.04	−3.48
	(0.2)	(0.3)	(0.3)	(0.4)

Cross-country panel data, Main sample. Regression constant not reported. Robust standard errors in parentheses.

see whether they change from positive to negative with rising levels of income, as predicted by the kernel regressions. In all regressions, the statistically significant coefficients are positive to income and negative to squared income. As expected, the explanatory power is low.

Column (1) of Table 12.2 provides the results for Pooled OLS, which serve as a point of reference. The marginal effects are calculated at income levels that can be directly compared with the income levels in Figure 12.2. The marginal income effects change as predicted by the kernel regression: positive at low-income levels and negative at high-income levels, and larger in absolute value at both ends (at $y = 7.3$ and 10.1) than near the peak of the hump (between 8.3 and 9.2). The negative coefficient of 0.008 at the high-income end implies a rate of convergence of about 1%.[6]

Column (2) reports results for the inclusion of time-fixed effects, which eliminates from the sample the effects of common shocks but retains the

---

[6] The convergence rate, λ, can be calculated from the estimated regression coefficient (b) as $\lambda = -\ln(1 + b)/t$, with $t = 1$ for annual growth rates.

cross-country variation. Like Pooled OLS, this specification produces a reasonable approximation of the growth path identified by the kernel regression: The marginal effects are estimated to be statistically significantly different from zero and have the right signs and relative sizes for both sides of the hump. The implied convergence rate at the high-income level is about 1.5%, but not much larger than the implicit divergence rate at the low-income level, which implies a net convergence rate close to zero.

The results change with the introduction of country-fixed effects in column (3). Eliminating the cross-country variation from the sample is like assuming that all countries are the same except for their income level, so it is almost by default that the statistically significant marginal income effects are all estimated to be negative. At the high-income level, the negative coefficient of –0.02 implies a convergence rate of about 2%, which is in line with results reported in the conditional convergence literature noted previously. Column (4) reports results for the inclusion of both country- and time-fixed effects. Not surprisingly, the marginal effects are much like the marginal effects estimated with country-fixed effects only.

Taken together, the results in Table 12.2 confirm the hump-shaped growth path of Figure 12.2 if the cross-country variation is maintained (columns (1) and (2)). In addition, they confirm the results of the conditional convergence literature if it is eliminated (columns (3) and (4)). Not controlling for obvious cross-country differences, except for the level of income, as in the first two specifications, will necessarily produce an omitted variables bias. But eliminating all cross-country variation, as in the latter two specifications, may be too much of a good thing, especially when assessing a potential pattern of long-run growth and development. After all, the long-run information appears to be in the cross-country variation of income levels, not in within-country variation of growth rates over time.[7]

The Grand Transition view relies on both cross-country and time series evidence. Treating the cross-country variation as a source of omitted

---

[7] Hall and Jones (1999) use this argument to motivate their cross-country regressions on the effect of institutions on long-run economic performance. Along the same lines, Frankel and Romer (1999) use cross-country regressions in *levels* to estimate the effect of trade on (long-run) growth. The combination of persistent country characteristics and non-persistent within-country growth rates, which has been emphasized by Easterly et al. (1993), also speaks against eliminating *all* cross-country variation from the sample, because otherwise nothing but regression to the mean may be left.

variables bias must lead to a rejection of the grand transition hypothesis for the sample at hand, because the within-country variation of growth rates in 1950–2010 does not suffice to capture the transition from a static to a modern steady state for individual countries. Maintaining the cross-country variation helps to identify a hump-shaped transition path both with kernel and panel regressions. The level of income only explains a tiny fraction of the observed variation in growth rates across countries and over time, but ignoring the Grand Transition pattern means missing a signal in the noise.

12.8 CONCLUSION

Kernel regressions based on cross-country panel data reveal a hump-shaped transition path for the growth rate. This empirical result contrasts with the prediction of a hyperbolic growth-income path derived from the workhorse model of growth empirics. The kernel regression results suggest that understanding long-run development calls for a two-sector model that can generate a hump-shaped growth-income path.

The simulation results referred to in Section 12.6 show that the hump-shaped path can be generated with a rather broad range of parameters and initial conditions, which determine the timing and the size of the hump. With obvious variation in initial conditions and possible variation of parameters across countries and over time, it becomes understandable why it has been difficult to identify a common pattern of long-run growth and development, especially with a model that imposes the restriction of a hyperbolic growth-income path. The kernel regressions reveal a common pattern of income dynamics that is overlaid by otherwise extremely noisy data; i.e., most of the enormous variation of observed growth rates remains unexplained.

The main empirical result is that the growth-income path is hump-shaped. This is supported by a number of robustness tests. If the long-run path of income can be considered as a transition from a traditional to a modern steady state, it follows by implication that the corresponding growth path must be hump-shaped. Such a growth path can be simulated based on a model that includes a traditional and a modern sector. Taken together, the hump-shaped growth-income path can be taken as the general pattern of long-run development.

13

Do Improvements of Institutions Harm Development?

The question in the headline has a divided answer: In the end, it is surely no, just as implied by the word "improvement." However, in the short run it is yes!

The potential growth of poor countries is high, as discussed in Chapter 12. LDCs (Less Developed Countries) can potentially grow by 7–9%. As shown, poor countries do catch up, but much more slowly than they should. This chapter proposes a new reason: Development causes an improvement of institutions as a result of the long-run transitions, such as the Democratic Transition (Chapters 4–7) and the Transition of the Economic System (Chapters 8 and 9). Better institutions do help development in the long run. However, people experience changes of institutions – even if they are improvements – as system instability, which harms investment and growth. In addition, the process of transition is rather erratic. The gross movements in institutional indices are often much larger than necessary, as seen from the nutshell histories of countries in Section 7.3.

The reader should keep in mind that this chapter covers institutional instability only. What is lost in generality is won in two ways: In sharpness of focus and in the understanding of causality, as it builds on the previous chapters that have analyzed precisely that.

TABLE 13.1. *Variables used in Chapter 13*

Variable	Definition
G^X-*ratio*	The gross over net changes in the institutional index, $X = P$ or F
Polity index from Chapters 4 to 7	
P, dP	P-index and its first difference. Political system index. dP are gross changes
zP	The fraction of years where P is zero, i.e., anarchy or temporary foreign domination
$\Pi^P(y_j)$	Democratic Transition. Gives the net change in political system
Fraser index from Chapter 9	
F, dF	F-index and its first difference. Economic system index. dF gives gross change
$\Pi^F(y_j)$	Transition of the Economic System. Gives the net change in economic system

dP and dF are calculated as the average numerical change per year.

The five sections of Chapter 13 proceed as follows: First, some stylized facts are provided (s1). An analysis of development over time shows (once again) the big peak in 1989–92 (s2). Then the large literature on development and political instability is surveyed (s3). Next follows a set of correlations and regressions analyzing the relation of average growth and the instability variables (s4). Finally, the implications of the results are presented (s5).

13.1 THE *G*-RATIO GIVING THE EXCESS VARIATION OF THE *P* AND *F* INDICES

Table 13.2 reports that the full transition requires a change in the political system index P of 14 points, and a change in the economic system index F of 2.8 points. The table also shows that the two indices change (much) more than that.

The P changes: For the 56 years covered, the net change is 5 P-points, which is 36% of the full change. However, this has required 23 P-points of gross movements, which is about 4.6 times as much as needed. Thus, there is substantial excess variation, and the changes show great variation: From zero in most western countries and in the countries on the Arab peninsula to more than 50 P-points in 19 countries. The top five are Turkey 69 (Figure 5.3b), Peru 72, Haiti 73, Pakistan 74, and Thailand 98 (Figure 5.3a), which is seven times the full transition.

The F-changes: For the 46 years covered, the net change is 1 F-point, which is also 36% of the full change, but this has required a gross change

TABLE 13.2. *Descriptive statistics and some calculations leading the G-ratio*

Variables y, P, dP, F, dF	Income (a)	Polity index (a)		Fraser index (b)	
(1) Range of data	Full data	Full data	Avl. data	Full data	Avl. data
(2) Average level 1960/1970	7.921	−0.34	−0.53	5.97	5.96
(3) Average level 2016	9.198	5.00	4.14	7.11	6.80
(4) Net change for period	1.277	5.34	4.65	1.19	0.84

Numbers in line (5) are from Table 13.1　　　　Some calculations for the average country

	Income (a)	Polity index (a)		Fraser index (b)	
(5) Change for full transition, to Table 13.6	4.5	14 from Chapter 4		2.8 from Chapter 9	
(6) Part of transition (4)/(5)	28%	24%	33%	43%	30%
(7) Years for a full transition	200	240	170	109	160

Changes for average country imputed for full period

Variable	Growth	$56 \times dP$	$46 \times dF$
(8) Gross numerical change	2.24	22.9	5.6
(9) *G-ratio* of excess change, to Table 13.6		$G^P \approx 4.5$	$G^F \approx 5.5$

Notes: (a) For the period 1960–2016. (b) For the period 1970–2016, where the first data are for 5-year periods.
Full data means that there are observations for all years. *Avl. data* means available data.

of 5.7 F-points. This also covers a great deal of variation. The top five are Rwanda 9.4, Zambia 9.5, Syria 9.7, Zimbabwe 9.9, and Nicaragua 10.5. If the data had covered the change from Soviet Socialism, more countries would have been in this category.

Thus, the inevitable transition is not a smooth process, but a process with substantial ***excess changes*** assessed as the ***G-ratio*** in row (9) of Table 13.2. The 14 P-points of the Democratic Transition normally provide gross changes of 14 $G^P \approx 60$ P-points in the average country, and the 2.8 F-points normally provide gross changes of 2.8 $G^F \approx 15$ F-points. As will be shown, this results in a substantial loss of growth, slowing down development to well below the potential.

The estimates shown in Section 13.4 require that the variables are roughly normal, so it is worth looking at the distributions of the P and F data as in Figures 13.1a and 13.b. It is clear that both institutional variables have non-normal distributions. The same applies to the two first difference series dP and dF. In order to make sure that results are robust

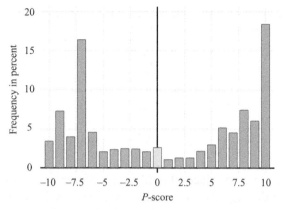

FIGURE 13.1a. Distribution of Polity scores

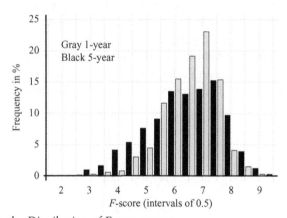

FIGURE 13.1b. Distribution of Fraser scores
The P-score of 0 is for no political system. The score of −7 was used for countries with Soviet Socialism. The F-scores are for the annual dataset and the 5-year spaced data

to the problematic distributions, Table 13.4 checks the basic pattern of correlations using rank correlations.

13.2 THE PATH OF VARIABILITY OVER TIME

The *first difference d*-scores are averaged per year for the period $t = 1, \ldots, k$ for country i as shown in Equation (13.1), but they can also be averaged across $i = 1, \ldots, n$ countries for year t as shown in Equation (13.2). This is done for $X = P$ and F:

$$dX_i = \sum_{t=1}^{k} |\Delta X_{it}|/k \qquad (13.1)$$

or

$$dX_t = \sum_{i=1}^{n} |\Delta X_{it}|/n \qquad (13.2)$$

Equation (13.2) produces the dP_t-scores depicted in Figure 13.2 and analyzed by the regressions in Table 13.3. The analysis shows a weak downward trend and a large peak rising no less than 1.5 polity points above the trend in connection with the demise of Soviet Socialism and the dissolution of the USSR and Yugoslavia, as covered in Chapter 3. Even when the new countries that emerged from the two federations are deleted, the peak still rises 0.8 points above the trend.

Table 13.3 shows the significance of the pattern in Figure 13.2. A trend of −0.014 results in a fall of 0.08 dP-points over the 5.8 decades, so it is no wonder that it is insignificant. The table shows that the trend and the peak do not interact. They are two independent phenomena.

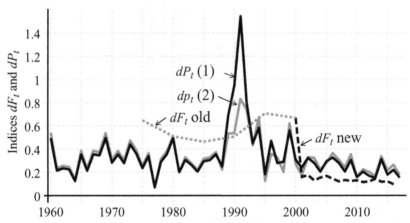

FIGURE 13.2. The first differences, dP_t and dF_t, for all years; see also Table 13.3 dP_t (1) is for all countries, while dP_t (2) excludes the 21 new countries that came into being in 1990; see Chapter 3. They all started with a large change. The curve remains similar when these countries are deleted, but the peak goes to 0.83 only. dFt old is for the period before 2000, where the F index had a 5-year time unit, while dFt new is for the period from 2000 onward, where the F-index is annual. Recall that the F-index did not contain the countries of the Soviet bloc.

TABLE 13.3. dP$_t$ *explained by trends and the post-socialist peak, 1988–93*

N = 5.8 decades		(1)	(2)	(3)	(4)
Decade		-0.01 (-0.5)	-0.01 (-1.6)	-0.01 (-1.6)	-0.04 (-0.4)
Dummy for year	1988		-0.04 (-0.4)		-0.04 (-0.4)
	1989		**0.39** (3.6)	**0.39** (3.6)	**0.39** (3.6)
	1990		**0.66** (6.0)	**0.66** (6.0)	**0.66** (5.9)
	1991		**1.26** (11.5)	**1.26** (11.5)	**1.25** (11.3)
	1992		**0.52** (4.7)	**0.51** (4.7)	**0.51** (4.6)
	1993		0.16 (1.5)		0.16 (1.4)
Constant		2.23 (0.6)	3.03 (1.8)	2.93 (1.7)	**0.29** (19.2)
R^2		0.005	0.800	0.790	0.789
R^2 adj		-0.013	0.771	0.770	0.764

Parentheses hold *t*-ratios. Coefficients are bolded if they are significant at the 5% level.

13.3 THE LITERATURE ON VARIABILITY
AND THE MISSING MIRACLE

This section covers the literatures on: *(a)* the effect of political instability on growth, *(b)* the effect of economic variability on growth, and *(c)* the missing growth miracle in most LDCs.

Ad (a). The relation between political instability and growth is discussed by a large literature, some of which has already been covered in Chapter 4. All kinds of political instability are found to reduce growth, but the relation is highly variable and often negligible. Much research shows that constitutional changes of governments in stable democracies have little effect on growth, as predicted by the median voter theorem, which applies in established democracies with a stable and well-defined single-dimensional issue space. Such democracies are mainly found in wealthy countries. A family of studies deals with the interaction of elections and economic policies (see Carmignani 2003 and de Haan and Klomp 2013). Such fluctuations have a small effect on the medium-term growth rate, although they may affect the public debt.

Most countries have not (yet) reached such stability, but it is still possible to study within-system instability using change of governments or even ministers as the instability indicator; see Aisen and Veiga (2013). Many authors do not distinguish the within-system and system variability, and some even say that the distinction is irrelevant (Alesina et al. 2006). Others, notably Jong-A-Pin (2009), study a wide range of instability measures.

It is worth noting the diversity of country cases. Argentina and Haiti have had many institutional changes and low growth but other countries, such as Thailand and Turkey, combine good economic development with even greater instability of the political system.[1]

Ad (b). Economic instability and growth are covered by an even larger literature, some of which was covered in Chapter 8. Most of the literature on the relation between economic systems and income or growth looks at the effect of Socialism vs capitalism, as covered by Chapter 3. It showed why the Soviet type of Socialism disappeared. In spite of high investment ratios, Soviet-type socialism produced a relatively low level of income and consumption and, in addition, low *P*-scores.

---

[1] The stories of the four countries Haiti, Argentina, Thailand, and Turkey are covered by Lundahl and Silé (2005), Tanzi (2018), Terwiel (2011), and Pope and Pope (2011), respectively.

A large literature analyzes the relation between changes in the economic system dF and growth. It typically analyzes the effect of particular events and types of reforms. The largest event is the change out of Socialism in 1988–95; see, e.g., Åslund (2002) or Gross and Steinherr (2004). In hindsight, the long-run effects have been largely beneficiary, but in the short to medium term there were great costs, which peaked at a loss of about 40% in GDP, and it typically took a decade to recover. Most of the literature deals with smaller cases, i.e. with the effect of trade liberalizations and other structural adjustments. They also tend to find a J-curve, of a downswing of a duration that depends on the size of the change, and a positive effect that eventually exceeds the downswing.[2]

Studies of the within-system instability analyze the longer-run consequences of economic fluctuations. A rather broad approach is Gavin and Hausmann (1998), who found that countries with high economic variability have low growth. Later, the literature has splintered into many sub-literatures dealing with the effect of specific types of instability/uncertainty on growth. Newer studies look at different types of uncertainty shocks and conclude that they affect growth, although sometimes only temporarily (Bloom 2009 and Basu and Bundick 2017). Another family of studies analyzes the effect of policy regimes and changes in such regimes. It defines a policy regime as a set of preferences for outcomes and policy instruments (Wilson 2000 and Fernández-Villaverde et al. 2015).

The mechanisms analyzed are most diverse; authors discuss, e.g., the link to the propensity to consume. However, the main link is the investment link, which has two parts:

$$\text{Instability} \Rightarrow \text{low investments} \Rightarrow \text{low growth} \qquad (13.3)$$

Many studies of the investment motive, since Borner et al. (1995), have pointed out that the predictability and transparency of political decisions are of great importance for the willingness to invest. System instability causes a loss of predictability and transparency and hence low investments. This is confirmed in many papers (at least) since Aizenman and Marion (1993).

Even more studies point to the second part of the link: Investment provides growth; see, e.g., Barro (1991). By combining the two parts, instability becomes a strong impediment to growth. It does not appear that there is a difference between instability of the political and economic

---

[2] The survey is small. The term "trade liberalization" produced almost 18,000 hits in google scholar, March 2020.

system in this theory. Both links in this theory apply rather generally to all types of uncertainty, so it might be difficult to sort out what is to the result of institutional instability.

Ad (c). As noted previously, most LDCs sorely miss growth miracles. This chapter explains the gap by means of the large system instability generated by the transition. The common explanation is that most LDCs have small isolated economies in the traditional steady state. The *gdp*-gap is about 50 times. Thus, a poor country with 50 million inhabitants has a GDP that is smaller than that of Denmark, and most LDCs have a smaller population. Denmark has a trade share of about one; i.e., the sum of import and export of goods and services is equal to GDP. A large trade share is indeed essential for development, but it is difficult to build a large export share. During the period of LDC-socialism, many countries did not even try, and they used trade restrictions as a device for tax collection and rent-seeking.

13.4 CAN SYSTEM INSTABILITY EXPLAIN INCOME AND GROWTH?

This section reports correlations in Table 13.4 and regressions in Table 13.5, analyzing the effect of system instability on development.

Table 13.4 analyzes three country samples: (A) is without OPEC and post-socialist countries, (B) is without post-socialist countries, and (C) is all countries. The table gives two "technical" results: The patterns in the three samples of the table are similar, but falling a little from (A) to (C) in most cases. The Kendall rank correlation shows much the same pattern as Pearson's correlation – there is no need to be concerned about the distribution of the series.

Table 13.4a reports the correlates to income: Rows (b) and (c) have a highly significant and consistent pattern. Rows (b) show that income is positively correlated to the levels of both indices. One reason for this correlation is the transition in the two system variables, from Figure 13.2. The next section shows that there are more reasons. Rows (c) report that income is negatively correlated to all three variability measures (dP, zP, dF) – especially to dF.

Table 13.4b reports the correlates to the growth rate: Rows (a) are the same as in Table 13.4a, and rows (b) have the same problem as the (a) rows. The correlations in rows (c) are (nearly) all negative and often significant. It is important that the short- and long-run connections are the reverse (just like in Chapter 10). Thus, the short-run connection does not aggregate to the long run. It has short-run costs to change the system, even when the changes have fine long-run consequences.

TABLE 13.4A. Cross-country correlations to the income level, y

Sample	Period 1: 1960–2016						Period 2: 2000–16					
Correlation	Pearson			Kendall			Pearson			Kendall		
Sample	(A)	(B)	(C)	(A)	(B)	(C)	(A)	(B)	(C)	(A)	(B)	(C)
N, countries	111	127	156	111	127	156	103	115	140	103	115	140
(a) g, growth	0.45	0.34	0.33	0.29	0.24	0.22	−0.02	−0.03	−0.01	−0.07	−0.07	−0.07
(b) P, Polity	0.69	0.45	0.44	0.50	0.35	0.36	0.44	0.22	0.24	0.44	0.32	0.36
F, Fraser							0.78	0.69	0.68	0.63	0.55	0.53
(c) dP, dif P	−0.39	−0.41	−0.36	−0.34	−0.35	−0.29	−0.40	−0.39	−0.40	−0.28	−0.29	−0.27
zP, P zero	−0.25	−0.24	−0.25	−0.25	−0.23	−0.20	−0.44	−0.43	−0.43	−0.15	−0.14	−0.12
dF, dif F							−0.59	−0.51	−0.46	−0.43	−0.37	−0.32

TABLE 13.4B. Cross-country correlations to the growth rate, g

Sample	Period 1: 1960–2016						Period 2: 2000–16					
Correlation	Pearson			Kendall			Pearson			Kendall		
Sample	(A)	(B)	(C)	(A)	(B)	(C)	(A)	(B)	(C)	(A)	(B)	(C)
N, countries	111	127	156	111	127	156	103	115	140	103	115	140
(a) y, income	0.45	0.34	0.33	0.29	0.24	0.22	−0.02	−0.03	−0.01	−0.07	−0.07	−0.07
(b) P, Polity	0.22	0.16	0.10	0.15	0.10	0.07	−0.15	−0.16	−0.14	−0.19	−0.20	−0.16
F, Fraser							0.02	−0.10	−0.05	−0.06	−0.13	−0.09
(c) dP, dif P	−0.18	−0.17	−0.19	−0.11	−0.09	−0.12	−0.14	−0.13	−0.15	0.02	0.05	0.04
zP, P zero	−0.07	−0.07	−0.09	−0.12	−0.11	−0.11	−0.34	−0.34	−0.33	−0.08	−0.08	−0.08
dF, dif F							−0.17	−0.06	−0.07	−0.02	0.05	0.06

Rows (a) are the same in the two tables. The three country samples (A), (B), and (C) are defined in the text. The Fraser index covers fewer countries, so period 2 is estimated for fewer observations. The correlations of P and F for period 2 are 0.50, 0.43, and 0.44 for samples A, B, and C.

237

Row (a) is the same in Tables 13.4a and b. It differs greatly for the two periods. Figures 13.3a and b show the scatters of the data used for the correlations. They both have the typical hump shape found in Chapter 12, and they even look similar, but the hump shape gives rather arbitrary results when the correlation enforces linearity. Thus, it illustrates the story about β-convergence told in Chapter 12.

The results from Table 13.4 are further analyzed by the regressions reported in Table 13.5. Table 13.5a compares explanations of income.

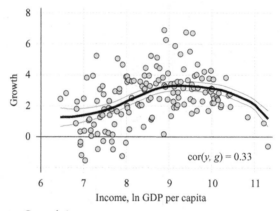

FIGURE 13.3a. Growth-income scatter, 1960–2016

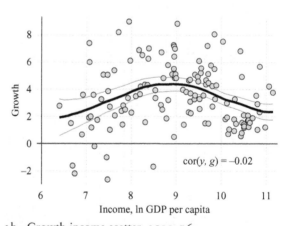

FIGURE 13.3b. Growth-income scatter, 2000–16

The kernel curve included has *bw* = 0.5. Seven outliers are deleted from the data for Figure 13.3b. This does not affect the form of the curve. The confidence intervals of the two curves overlap. However, a linear approximation gives a positively sloped curve for Figure 13.3a and a negative one for Figure 13.3b as in rows (a) of Table 13.4

TABLE 13.5a. *Cross-country regressions explaining income, y*

		Full period 1960–2016			Period from 2000–16	
		(Reg 1)	(Reg 2)	(Reg 3)	(Reg 4)	(Reg 5)
(a)	g, growth	0.13 (3.1)		−0.09 (−3.2)		−0.09 −(2.4)
(b)	P, Polity	0.08 (7.2)	0.09 (7.3)	−0.02 (−1.3)	−0.01 (−0.5)	0.04 (2.2)
	F, Fraser	n.a.	n.a.	0.78 (7.3)	0.85 (7.9)	
(c)	dP, dif P	−0.80 (−4.2)	−0.90 (−4.7)	−0.11 (−0.8)	−0.09 (−0.7)	−0.47 (−2.7)
	zP, P zero	−1.05 (−1.2)	−1.14 (−1.2)	−0.96 (−3.3)	−0.71 (−2.4)	−1.63 (−4.1)
	dF, dif F	n.a.	n.a.	−3.59 (−2.9)	−2.55 (−2.0)	
(d)	Com/Post	0.44 (1.9)	0.61 (2.6)	0.63 (3.1)	0.32 (1.7)	0.45 (1.7)
	OPEC	1.18 (5.1)	1.26 (5.3)	1.63 (6.6)	1.54 (6.1)	1.05 (3.1)
	n, per country	−0.00 (−0.4)	0.00 (0.1)	0.08 (3.1)	0.06 (2.3)	0.02 (0.5)
	Constant	8.50 (19.2)	8.62 (19.0)	3.43 (3.8)	2.80 (3.1)	8.98 (17.4)
	N, countries	156	156	140	140	140
	R^2	0.480	0.447	0.664	0.638	0.341
	R^2 adj.	0.455	0.424	0.641	0.616	0.306

TABLE 13.5b. *Cross-country regressions explaining growth, g.*

		Full period 1960–2016		Period from 2000–16		
		(Reg 1)	(Reg 2)	(Reg 3)	(Reg 4)	(Reg 5)
(a)	*y*, income	**0.47 (3.1)**		**−0.85 (−3.2)**		**−0.49 (−2.4)**
(b)	*P*, Polity	−0.01 (−0.6)	0.03 (1.1)	**−0.14 (−3.2)**	**−0.13 (−3.0)**	**−0.11 (−2.6)**
	F, Fraser	n.a.	n.a.	−0.12 (−0.3)	**−0.84 (−2.5)**	
(c)	*dP*, dif *P*	−0.39 (−1.0)	**−0.81 (−2.2)**	−0.32 (−0.7)	−0.24 (−0.5)	−0.17 (−0.4)
	zP, *P* zero	−0.17 (−0.1)	−0.70 (−0.4)	**−3.55 (−3.9)**	**−2.94 (−3.2)**	**−3.92 −(4.1)**
	dF, dif *F*	n.a.	n.a.	**−14.50 (−3.7)**	**−12.33 (−3.1)**	
(d)	Com/Post	**1.01 (2.2)**	**1.29 (2.9)**	**3.86 (6.8)**	**3.58 (6.1)**	**3.31 (5.7)**
	OPEC	0.04 (0.1)	0.63 (1.4)	**2.35 (2.7)**	1.04 (1.3)	1.40 (1.7)
	n, per country	**0.03 (2.1)**	**0.03 (2.1)**	**0.29 (3.6)**	**0.24 (3.0)**	**0.19 (2.4)**
	Constant	**−3.12 (−2.0)**	0.93 (1.1)	**9.87 (3.4)**	**7.48 (2.6)**	**5.10 (2.3)**
	N, countries	156	156	140	140	140
	R²	0.152	0.098	0.400	0.354	0.332
	R² adj.	0.112	0.062	0.359	0.314	0.297

Sections (a) to (c) correspond to the rows in Table 13.4. Parentheses hold *t*-ratios. Coefficients are bolded if they are significant at the 5 % level.

The coefficient to growth still changes from period to period, but now the coefficient is smaller. It also appears that Fraser, F, and its first difference, dF, are powerful variables destroying the coefficients of Polity, P, and its first difference, dP. Economic freedom has a positive coefficient, while its variability has a large negative coefficient.

Table 13.5b compares explanations of the growth rate. All 12 estimates of coefficients to dF, dP, and Z^P in Table 13.5a and the same 12 estimates in Table 13.5b are negative, and most are significant. This result is consistent with the theory that increasing variability causes decreasing growth. Note that the dF-variable is much stronger than the dP^P-variable.

The remaining coefficients provide strong indications of confluence, notably between income and the Fraser index. Still, two results stand out: While the Fraser index has a positive coefficient to income, changes in the index have substantial negative effects. Thus, while liberalization has good effects in the long run, it is expensive in the short run – and vice versa for an increase in the level of regulation. In addition, it is nice to see that the post-socialist countries have relatively high growth. Thus, while the change from Socialism was expensive in the short to medium term, it resulted in higher growth during the recuperation period.

The zP-variable measures the fraction of years with anarchy and temporary foreign occupation. Such years are not present in most countries, but when they are, they are quite large. It is rather expensive measured in lost income and growth to go through periods of anarchy.

This section provides two parameters measuring the effect of instability: For political instability, it is the coefficient on dP that is about -0.5. For economic instability it is the coefficient on dF that is about -13.

13.5 CONCLUSIONS

This chapter has provided various estimates of components of the cost of the Grand Transition. They are summarized in Table 13.6. The estimates are uncertain – notably the ones in rows (2) and (3) – however, it is still clear that they show substantial costs.

The minimum of just above 40 percentage points is reached when only the changes necessary for the transition are made. It is a small loss when distributed over a couple of centuries. However, most countries take a roundabout road to development, and this means that the changes are much larger than necessary. This means that the loss is much larger. On average it is about 230 percentage points, which over 1–2 centuries is 1.1–2.3 percentage points per year.

TABLE 13.6. *The costs of the Grand Transition, at best and on average*

$X = P$ or F	P-index, from		F-index, from		Total loss
(1) Full transition	14 points	Table 2	2.8 points	Table 2	
(2) G^X, excess changes	4.5 times	Table 2	5.5 times	Table 2	
(3) Effect of dX	−0.5	Last section	−13	Last section	
(4) Total (1) × (2) × (3)	−31		−200		−230
(5) Minimum (1) × (3)	−7		−36		−43

However, think of the potential miracle growth that may make countries go through the Grand Transition in half a century. This is clearly impossible if countries go through the normal amount of institutional changes that provide a loss of 230 percentage points, which, when distributed over 50 years, is 4–5 percentage points per year.

The findings in this chapter confirm the standard result in the literature that system instability harms investment and hence growth. Thus, it tells a story of growth that applies its own brakes in middle-income countries. The prevailing opinion of the East Asian growth miracle is that it should be explained by the growth premium reached from transfers of resources – notably labor – from the traditional to the modern sector. The chapter argues that this transfer is normally quite problematic, as many countries experience (high) institutional instability, which generates uncertainty that harms investment.

Thus, the growth miracle may rather be that the political systems of these countries were sufficiently stable to limit the necessary economic system reforms until the good effects of the changes became visible to the majority of the population before the countries democratized.[3] They also managed to use the world market to overcome the limitations of the domestic market, so that the modern sector could expand rapidly.

---

[3] It is also worth noting that one of the most thoughtful and successful practitioners of development, Lee Kuan Yew, often claimed that political stability is a key to development. Lee Kuan Yew ruled Singapore for all the 45 years of "miracle" growth, where he practiced what he claimed.

14

Conclusions

This book applies a grand perspective: Cross-country and long-run. In this perspective, much that is otherwise important becomes small details. However, the perspective allows us to see a general Grand Transition "underlying" pattern that often escapes notice. In this perspective, the various sectoral transitions – such as the Democratic and Religious transitions – are easy to understand.

Thus, this book has shown that the process of development has a lot of endogeneity in the long run. It started with the well-known observation that countries have two basic steady states, the traditional and the modern, where the standards of living differ by 50 times, so that income differs by 4 log points. In both steady states, all relations in the socio-economic structure are (rather) stable, but very different. Thus, the Grand Transition involves massive structural change, which includes transitions of all institutions. While it is difficult to predict when these changes occur, they lead to much the same development in the end.

The pattern found asks if it makes sense to demand good governance in the form of *democracy* and *honesty* in poor countries. It would surely be welfare enhancing if it could be done, but the analysis suggests that it is unlikely to be maintainable. India has managed to keep one of the two, but most poor LDCs have neither democracy nor honesty. However,

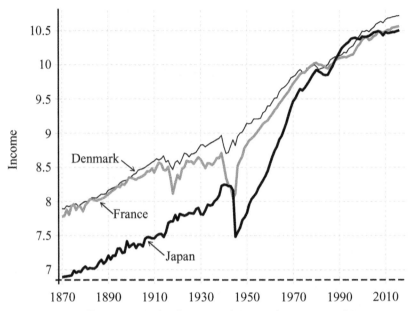

FIGURE 14.1. The economic development of Denmark, France, and Japan

development is a process that causes both democracy and honesty. The analysis suggests that it is easier to put the horse in front of the cart than vice versa.[1]

14.1 AN ILLUSTRATION

This book has shown that development shapes institutions. This message is illustrated in Figure 14.1 by three countries in different cultural areas, Northern and Southern (Latin) Europe and East Asia. They all had an old feudal/royalist system 250 years ago: (i) Denmark had a peaceful and gradual reform process leading to the abolition of feudalism and to democracy. (ii) France crushed royalism and feudalism by means of a large bloody revolution, and has had a great deal of system zigzag since then (see Figure 6.5c). (iii) Japan was a traditional isolationist system on a distant

---

[1] It is like the people who look at the agricultural transition depicted in Figure 1.1a and conclude that the causality is from the fall in the share of agriculture to development. This conclusion has led to amazingly harmful policies.

TABLE 14.1. *The seven institutional variables in the three countries, 2016*

	P, Polity	*CL*, Civil Liberties	*PR*, Political Rights	*B*, Ownership	*F*, Fraser Index	*T*, Corruption	*R*, Religiosity
Denmark	10	1	1	29.75 (a)	7.77	9.0	30.5 (a)
France	9	1	1	9.29 (a)	7.25	6.9	20.2 (a)
Japan	10	1	1	21.9	7.49	7.2	19.4

Note: (a) indicates that the last WVS wave had no data, so the last available are given.

island with late reforms (just before the data started). The reforms took time, and then followed a period of globalization and a rapid catch-up.

For the last 150 years, France and Denmark have had a very similar log-linear growth path. Japan started late, but caught up – following a rapid transition path. For the last 40 years, the three countries have experienced virtually the same development. Given the uncertainty of measurement of the *gdp* and the PPP conversion, there is no significant difference.

Table 14.1 shows that the three countries' institutions have become rather similar as well. The measures are aggregate and rather crude, and many details are surely different, but it is clear that each country is much more similar to either of the other two countries than it is to itself 200 years ago. When you travel from one country to the next, the three countries seem very different indeed. However, once you start to think about the differences, you will probably agree that most are small – often very charming – cultural traits and conventions that are slowly vanishing.

14.2 DEVELOPMENT ITSELF AS THE EXPLANATION

Throughout the book, institutions (X) have been explained by means of income, y, i.e., $X = \Pi^X(y)$, which is the transition in X in a long-run or wide cross-country perspective. It has been stressed that this is a reduced form. The analysis suggests that many other socioeconomic variables (incl. welfare goods) have transition paths – the ones examined certainly do. Thus, it is easy to replace income with a handful of other development indicators in the estimates. Development is a process with a lot of *confluence*.

Think of the Human Development Index, where leading social scientists for the last 30 years have tried to find a better measure for development than income. It is part of the research agenda that the HD-Index should be different from income. In spite of major efforts, the researchers keep finding measures that have a correlation of at least 0.95 to income. When income goes up, people will purchase healthcare, education, and social security, and try to acquire governments that provide these welfare goods. It is clear both that development requires education and that education can "explain" development. We can explain, e.g., the Democratic Transition by the level of education, but this is almost the same as explaining it by income.[2]

---

[2] Several researchers have tried to find an independent contribution of education in models explaining the political system, but it is tricky given that income is a fine variable "explaining" education; see Murtin and Wacziarg (2014).

When we find that causality is from development to the institutional variable, this means that many policies are endogenous in a larger perspective. The pressures of development end up defeating the policies pursued if these policies are inconsistent with development. The reader may think of New Zealand or Uruguay, both of which for a long time followed policies of "stop the world I want to get off,"[3] but in both cases the policy broke down under the pressures of development in the rest of the world.

A much larger example is the USSR (as already discussed), where a highly ideological regime tried very hard to create an alternative model. The efforts were truly heroic and very expensive for the population, with about 20 million killed, and a low level of consumption of anything but steel. Today, Russia has approximately the same gap to the West as it had a century ago. Finland broke out of Russia in 1918, when, as the Finnish province, it had a standard of living of about 80% of the Russian part of the USSR in Maddison's data. Today, Finland has the same standard of living as the rest of Northern Europe, and though Finnish development has seen some crises, the social costs have been much smaller (relatively) than the Russian ones. It is likely that Russia could have had similar development as Finland, and saved most of the enormous costs.

14.3 WHAT HAPPENED TO EXOGENEITY?

The argument up to now comes close to saying that everything is explained by everything else. Given that development has a large endogenous element, exogeneity becomes a rather blurry concept, like a handful of fine sand that slips through the fingers.

Perhaps the solution is the concept of a *triggering event*. Chapter 6 looked at the triggering event that led to changes in the political system – the analysis had the great advantage that political systems change rarely and in jumps, so it is fairly easy to identify the larger jumps. It is not so easy to identify the triggering events. My attempt revealed that the triggers for the larger jumps were very diverse, and most were exogenous or practically so. However, once they changed, most changes in the political

---

[3] Both countries are fertile and have a fine climate. For a long time, they pursued policies of de-globalization, with deep protection leading to low growth, short working hours, early pensions, etc. New Zealand carried out a large-scale structural adjustment in the mid-1980s – increasing the Fraser index by 2½ points. Uruguay has also re-globalized but more slowly.

system were toward the transition path. There was still a substantial random element in the changes, and they often overshot the path. Thus, we reached The Jumps Model, where the transition path worked as an attractor for system jumps caused by random shocks. It was argued that the transition path resulted from the Grand Transition, notably the transitions in agriculture and religiosity that undermined two of the three pillars of the traditional power structure.

It is more difficult to find out when the economic system changes, as it takes more time, and measurement is more difficult. However, my assessment is that we are dealing with similar mechanisms, where the changes are started by rather random triggering events, and they often take countries in the direction of other countries at the same level of development.

The concept of triggering events means that exogeneity occurs as sparks that are widely distributed throughout the politico-economic system. This explains why causality is such an elusive concept. We have tried to get a handle on causality, using four types of tests, the most formal one of which is the DP-test using pre-historical data for the development potential of countries as the instruments in TSIV-regressions. We have found that in most cases the instrumented income explains the cross-country pattern of institutions (almost) as well as income itself.

The pre-historical DP-data only covers half of the countries, and the explanatory power is less than half of the variation. However, I do find that income is a powerful variable explaining the various institutional variables, so it is still an important result that the main causal direction is from income in the long run, but there is of course still a great deal of space left for other explanations, especially in the short run.

14.4 IS SOMETHING NEW COMING UP?

Section 4.8 referred to Fukuyama's (1992) socioeconomic bestseller "The End of History." The idea was that modern society in the West and in a handful of East Asian countries has now reached such a high level of wealth and economic and political stability that it is difficult to imagine that future historians will have much to tell about modern countries of our time.

My country is a typical case. Throughout history, Denmark has had many wars with Sweden and Germany. The last war with Sweden was The Great Northern War that ended in 1720. Since then, there have been tensions in connection with the Napoleonic War, but for the last 200 years, tensions have vanished. The last war with Germany was in 1864. This was just before German unification, and it dealt with the complex Schleswig-Holstein Question. Since then, Denmark was occupied by Germany during the Second World War, but for the last 75 years, tensions have vanished. After the end of the Soviet empire, few Danes feel threatened by any foreign power. It is much the same for the majority of modern countries.

Thus, one may ask: Is it really the end of history? Or are we moving toward something else? Many observers are arguing that we are seeing new fault-lines causing tensions both in the economic and political sphere. Two such lines are visible,

(i) The first is mass migration from the third world, notably Muslims, who find it difficult to accept modern secular society. This has created some backlash of populist parties that are anti-foreign and anti-elite. In most modern states, such parties have reached a level of about 20% of the vote. To accommodate and fence in the backlash, immigration to the West has been strongly curtailed, and after another couple of generations, most of the great-great grand-children of original immigrants will probably be integrated. In addition, as more countries become wealthy, there will be fewer countries from which immigrants will leave, and more countries to which they will want to go.

(ii) The second is that threatening climate changes have created a mass movement for "systemic change." It is not at present clear how large the changes need to be. At present, it appears likely that they may include a higher level of social control, but in the longer run most of the adjustment may be handled by the market and technological change.

Consequently, I see little reason to believe that modern institutions will be unable to handle both of these fault–lines, even if it will take some time.

To write this book, I have looked through the politico-economic history of a great many countries. I have been left with a strong impression of the failure of all attempts to find a short cut to development. Some countries have managed to grow quickly, but then they have followed rather orthodox policies based on export to the world market. That is, South Korea has been much less adventurous in its economic strategy than Argentina. Thus, Argentina started as a successful exporter, but since the Crisis of the 1930s, it has experimented with many kinds of policies, which are often referred to as Latin American Structuralism and Populism. Both concepts are slippery and have produced a whole set of unorthodox development experiments, of which none have been successful. It is difficult, from afar, to understand what Hugo Chavez (of Venezuela) – and his successor – was/is trying to accomplish.

This does not mean that countries do not benefit from a public sector that provides a good level of the three big welfare goods: education, healthcare, and social protection. Most successful countries do have a balance between the private and the public sector, where the public sector has a size that can be financed from taxes. It is difficult to collect taxes in the LDCs, and narrow taxes can easily become harmful, so it is essential that taxes are broad, but this is all a huge story that exceeds the themes of this book.

14.5 INEVITABLE CHANGES AND REMAINING DIFFERENCES

The Grand Transition is a change that has to occur in order for development to succeed. It starts with a difficult divergence from the traditional steady state, and ends with a convergence to the modern steady state. As far as I know, this occurs for all variables. The literature has demonstrated that it happens with variables for the economic structure and for the main demographic variables, as well as for variables measuring the level of education, urbanization, etc.

This book has demonstrated that it is also the case for variables measuring institutions. The Democratic Transition is as strong as the Demographic Transition, and the Transition in the Economic System is almost as strong as the Agricultural Transition. To become wealthy and stable, a country has to go through a set of institutional transitions. For each socioeconomic variable, the transition represents the inevitable net change that has to happen.

We all like to think that countries can choose their system and that a range of choices is available. The Grand Transition view argues that the choice is fairly narrow. Most countries take a rather roundabout path to the goal, so they go through gross changes that are large relative to the net changes necessary. The G-ratio measures the ratio of gross to net changes. Chapter 13 has demonstrated that high G-ratios come with considerable costs.

References

The papers on which this book is based have twice as many references, but in several instances I have found meta-studies or recent surveys that have allowed me to limit references.

Acemoglu, D., Johnson, S., Robinson, J. A., 2005. Institutions as the fundamental cause of long-run growth. Chapter 6, 385–472 in Aghion and Durlauf (2005)

Acemoglu, D., Johnson, S., Robinson, J. A., Yared, P., 2008. Income and democracy. *American Economic Review* 98, 808–42

Acemoglu, D., Naidu, S. Restrepo, P., Robinson, J. A., 2019. Democracy does cause growth. *Journal of Political Economy* 127, 47–100

Aghion, P., Durlauf, S., eds., 2005, 2014. *Handbook of Economic Growth*. Four volumes. North-Holland, Amsterdam

Aidt, T. S., 2003. Economic analysis of corruption: A survey. *Economic Journal* 113 (491), 632–52. Also Chapter 3 in Dutta and Aidt (2016)

Aidt, T. S., Franck, R., 2015. Democratization under the threat of revolution: Evidence from the great reform act of 1832. *Econometrica* 83, 505–47

Aidt, T. S., Jensen, P. S., 2014. Workers of the world, unite! Franchise extensions and the threat of revolution in Europe, 1820–1938. *European Economic Review* 72, 52–75

Aisen, A., Veiga, J. F., 2013. How does political instability affect economic growth? *European Journal of Political Economy* 29, 151–67

Aizenman, J., Marion, N., 1993. Policy uncertainty, persistence, and economic growth. *Review of International Economics* 1, 145–63

Alesina, A., Özler, S., Roubini, N., Swagel, P., 2006. Political instability and economic growth. *Journal of Economic Growth* 1, 189–211

Andersen, T. B., Jensen, P. S., 2019. Preaching democracy. *Journal of Comparative Economics* 47(3), 525–40

Andvig, J. C., Moene, K. O., 1990. How corruption corrupts. *Journal of Economic Behavior and Organization* 13, 63–76. Also Chapter 16 in Dutta and Aidt (2016)

Arrow, K. J., 1963. *Social Choice and Individual Values* (2nd ed.). Yale University Press, New Haven, CT

Åslund, A., 2002. *Building Capitalism. The Transformation of the Former Soviet Bloc*. Cambridge University Press, Cambridge

Azariadis, C., Stachurski, J., 2005. Poverty traps. Chapter 5, 295–384 in Aghion and Durlauf (2005)

Azzi, C., Ehrenberg, R., 1975. Household allocation of time and church attendance. *The Journal of Political Economy* 83, 27–56

Barro, R. J., Sala-i-Martin, X., 1995, 2004. *Economic Growth*. MIT Press, Cambridge, MA

Basu, S., Bundick, A., 2017. Uncertainty shocks in a model of effective demand. *Econometrica* 85, 937–58

Berger, H., Spoerer, M., 2001. Economic crises and the European revolutions of 1848. *Journal of Economic History* 61, 293–326

Binswanger, H. P., Deininger K., Feder, G. 1995. Power, distortions, revolt and reform in agricultural land relations. Chapter 42, 2659–2772 in Behrman, J., Srinivasan, T. N., eds., *Handbook of Development Economics*, Vol 3B. North Holland, Amsterdam

Bjørnskov, C., 2010. How does social trust lead to better governance? An attempt to separate electoral and bureaucratic mechanisms. *Public Choice* 144, 323–46

Bjørnskov, C., Paldam, M., 2012. The spirits of capitalism and socialism. A cross-country study of ideology. *Public Choice* 150, 469–98

Blaug, M., 1997. *Economic Theory in Retrospect*, 5th ed. Cambridge University Press, Cambridge

Bloom, N., 2009. The impact of uncertainty shocks. *Econometrica* 77, 623–85

Blume, L., Müller, J., Voigt, S., 2009. The economic effects of direct democracy: A first global assessment. *Public Choice* 140, 431–61

Bond, S. R., Eberhardt, M., 2013. *Accounting for Unobserved Heterogeneity in Panel Time Series Models*. Mimeo, Oxford and Nottingham

Borner, S., Brunetti, A., Weder, B., 1995. *Political Credibility and Economic Development*. Macmillan, London

Borooah, V. K., Paldam, M., 2007. Why is the world short of democracy? A cross-country analysis of barriers to representative government. *European Journal of Political Economy* 23, 582–604

Carmignani, F., 2003. Political instability, uncertainty and economics. *Journal of Economic Surveys* 17, 1–54

Cheibub, J. A., 1996. What makes democracies endure? *Journal of Democracy* 7, 39–55

Chenery, H. B., Syrquin, M. 1975. *Patterns of Development 1950–1970*. Oxford University Press, Oxford

Chenery, H., Srinivasan, T. N., eds. 1988. *Handbook of Development Economics*. Two volumes, North-Holland, Amsterdam

Christoffersen, H., Beyerler, M., Eichenberger, R., Nannested, P., Paldam, M., 2014. *The Good Society. A Comparative Study of Denmark and Switzerland*. Springer-Verlag, Berlin

Christoffersen, H., Paldam, M., 2006. Privatization in Denmark, 1980–2002. Chapter 4, pp. 117–40 in Köthenburger et al. (2006)

Clark, G., 2007. *A Farewell to Alms: A Brief Economic History of the World.* Princeton University Press, Princeton, NJ

Colagrossi, M., Rossignoli, D., Maggioni, M. A., 2019. Does democracy cause growth? A meta-analysis of 2000 regressions. *European Journal of Political Economy*, https://doi.org/10.1016/j.ejpoleco.2019.101824

Coppedge, M., Gerring, J., Knutsen, C. H., Lindberg, S., Teorell, J., Altman, D., Bernhard, M., Fish, M. S., Glyn, A., Hicken, A., Lührmann, A., Marquardt, K. L., McMann, K., Paxton, P., Pemstein, D., Seim, B., Sigman, R., Skaaning, S-E., Straton, J., Cornell, A., Gastaldi, L., Gjerløv, H., Mechkova, V., von Römer, J., Sundström, A., Tzeglov, E., Uberti, L., Wang, Y-t., Wig, T., Ziblatt, D., 2020. V-Dem Codebook v10. Varieties of Democracy (V-Dem Project). University of Gothenburg V-Dem Institute

Danmarks Kirker, http://danmarkskirker.natmus.dk/

Diamond, J., 1997. *Guns, Germs, and Steel: The Fates of Human Societies.* Norton, New York

Ditzen, J., 2016. XTCD2: module to perform Pesaran's (2015) test for weak cross sectional dependence in panel data. Available for download in Stata

Doucouliagos, H., Paldam, M., 2009. The aid effectiveness literature. The sad result of 40 years of research. *Journal of Economic Surveys* 23, 433–61

Doucouliagos, H., Ulubaşoğlu, M. A., 2008. Democracy and economic growth: A meta-analysis. *American Journal of Political Science* 52, 61–83

Durkin, J. T., Greely, A. M., 1991. A model of religious choice under uncertainty: On responding rationally to the nonrational. *Rationality and Society* 3, 178–96

Dutta, J., Aidt, T. S. eds., 2016. *Corruption and Economic Development.* The International Library of Critical Writings in Economics series, vol. 324, Edward Elgar, Cheltenham

Easterly, W., Kremer, M., Pritchett, L., Summers, L., 1993. Good policy or good luck? Country growth performance and temporary shocks. *Journal of Monetary Economics* 32, 459–83

Eberhardt, M., 2012. Estimating panel time series models with heterogeneous slopes. *Stata Journal* 12, 61–71

Economist, https://ukshop.economist.com/collections/the-economist-historical-archive-1

Ekelund, R. B., Hébert, R. F., Tollison, R. D., 2006. *Marketplace of Christianity.* MIT Press, Cambridge, MA

Engerman, S. L., Sokoloff, K. L., 2008. Debating the role of institutions in political and economic development: Theory, history, and findings. *Annual Review of Political Science* 11, 119–35

Fernández-Villaverde, J., Guerrón-Quintana, P., Kuester, K., Rubio-Ramírez, J., 2015. Fiscal volatility shocks and economic activity. *American Economic Review* 105, 3352–84

Finke, R., Iannaccone, L. R., 1993. Supply-side explanations for religious change. *Annals of the American Academy of Political and Social Science* 527 May, 27–39

Frankel, J. A., Romer, D., 1999. Does trade cause growth? *American Economic Review* 89, 379–99

Fraser Index of Economic Freedom, 2020. www.fraserinstitute.org/studies/economic-freedom

Freedom House, 2020. https://freedomhouse.org/countries/freedom-world/scores

Fukuyama, F., 1992. *The End of History and the Last Man*. Many editions

Galor, O., 2011. *Unified Growth Theory*. Princeton University Press, Princeton, NJ

Gavin, M., Hausmann, R., 1998. Macroeconomic volatility and economic development. Chapter 4, 97–116 in Borner, S., Paldam, M., eds., 1998. *The Political Dimensions of Economic Growth*. Macmillan, London and New York, see also IDB(1995)

Gollin, D., 2014. The Lewis Model: A 60-year retrospective. *Journal of Economic Perspective* 28(3), 71–88

Gross, D., Steinherr, A., 2004, 2009. *Economic Transition in Central and Eastern Europe: Planting the Seeds*. Cambridge University Press, Cambridge

Gründler, K., Krieger, T., 2016. Democracy and growth: Evidence from a machine-learning indicator. *European Journal of Political Economy* 45, 85–107

Gründler, K., Potrafke, N., 2019. Corruption and economic growth: New empirical evidence. *European Journal of Political Economy* 60 article 101810

Gundlach, E., Paldam, M., 2009a. A farewell to critical junctures: Sorting out long-run causality of income and democracy. *European Journal of Political Economy* 25, 340–54

2009b. The transition of corruption: From poverty to honesty. *Economic Letters* 103, 146–48. Also chapter 27 in Dutta and Aidt (2016)

2010. The agricultural, demographic and democratic transitions. Two estimation models with the reverse results. http://martin.paldam.dk/Papers/GT-Main/5-Three-transitions.pdf

2012. A model of the religious transition. *Theoretical Economics Letters* 2012, 419–22

2020. A hump-shaped transitional growth path as a general pattern of long-run development. *Economic Systems* 44(3) article 10825

Gutmann, J., Paldam, M., 2020. Four measures of corruption. Appendix 2 to Paldam (2021a)

Gwartney, J., Lawson, R., Block, W., 1996. *Economic Freedom of the World: 1975–1995*. Fraser Institute, Vancouver, B.C. First annual publication of the Fraser index

Gwartney, J., Lawson, R., Grubel, H., de Haan, J., Sturm, J.-E., Zandberg, E., 2009. *Economic Freedom of the World: 2009 Annual Report*. Fraser Institute, Vancouver

Gwartney, J., Lawson, R., Hall, J., Murphy, R., 2018. *Economic Freedom of the World 2018 Annual Report*. Fraser Institute, Vancouver

Haan, J. de, 2007. Political institutions and economic growth reconsidered. *Public Choice* 131, 281–92

Haan, J.,de, Klomp, J., 2013. Conditional political budget cycles: A review of recent evidence. *Public Choice* 157, 387–410

Hall, R. E., Jones, C. I., 1999. Why do some countries produce so much more output per worker than others? *Quarterly Journal of Economics* 114, 83–116

Harris, J. R., Todaro, M. T., 1970. Migration, unemployment and development: A two-sector analysis. *American Economic Review* 60, 126–42

Heidenheimer, A. J., Johnson, M., LeVine, V., eds., 1989. *Political Corruption: A Handbook*. Transaction Publishers, New Brunswick, NJ

Hibbs, D. A. Jr., Olsson O., 2004. Geography, biogeography, and why some countries are rich and others are poor. *Proceedings of the National Academy of Sciences of the United States* (PNAS) 101, 3715–74

Higgins, B., 1959. *Economic Development. Principles, Problems, and Policies*. Constable and Co., London

Iannaccone, L. R., 1998. Introduction to the economics of religion. *Journal of Economic Literature* 36, 1465–95

IDB, 1995. Overcoming volatility. Part 2 pp. 189–258 in *Inter-American Development Bank, Economic and Social Progress in Latin America 1995 Report*, see also Gavin and Hausmann (1998)

Inglehart, R., Basáñez, M., Díez-Medrano, J, Halman, L., Luijks, R., eds. 2004. *Human Beliefs and Values. A Cross-cultural Sourcebook Based on the 1999-2002 Value Surveys*. Siglo XXI Editiones, México DF

Inglehart, R., Basáñez, M., Moreno, A., eds. 1998. *Human Values and Beliefs. A Cross-Cultural Sourcebook*. Michigan University Press, Ann Arbor, MI

Jones, C. I., Vollrath, D., 2013. *Introduction to Economic Growth*. 3rd ed. WW Norton, New York

Jong-A-Pin, R., 2009. On the measurement of political instability and its impact on economic growth. *European Journal of Political Economy* 25, 15–29

Kiszewski, A., Mellinger, A., Malaney, P., Spielman, A., Ehrlich, S., Sachs, J. D., 2004. A global index of the stability of malaria transmission based on the intrinsic properties of anopheline mosquito vectors. *American Journal of Tropical Medicine and Hygiene* 70, 486–98

Knack, S., 2002. Social capital and the quality of government: Evidence from the States. *American Journal of Political Science* 46, 772–85

Knack, S., Keefer, P., 1995. Institutions and economic performance: Cross-country tests using alternative institutional measures. *Economics and Politics* 7, 207–27

Köthenburger, M., Sinn, H.-W., Whalley, J., eds., 2006. *Privatization Experiences in the European Union*. MIT Press, Cambridge, MA

Kroeze, R., Vitória, A., Geltner, G., eds., 2018. *Anticorruption in History. From Antiquity to the Modern Era*. Oxford University Press, Oxford

Krueger, A. O., 1974. The political economy of the rent-seeking society. *The American Economic Review* 64(3), 291–303

  1990. Government failures in development. *Journal of Economic Perspectives* 4(3), 9–23

Kuznets, S., 1965. *Economic Growth and Structure. Essays 1954–64*. Norton, New York

  1966. *Modern Economic Growth*. Yale University Press, New Haven, CT

  1968. *Towards a Theory of Economic Growth*. Yale University Press, New Haven, CT

Lambsdorff, J. G., 2007. *Institutional Economics of Corruption and Reform. Theory, Evidence and Policy.* Cambridge University Press, Cambridge

Laursen, K., Paldam, M., 1982. The dynamics of the world's income distribution 1955–2000. *Nationaløkonomisk Nationaløkonomisk Tidsskrift*, special issue, 135–46

Leff, N. H., 1964. Economic development through bureaucratic corruption. *American Behavioral Scientist* 8, 8-14, and in Heidenheimer et al. (1989), Chapter 24, 389–403, and Chapter 23, 553–59 in Dutta and Aidt (2016)

Lewandowski, P., 2007. 'PESCADF': Module to perform Pesaran's CADF panel unit root test in presence of cross section dependence. Warsaw School of Economics, Institute for Structural Research, Poland.

Lewis, A., 1954. Economic development with unlimited supply of labour. *The Manchester School* 22, 139–91

Leys, C., 1965. What is the problem about corruption? *Journal of Modern African Studies* 3, 215–30, and in Heidenheimer et al. (1989), Chapter 5, 51–66

Lipford, J., McCormick, R. E., Tollison, R. D., 1993. Preaching matters. *Journal of Economic Behavior & Organization* 21, 235–50

Lipset, S. M., 1959. Some social requisites of democracy: Economic development and political legitimacy. *American Political Science Review* 53, 69–105

1994. The social requisites of democracy revisited: 1993 presidential address. *American Sociological Review* 59, 1–22

Lucas, R. E. Jr., 2009. Trade and the diffusion of the Industrial Revolution. *American Economic Journal: Macroeconomics* 1, 1–25

Lundahl, M., Silé, R., 2005. Haiti: Nothing but failure. Chapter 14, 272–301 in Lundahl, M., Wyzan, M. L., eds., 2005. *The Political Economy of Reform Failure*. Routledge, London

Maddison Project Database, version 2018. ggdc.net/maddison/maddison-project/home.htm

Maddison, A., 2001. *The World Economy: A Millennial Perspective.* OECD, Paris

2003. *The World Economy: Historical Statistics.* OECD, Paris

Malthus, T. R., 1798. *An Essay on the Principle of Population.* Many editions and reprints

Marshall, M. G., Gurr, T. R., Jaggers, K., 2018. *Polity^{TM} IV project. Political Regime Characteristics and Transition. Dataset Users' Manual.* Center for Systemic Peace. Regular updates available from the Polity home page

Masters, W. A., McMillan, M. S., 2001. Climate and scale in economic growth. *Journal of Economic Growth* 6, 167–86

McArthur, J. W., Sachs, J. D., 2001. Institutions and geography: Comment on Acemoglu, Johnson, and Robinson 2000. NBER Working Paper no. W8114.

McCleary, R. M., Barro R. J., 2006. Religion and economy. *Journal of Economic Perspectives* 20, 49–72

Megginson,W. L., Netter, J. F., 2001. From state to market: A survey of empirical studies on privatization. *Journal of Economic Literature* 49, 321–89

Méon, P.-G., Sekkat, K., 2005. Does corruption grease or sand the wheels of growth? *Public Choice* 122, 69–97

Méon, P.-G., Weil, L., 2010. Is corruption an efficient grease? *World Development* 38, 244–59. Also chapter 24 in Dutta and Aidt (2016)

Murtin, F., Wacziarg, R., 2014. The democratic transition. *Journal of Economic Growth* 19, 141–81

Nannestad, P., Paldam, M., 1994. The VP-function: A survey of the literature on vote and popularity functions after 25 years. *Public Choice* 79, 213–45

1997. The grievance asymmetry revisited: A micro study of economic voting in Denmark, 1986–92. *European Journal of Political Economy* 13, 81–99

North, D. C., 2005. *Understanding the Process of Economic Change.* Princeton University Press, Princeton, NJ

Nove, A., 1977. *The Soviet Economic System.* Allen & Unwin, London

Olsson, O., Hibbs Jr, D. A., 2005. Biogeography and long-run economic development. *European Economic Review* 49, 909–38

Opfinger, M., 2011. Religious market theory vs. secularization: The role of religious diversity revisited. Department of Economics. Working paper, Leibniz University, Hanover

Paldam, E., Paldam, M., 2018. The political economy of churches in Denmark, 1300–2015. *Public Choice* 172, 443–63

Paldam, M., 1997. *Dansk U-Landshjælp. Altruismens Politiske Økonomi.* Aarhus Universitetsforlag, Aarhus

2001. Corruption and religion. Adding to the economic model. *Kyklos* 54, 383–414

2002a. The cross-country pattern of corruption: Economics, culture and the seesaw dynamics. *European Journal of Political Economy* 18, 215–40

2002b. *Udviklingen i Rusland, Polen og Baltikum. Lys Forude efter Ændringen i det Økonomiske System.* Aarhus University Press, Aarhus

2009a. An essay on the Muslim Gap. Religiosity and the political system. Chapter 10, 213–42 in Wintrobe, R., Ferrero, M., eds. *The Political Economy of Theocracy.* Palgrave, New York

2009b. The macro perspective on generalized trust. Chapter 21, 354–78 in Svendsen, G. T., Svendsen, G. L. H., eds., 2009. *Handbook of Social Capital. The Troika of Sociology, Political Science and Economics.* Edward Elgar, Cheltenham

2013. The political economy of Dutch Disease – a survey. Chapter 10, 179–96 in Cabrillo, F., Puchades, M., eds., *Constitutional Economics and Public Institutions.* Edward Elgar, Cheltenham

2017a. The cycle of development in Africa: A story about the power of economic ideas. 497–525 in Christensen, B. J., Kowalczyk, C., eds. *Globalization. Strategies and Effects.* Springer, Berlin

2017b. An economic perspective on the Reformation and the downscaling of the Church in Denmark, 1450–1650. Working paper available from martin. paldam.dk/GT-Religion.php

2018. A model of the representative economist, as researcher and policy advisor. *European Journal of Political Economy* 54, 6–15

2020a. A study of triggering events. When do political regimes change? *Public Choice* 182, 181–99

2020b. The Democratic Transition – the Story of the Long run. Conference paper. Available from http://martin.paldam.dk/Papers/GT-Main/14-DemTrans.pdf

2021a. The transition of corruption. Institutions and dynamics. *European Journal of Political Economy* 67(2), article 101952

2021b. Measuring democracy. How Different Is the Polity and the V-Dem Indices? Pt. working paper. Available from http://martin.paldam.dk/Papers/GT-Main/15-V-Dem-Polity.pdf

Paldam, M., Gundlach, E., 2008. Two views on institutions and development: The Grand Transition vs the Primacy of Institutions. *Kyklos* 61, 65–100

2012. The democratic transition: Short-run and long-run causality between income and the Gastil index. *The European Journal of Development Research* 24, 144–68

2013. The religious transition. A long-run perspective. *Public Choice* 156, 105–23

2018. Jumps into democracy. Integrating the short and long run in the democratic transition. *Kyklos* 71, 456–81

Parker, D., Saal, D., eds., 2003. *International Handbook on Privatization.* Edward Elgar, London

Pejovich, S., ed., 1997. *The Economic Foundations of Property Rights. Selected Readings.* Edward Elgar, Cheltenham

Pesaran, M. H., 2006. Estimation and inference in large heterogeneous panels with a multifactor error structure. *Econometrica* 74, 967–1012

2015. Testing weak cross-sectional dependence in large panels. *Econometric Reviews* 34, 1089–1117

Pesaran, M. H., Shin, Y., Smith, R. P., 1999. Pooled mean group estimation of dynamic heterogeneous panels. *Journal of the American Statistical Association* 94, 621–34

Pesaran, M. H., Smith, R. P., 1995. Estimating long-run relationships from dynamic heterogeneous panels. *Journal of Econometrics* 68, 79–113

Pipes, R., 1999. *Property & Freedom.* Harvill Press, London Polity home page www.systemicpeace.org/polityproject.html

Pope, H., Pope, N., 2011 3rd ed. *Turkey Unveiled: A History of Modern Turkey.* Overlook Duckworth, New York

Puchades-Navarro, M., Montoro, J. D., 2009. Religious decline and public expenditure. Presented at the European Public Choice Society Meeting, Athens

Ranis, G., Fei, J. C. H., 1961. A theory of economic development. *American Economic Review* 51, 533–65

Rostow, W. W., 1960. *The Stages of Economic Growth: A Non-Communist Manifesto.* Cambridge University Press, Cambridge

Solow, R. M., 1956. A contribution to the theory of economic growth. *Quarterly Journal of Economics* 70, 65–94

1970, 2000. *Growth Theory. An Exposition.* Oxford University Press, Oxford

Soto, H. de, 2000. *The Mystery of Capital. Why Capitalism Triumphs in the West and Fails Everywhere Else.* Black Swan Books, London

Stark, R., Iannaccone, L. R., 1994. A supply-side reinterpretation of the "secularization" of Europe. *Journal for the Scientific Study of Religion* 33, 230–52

Tanzi, V., 2018. *Argentina, from Peron to Macri: An Economic Chronicle*. Jorge Pinto Books, Bethesda, MD

Terwiel, B. J., 2011. *Thailand's Political History. From the 13th Century to Recent Times*. 2nd ed., River Books, Bangkok

Transparency International, the TI index www.transparency.org/

Treisman, D., 2000. The causes of corruption: A cross-national study. *Journal of Public Economics* 76, 399–457

Ugur, M., 2014. Corruption's direct effects on per-capita income growth: A meta-analysis. *Journal of Economic Surveys* 28(3), 472–90

Uslaner, E. M., 2002. *The Moral Foundation of Trust*. Cambridge University Press, Cambridge

Weber, M., 1904/05. Die Protestantische Ethik und der "Geist" des Kapitalismus. *Archiv für Sozialwissenschaft und Sozialpolitik* 20, 1–54 and 21, 1–110. Many reprints and translations

Wilson, C. A., 2000. Policy regimes and policy changes. *Journal of Public Policy* 20, 247–77

World Bank, 1995. *Bureaucrats in Business: The Economics and Politics of Government Ownership*. Oxford University Press, Washington, DC

World Development Indicators http://devdata.worldbank.org/dataonline/

WVS, World Values Survey, www.worldvaluessurvey.org

Index